# From Normandy to Auschwitz

# From Normandy to Auschwitz

Paul le Goupil

Pen & Sword
**MILITARY**

First published in France in 1991 as
*Un Normand dans... Itinéraire d'une guerre, 1939–1945* by
Éditions Tirésias – Michel Reynaud

First published in Great Britain in 2018 by
Pen & Sword Military
an imprint of
Pen & Sword Books Ltd
47 Church Street
Barnsley
South Yorkshire
S70 2AS

English Translation Copyright © Francis Yerbury 2018

ISBN 978 1 52672 191 4

The right of Paul le Goupil to be identified as Author of this work has been asserted
by him in accordance with the Copyright, Designs and Patents Act 1988.

A CIP catalogue record for this book is
available from the British Library.

Printed and bound in England by TJ International Ltd, Padstow, Cornwall

Pen & Sword Books Limited incorporates the imprints of Atlas, Archaeology, Avia-
tion, Discovery, Family History, Fiction, History, Maritime, Military, Military Clas-
sics, Politics, Select, Transport, True Crime, Air World, Frontline Publishing, Leo
Cooper, Remember When, Seaforth Publishing, The Praetorian Press, Wharncliffe
Local History, Wharncliffe Transport, Wharncliffe True Crime and White Owl.

For a complete list of Pen & Sword titles please contact
PEN & SWORD BOOKS LIMITED
47 Church Street, Barnsley, South Yorkshire, S70 2AS, England
E-mail: enquiries@pen-and-sword.co.uk
Website: www.pen-and-sword.co.uk

# Contents

# Translator's Preface

*'That which has happened is a warning. To forget it is guilt. It must be continually remembered. It was possible for this to happen, and it remains possible for it to happen again at any minute. Only in knowledge can it be prevented.'*

*Karl Jaspers.*

*'...we become aware that to escape from Auschwitz is no small fortune.'*

*Primo Levy*

Paul Le Goupil's memoir moved me to translate it in its entirety, in the spirit of Jaspers' call to the duty of collective memory. I am grateful to the author for many elucidations of his story. We both live in Normandy, the territory marked literally and figuratively by occupation, and the act of liberation from oppression. His resistance is of the unseen kind, that of the Pen against the Sword. Thousands of French men and women silently slipped sand into the cogs of the Nazi machine, often paying with their lives, but their actions deserve the opposite of silence. His complete book covers the years 1939 to 1945, however his participation in resistance began during his first year as a teacher, and he has authorised this brief summary of the early years to better match the editorial remit of 'Pen and Sword'.

Francis Yerbury
Caen la mer
March 2017

The author has indicated certain names by initials only, in order not to prejudice them or their families.

# From Carefree to Curfew

When church bells tolled in the afternoon of Sunday 3 September 1939, hunting, one of Paul's passions, apart from his accordion and fishing, was postponed and did not resume until September 1945. What happened in between is related here thanks to diaries, notes and his memory, as far as possible. Two generations of his family had already experienced war with Germany, or 'Prussians' as his sharp-tongued great aunt always called them having witnessed them in 1871. His father was a gendarme, but Paul had decided to become a teacher, training at the École Normale (EN) in Rouen where they lived. There he spent the winter of the phoney war meeting students from other regions with different characters and political views, which gave rise to much debate. They combined studies with light-hearted fun until the catastrophe of the German invasion in May 1940, when he went west as a refugee by bicycle to family in the Cotentin. Narrowly escaping execution at the hands of an overzealous territorial guard he arrived in his relatives' rural world and set about being useful in the many farm chores. In due course German troops occupied their land and buildings, and while he worked the farm their occupiers busied themselves practising for the invasion of Britain in rubber boats! He was reunited with his mother and enjoyed fishing, but he was gripped by a sense of loneliness as a refugee and was happy to put his bike on a train back to Rouen.

The centre of the EN building became a shrine to Hitler and classes became dull platforms of Pétainist dogma, which Paul rejected – thus his anti-Pétainist end-of-year exam answers obliged him to take a resit. For a break he worked in a summer camp, also run in Pétainst spirit. Discouraged and disgusted, he resat the examinations, towed the line and was admitted to the final year.

People's lives in his second year were marked by cold and hunger; they made flour with a coffee grinder! His diary for that year is full of references to shortage of basic food, which he frequently remedied by transporting items. Nevertheless the trainee teachers did manage to organise a blow-out meal before going on practicals which included sport. He emerged fitter, but unaffected by the new doctrine. The lack of food brought with it a downturn in the atmosphere between occupying troops and the population. The slogan 'The Boche take the lot' could be heard in shop queues and tracts began to be handed out. Furthermore isolated attacks on German soldiers and the more frequent train derailments resulted in reprisals, executions, deportations, earlier curfews, bans on cycling, and the closing of theatres and cinemas.

As resistance developed, so did measures against it. One incident shows the conflict resulting from his father's function as a gendarme: investigating ration card trafficking he was able to identify the person denouncing it. The handwriting of the letter of denunciation was identifiable as that of the notes of Paul's teaching supervisor!

But, with or without the Kommandatur's permission, he managed to travel to visit friends, to ferry food, to attend a wedding, often on his bike, now expensive to maintain, by which means he went to spend September 1942 in the Cotentin before beginning his chosen career.

# Chapter 1

# Novice Teacher and Novice Resister

I went back to Rouen without difficulty to take up my first teaching post. I had just been allocated to the Jean Jaurès School at Grand Quevilly, a school, comprising twelve classes, located less than ten minutes from my home by bicycle.

According to the established traditions which have not changed, the last one into a school got the job that no one else wanted, which was therefore the least attractive. So they gave me the worst primary infants class. I had to teach reading to kids of ages ranging from 6 to 9 as some had repeated their year more than once. The social background was basically working class, including many Portuguese, and was especially underprivileged. Those children were for the most part undernourished, thin, tired and flea- and tick-ridden. On advice from my colleagues faced with the same scenario, I placed the flea victims and the tic victims on opposite sides of the class. We and the school principal too redoubled our advice to their families and gave out free medication against the scourges, but most of the time we came up against the prejudices of those times. For some parents, ticks were caused by bad wartime bread: it was 'bread tick'. As for fleas, they thought that the flea nest had burst. Some mothers explained to me that everyone has a flea 'nest' on his scalp and that in case of weak health or illness the shell of this nest bursts, allowing the fleas to free range in the hair.

Immigrant families whose fathers' lungs were exposed to their work in chemical factories did not have the benefit of a high resistance in terms of health. Under the circumstances I caught fleas a few times and passed them on to my mother and sister. Twice I had to go to the hospital to get rid of ticks by taking sulphur baths.

Many of the children's only food was the school canteen lunch meal and the four pm biscuits provided by the Secours National. We even wondered if they were consumed in class as we became aware that some parents, fortunately only a minority, insisted on pain of punishment that the biscuits be brought home to be resold. There was a high level of absenteeism; one main reason given was the lack of shoes, so the Secours National made a few pairs available to us. Sometimes they suffered the same fate as the biscuits and were not to be seen on the feet of our schoolchildren.

I can still recall a French family which exploited its children. The mother and father did not work and also drank. To get money they had trained their children to pick up cigarette butts. Two of them, aged 7 and 9, being unable to read were enrolled in my class, but I did not see much of them. I noticed that the elder, whenever I made a brusque gesture, covered his head with his two arms as if to protect himself. As I gained his confidence he recounted to me how his parents made him collect the butts from the terraces of the main Rouen cafés such as La Bourse, Le Victor etc. If the crop was thin he was beaten. The father dried the tobacco, remixed it, and with a gadget made new cigarettes which he resold on the black market or exchanged for wine. The headmaster notified this case to the police and there was an enquiry.

Under such circumstances the results were poor and when I left that class in June, only sixty per cent of the children were able to read. The head teacher, a wounded veteran of the Great War (1914–18), full of vigour, did his utmost to defend his young teachers. There were three of us novices. He acted as a buffer and never hesitated to take our side against parents who had short fuses under the circumstances at that time. A novice teacher is always an easy target.

I made new friends such as Rousseau, a novice like me, with us as a replacement teacher. We had the same views concerning the war. However he thought we should get involved actively to rid us of the Boche. An older colleague taught me the art of finding mushroom delicacies in the Essarts forest. I avoided talking politics with him, to maintain friendly relations as he had Pétainist leanings.

During holiday breaks I would meet up with EN pals who were posted to jobs in the Rouen area, at the Chrysanthème café or in Rue Grand Pont. Above all I visited the sister of one of them, Charley, as he was in a sanatorium, to get some news of him. Having been an ardent young anti-Nazi in the young socialists he thought that by explaining it to German soldiers, he could persuade them to fight Nazism. To this end he had set himself the task of learning German. Being malnourished like so many EN students and living in a hovel, one day he suffered a pulmonary haemorrhage. His sister Marie had quit teaching to enrol in the midwifery school of the Hospice Général de Rouen and seemed better suited to that profession. She was some years older than me and was well educated, endowed with maturity and a sense of proportion, and set on an even keel, all of which drew me to her. I thought of her more as a pal than as a woman. I invited her home sometimes for a good meal.

Towards the end of October she brought me some leaflets of the clandestine Communist Party and some copies of *L'Humanité*.[1] One pamphlet, by Gabriel Péri, who was shot by the Germans in December 1941, was entitled 'No! Nazism is not socialism'. That was the first time since the paper called Jaurès that I had read clandestine texts. I handled them with respect and read them, mindful of the courage of the militants who wrote, printed and distributed those publications that made me rethink the words of my friend Rousseau on the need to be active in order to rid ourselves of the Boche.

Some days later I met Marie Louise at the Café de la Bourse and she invited me to dinner at her home. Then she asked me if I had read the documents she had entrusted me with. We discussed the Péri pamphlet which I found a bit heavy going and lacking in concision. Then with a different tone of voice, as if fearing rejection, she asked me if I wanted to distribute a packet of newspapers and tracts. I felt obliged to accept. It comprised forty copies of *L'Humanité*, tracts and pamphlets of the CP (Communist Party). She seemed to be relieved to be rid of that packet which she wrapped up in the *Journal de Rouen* newspaper. I did not show it but it gave me quite a shock. I went home like a zombie with my parcel under my arm and on arrival I hid it on top of my chest of drawers and then, being worried about it, I moved it and hid it under the wood store in the laundry.

I felt as if I was Jean Valjean[2] with the coin in his hand. This packet was like a bomb which marked the end of the happy days when my major preoccupations were cinema and upcoming holidays. Of course half my diary was devoted to the war and I traced the lines of the Russian front on the Vidal-Lablache atlas. I listened to the BBC, Suisse Romande radio, Radio Moscow, but I was an armchair strategist, a spectator, a pundit in the Café du Commerce. This time the war caught up with me and I was implicated. It had grasped my hand and would not let me go, except as a coward or backslider. That evening my parents noticed my stress but I pretended to have a migraine so as to retire to my room and think things over. Those pamphlets presented me with three scenarios. To burn them, to distribute them or to get someone else to do so. The thought of the sacrifices of those who had got them into my hands ruled out the first option. As for the third I did not know of anyone capable of doing it. So I was left with the option of distributing them myself.

Next day at lunchtime I took the packet to school with a view to throwing them around when it was dark in the evening on my way home. I used to stop at a café in Grand Quevilly. It was a meeting point for domino, card and chess-players. It was where I got to know a member of the Rouen chess club, a strong player who taught me openings, how to develop the pieces and build up attacks with them. From time to time I managed to win a game. In those days it was dark when I got home.

I talked to Rousseau about the papers and offered him a few copies. He confided to me that he belonged to a resistance group and he took my entire bundle to distribute in his district. I must admit I was relieved as if freed from servitude and that evening my appetite was better.

Some days later Marie Louise came to the house with an even larger bundle in her bag. She asked me how the hand-outs had gone but I did not let her in on my solution. This time I was not afraid. I gave a small packet to Rousseau and after a short chess game I threw out small handfuls on the Boulevard Stanislas Girardin, at the Bruyères roundabout and at La Villanette. It was with a sort of elated anger that I opened my jacket to send the tracts flying through the air. I even regretted giving so many of them to my colleague, so easy and intoxicating did it seem. This action made me feel easier with my self image, although deep down I already knew that the price to be paid would be high.

From this time on my life did not outwardly change. I still went to the cinema three times a week; I went for a drink with friends, boy or girl, but little by little I latched on to the Resistance. Marie Louise gave me other packets of 'material' as it was called, then she asked me if I wanted to meet someone in the organisation. She gave me to understand that towards the end of November I should be at such and such a time at the Sainte Lucie roundabout. At that time Grand Quevilly was not as it is now, and this junction was almost deserted. I turned up at precisely the appointed hour. Then I saw a young man of about 25 arriving on foot casually pushing his bicycle. He hesitated a little and uttered the password, 'Have you got the time please?' to which I was to reply, 'Sorry but I haven't got my watch.' He shook my hand and we chatted while pushing our bikes along.

He said he was a member of the 'Front National'. He explained that, once founded by the Communist Party, the movement was now independent, with the aim of uniting all those who wanted to get rid of the Boche, regardless of political or religious affiliations. The first task was to recruit two or three friends to form a cell, which in turn would try to enrol two or three others that I would not know. In this way the organisation was shielded so that when a cell was arrested the rest was protected. Further to recruitment the major tasks were the distribution of newspapers and tracts, opposition to secondments to Germany, the search for hiding places, and supply of food for fugitives. I declared myself to be in agreement with the aims of the organisation and considered myself as a full member. We discussed politics and I quickly realised he was a communist.

He passed me a big packet of material to distribute in Petit and Grand Quevilly and fixed a subsequent meeting for two weeks later. The next time the package he handed me did not contain the *Humanité* newspaper, but papers of the Front National called *L'espoir*,[3] the paper of young Normandy patriots, and some pamphlets written by women's committees demanding better food, one of them specifically criticising the bad quality of food served in municipal canteens. This time I gave only one copy of each tract to Rousseau and delivered the rest myself by bicycle, throwing them as usual and going via different districts to avoid being spotted. The following morning I took the same route to go to work and was gratified to see that, apart from some which had fallen in the gutter and got wet, everything had been picked up.

On 12 December, my twentieth birthday, there was an air raid. My diary entry reads, 'On Saturday noon just before I reached school the air raid warning sounded. Six of us colleagues were chatting in the school yard when six British fighters appeared very high, glinting in the sunlight. Suddenly could be heard a low rumbling like a train crossing a metal bridge. It was a squadron of American heavy bombers escorted by fighters; we could count fifteen flying at about 3,000 metres in close formation emerging from a cloud. We immediately gathered the children under the awning as we did not have a shelter. No bombs fell from the aircraft. They flew over the power station majestically followed by sixteen more. The shouts of the children under the shelter were drowned out by the sound of heavy machine gun fire and then the planes disappeared behind the hill at Canteleu, appearing to veer slowly towards Le Havre. The heavy machine gun fire could be heard for a few more minutes, then silence fell and the children went into class as the all clear sounded. According to witnesses no bombs were dropped. Around five pm when classes let out I learned that some fell on Caen Avenue and around the Trianon cinema in Sotteville. Not one hit a military target as I was able to see for myself on the spot. Only residential buildings were hit. A large crowd came to see the damage. It was a sorry sight. A dozen huge craters of more than 12 metres in diameter have destroyed most houses in the sector. Everywhere, windows are broken, tiles ripped off, earth upturned and piles of debris. Fortunately, considering the damage, the number of victims is not high (18 dead and 56 wounded). Another cluster of bombs fell on the far end of Avenue Jean Jaurès, destroying a factory making bolts and damaging a block of worker flats. Then there were others that fell on Saint Etienne, including a worker district in Darnétal, in the fields of Notre Dame de Franqueville, and a mental hospital. We counted no less than 132 bomb hits of at least one ton. The raid was a total failure despite the presence of 45 bombers and 300 fighters. It was the third time the Flying Fortresses had come over for nothing. There are several possible explanations for the failure of this raid: the Americans were under attack from German fighters from Vernon, and had to release their loads willy nilly which is how some fell on fields. Or perhaps because it was cloudy, which prevented the American aircraft from seeing their targets. Finally, there are adverse wind currents in the Rouen area which are a hazard for flyers. Whatever the reason that makes three useless raids and that beats all records. But alas they will return.'

Over Rouen and Le Havre however there were sadly many other such errors.

Some days later I went to see Louis Miton who had been allocated with his wife to some backwoods place in the Somme département in Frettemolle where none of the roads were metalled. After Serqueux the train crossed a plain dotted with bomb craters which had destroyed square kilometres of fields. Louis told me it was the result of a failed attack on the German airfield at Poix. With my friends we spent a very pleasant day, above all a gastronomic one. I remember demolishing almost all of a bowl of chocolate mousse. Since electricity was patchy Louis had, to solve the problem of heating, hooked up a pirate connection onto the electricity cable, which he disconnected each morning.

The year ended on an optimistic note as far as military operations went. All of us, that is my friends, colleagues, my National Front contact, thought that the war had reached a turning point and that landings would take place in the spring of 1943.

I decided to go to Illiers for my end-of-year holidays. This time I stayed with Jean's parents on the outward and return journeys; they had let out their hotel and were living in a small apartment in Rue de Reuilly in Paris. During that stay I had much more difficulty than usual in finding food. The piles of beans from the farms of the Beauce were just a distant memory since the service of Food Supply had taken control of them. Nevertheless I managed to fill my suitcases with the help of my uncle, and by knocking on several doors. On passing back through Paris I left some of those food stocks for Jean's parents. I had to take a bus as I could not get a ticket for the Paris–Le Havre express. There was such a queue for trains that, to get an express ticket, you had to pick up your ticket at least two weeks in advance.

I spent the last days of my holidays at Goderville at the home of Jean who lived there with his girlfriend and her parents. I talked to him a little about my commitment to the Front National but he remained just as anti-communist. He considered the Front National militants as fodder for the Communist Party which pulled the strings and exploited them. His stance on the war had not shifted. For him it was an imperialist action and only benefitted the bourgeoisie.

On returning to Rouen station, the passengers faced a reception committee consisting of German military police (Feldgendarme), Gestapo members and German soldiers searching people and checking IDs, as the day before there had been an attack against an officer of the Kommandatur. It passed off alright for me, which was not the case for some others who were taken away by truck, for unknown reasons.

I made notes in my diary on the fourteen trips I made that year and added, 'What will this year mean? Maybe I will do Something Big, the Last Act.'

I continued to meet my Front National contact in the district of Grand-Quevilly-Extension or on the road leading to Grenet's farm. We discussed things; he passed on newspapers and tracts to me and asked me about various things. Our relationship did not progress as if he had orders to observe and report on my intentions. The reason, as I found out later, was that I was the son of a cop. I found it easy to live with this test of loyalty which did not cause me any problems.

I went through my father's briefcase while he slept in case I might come across any information about the resistance. One day I came across lists written in pencil of about twenty names and addresses with annotations such as 'area chief belonging to cell such and such'. Most lived in Sotteville, Déville or Maromme. These lists had probably been drawn up in police stations as they were not in my father's handwriting. He must have been put in charge of an enquiry into Communist Party militants. I copied out the names and addresses and passed them on to my contact whom I was to meet the following day. The next week I asked him what had happened about it and he replied that they were old lists and that many of the people had been arrested some months before or had left without leaving an address. However he had been able to warn two friends, male and female.

Towards the end of 1943 there was the affair of the wife of the pharmacist in Grand Quevilly. She was a graduate of the EN from 1937 to 1940 and I met her at a dance. She had married a pharmacist in Grand Quevilly and had been appointed to Marie Curie School. One evening when classes let out, a militant from the Union of French Women was handing out pamphlets against secondments to Germany, to mothers picking up their children, as well as to schoolchildren. The schoolteacher had had the militant arrested, I know not why, since she was not a known Pétainist, and had held onto her arm until the arrival of the police whose station was quite near. The woman got eight years hard labour. Those around the teacher were very upset and soon she retired from teaching and assisted her husband as cashier. She rarely ever went out for fear of reprisal. One evening as she was closing the pharmacy someone came in and shot her twice fatally and left by bicycle with an accomplice acting as look-out.

I thought this death was too high a price to pay, perhaps because I knew the victim, but my Front National contact, to whom I spoke about it and who seemed well informed, did not share my view. He thought such an execution would serve as an example to deter potential informants.

On 16 February 1943 I made a note of the news in my diary. The third item, unbeknown to me was to change my life:

'1. Imposition of a metal tax. Anyone not returning copper or tin will be fined 130 to 180 francs by way of compensation per kilo.
2. Census of men between 20 and 30 in order to deprive those who avoid it of their ration cards.
3. Creation of the STO[4] for young people born in 1920, 21, 22. This is designed to affect civil servants, students and lay-abouts.

These three measures show how Laval is doing everything to help the Germans.'

My probation period must have been complete as my contact let me know that an official of the organisation wanted to see me. He set up a rendez-vous at the number 12 bus stop near the Vache Noire café in Rue d'Elbeuf. On the given day he was there accompanied by a man of about 30; he was stocky, sharp featured, and wore thick lens glasses and a leather jacket. My contact introduced him as Roland and then left us. I never saw him again and never knew what became of him.

Roland and I talked for a long time strolling along the side reserved for trams. He talked to me about the Front National and its aims, repeating the notions presented by my contact in Quevilly-Extension.

But I had done some thinking since my first encounter and, given my admiration for the Red Army and my very left wing views, the Front National did not seem to match my revolutionary ideal. I thought that the Resistance and the liberation of France should give rise to a social revolution. I cut in and told him I would prefer to be an active Communist Party militant. Then I saw him light up with a big smile. He warmly took my hand and said, 'I myself am a communist. I'll think it over but I believe you will be more useful to us elsewhere. We lack organisers in the FPJ [Front Patriotique de la Jeunesse].'

We continued our discussion and he explained to me that the FPJ was to the Young Communists what the Front National was to the Communist Party. At that point in the conversation he said to me, 'From now on I will be your contact and not the cobbler friend.'

In this way I learned by chance that my first contact was a cobbler probably living in Quevilly-Extension. If I had been an informer this piece of information would have been fatal for him. Before leaving, Roland gave me a rendezvous for two weeks later.

In my diary I wrote more and more often of my anti-German and anti-Vichy sentiments, especially in view of the threat of my compulsory departure for Germany which was clearly on the cards. Thus the entry for 26 February 1943 reads,

'Home front situation. Laval is carrying out his threat to call up the classes of '40-'41-'42 for compulsory labour. Only a bullet can stop him. An announcement has been put in the papers. Wednesday and Thursday I went to the sign-up. Young people fall into three categories

— Farm workers who stay in their job
— Workers in France
— Workers in Germany

'The last group is to be the biggest. Teachers are not to be exempted at least not at the moment. I still hope to stay however.

'Laval and the Germans are going to suck out all the nation's youth between 18 and 30 and deport them to Germany in anticipation of the invasion. The home front situation is becoming tenser. We must hang on but how many months longer? Til the end of August, say six months? When will the landings take place? How to hang on six months, half a year? That's the rub!'

And on 27 February, still preoccupied with this problem I continued...

'Home front: the classes affected are under growing threat. The two Rousseau brothers, one being my colleague from Jean Jaurès, called up along with 32 of their friends in town had a second rigorous test with x rays and will probably be sent off in spite of all their efforts not to be. Word is going around that printed forms for the classes of '43 and '44 are ready and that those on the lists up to age 30 will leave within two weeks and that men up to 50 will suffer the same fate. What should we believe? One thing is certain. Our class years are in their sights and no exemption will be granted for teachers.'

I was going through ups and downs as in addition to the threat of departure and to my resistance activities I was going out with an apprentice hairdresser with beautiful black eyes – Réjane. Up until then I had had lots of flirtations of no consequence but this time I was smitten. I was at sixes and sevens all the more so as my yearning for her was as yet not mutual.

Roland entrusted me with, in addition to the distribution of tracts and newspapers, the sale of liberation bonds to help fund the Front National. They were issued in values of five, ten, and twenty francs. He said to me, 'It's a way of making contact. When you sell them you can explain the aims of the movement and sometimes the buyer will go from being a sympathiser to becoming a member.'

I sold a few of these bonds among my acquaintances. Most of them seemed bothered. They would slip me five or ten francs, tear up the bonds and avoid me from then on. I lost a few friends that way.

Our family doctor, a resident of Sotteville, often called at home as my sister was being treated following an infection. When he called he chatted to my father, not missing an opportunity to vent his anger against the 'lousy Boches', and that he would not forget them on the day of the invasion. I thought he would make an ideal recruit for the Front National and one afternoon I went for an appointment. I waited almost two hours as he had a lot of patients. When my turn came I offered him some bonds. He turned pale, held out a hefty franc note, refused to take them and said, 'Above all, don't mention my name anywhere. Forget your visit here. You don't know me. You're brave to do what you're doing Paul, but it's suicidal… I have a family to support and I can't take risks. Don't come back here. It's too dangerous!'

I did not hold it against him. I felt the same unease when Marie Louise suggested that I hand out tracts. It was all the more significant as I found out later that he had treated injured FTP[5] members, which took much more commitment than buying solidarity bonds. This experience gave me food for thought and I no longer tried to enlist the support of people without sounding them out first. I waited for them to make the first moves. I stopped selling bonds, pointing out to Roland that the procedure had the disadvantage of exposing the seller, putting him at the mercy of an informer or a loose talker.

At the beginning of March Roland introduced me to the main FPJ contact, Gilbert (I cannot remember his pseudonym). He was tall, blond, a little older than me, and a tenacious guy who knew how to galvanise his listeners. For him it was a piece of cake: the landings were imminent, the FPJ was growing in strength from week to week and he could foresee an army of young people on the heels of the Boche. He was thinking of putting me in charge of the movement at département level as he was to become inter-regional head, which meant being in charge of seven départements.

'But there's a problem,' he said. 'Your father is a cop and the lads are suspicious of the son of a cop.'

So it was Roland, as he later confirmed, a Communist Party representative who in this role wore the hats of the Communist Party and the Young Communists, but also the Student Communists, the FPJ, the FN, the UFF (the Union of French Women), the SP (Secours Populaire – the People's Aid), and the Franc Tireurs and Partisans (FTP), who out of concerns about security was holding back my rise to higher responsibilities.

The pace of departures for Germany was hotting up. There were queues at the door of the labour office. One received a notice to attend there. Then one received a work permit and a travel warrant. Together with a neighbour in the postal service we were the only ones of the class of '42 not to be called up. I breathed a sigh of relief once more.

On 10 March I went to the right bank railway station to go to Goderville to see Jean, my EN friend from Le Havre whose parents ran a hotel, and his ladyfriend. He too had managed to defer draft. On the way there I saw a station full of conscripts accompanied by their families from all social backgrounds. On Thursday evening on my return journey about twenty young men were waiting for the Paris train at Bréauté-Beuzeville station. They were mostly bakers, butchers or those in skilled trades.

In Rouen the civil service tried to gain time to block the departure of their staff. At the Academic School Board word was going around (one of many at that time) that a list of fifty-two probationers, with the addition of eight qualified teachers, was ready.

Gilbert produced more tracts urging young people not to go. They were distributed in the evening near the station and inside it, and I participated in that several times. Gilbert told me of speakers (he advised me never to be one). A friend arrived at the station during the rush hour or in front of a factory with an empty tool box on his shoulder, protected by several FTP members. He put his tool box down, stood on it and gave a speech of some minutes, urging young people not to go. Then tracts were scattered and in the ensuing mêlée he would flee, protected by his friends.

At Gilbert's instigation I drafted a tract to incite teachers not to go. Five hundred copies were printed and sent to fifty young teachers and probationers whose addresses we had. The remainder were handed out with other tracts at school gates.

On 28 March there was another allied raid on Sotteville which I related thus:-

'Sunday midday: siren. Low rumbling sound of US squadrons. We count 72 four-engined planes. Whistle and whine of bombs falling in clusters. The whistling is so strong that it covers the sound of the explosions. I lay down without emotion but with just a nip of fear. Then a louder roar of huge planes. Some distant machine gun fire, then nothing. But we hear explosions over Sotteville, first isolated crunches then a continuous rolling barrage like a military front. An ammunition train blows up at the station. After the raid the sky is full of clouds of dust and a pall of smoke. During the afternoon I go up Saint Catherine rise with my sister and a neighbour. It was a sight worth seeing. A whole section of Quatremare workshops was ablaze. Many trains belched steam and flames. From time to time white plumes of steam were rent by a big black outburst followed by the sound of an explosion some seconds later. A shell had just burst. Sometimes a tanker wagon full of fuel oil or petrol burst into a high red torch of flame. Near the devastated area a locomotive manoeuvres regardless of the danger. The fields around are cratered with enormous ochre coloured holes which contrast with the pale green of the flat land. Many residents come up like us to see the extent of the damage.

'The sight is more terrible viewed close up than at a distance and the full horror of war is clear to see. Square miles of houses are flattened by bombs; whole working class districts built around workshops are blown to pieces and crushed. The mental asylum and the cycle stadium were also seriously damaged. The workshops themselves received some direct hits and wisps of smoke emerged from their damaged roofs. It will take months to repair. The raid was a success but alas we mourn about one hundred dead.

'If we try to obtain a surface area calculation of the devastated area we end up with a rectangle of at least 2 kilometres long by 800 metres wide on the side of the hill overlooking Amfreville-la-Mi-Voie bordering on the cycle track on one side and the mental institution on the other, the workshops and the station being at the centre. Again this time there are more than 400 hits but the bombs are much more centred on the target. The raids are more destructive and effective. This summer the situation will be unbearable. A simple course error, unfavourable cloud, or an air battle would mean that hundreds of bombs will flatten residential areas.'

At the beginning of April, following the havoc caused by this bombing, the parents of the children at my school were informed that they could have their children evacuated with aid from the city, to zones less at risk. (At Grand Quevilly there were a power station, several factories supplying the Germans, and shipyards). The children would be placed in school camps or with host families, at a cost of between 15 and 21 francs per child per day for families earning more than 3,500 francs per month (a small minority) and at no cost for the remainder. The support organisation was based on a ratio of three teachers to one hundred kids.

Fortunately for me this campaign was not a success, as I did not want to end up in the backwoods. Of the 500 pupils enrolled at school only twenty signed up for camp and sixty let it be known that they would find shelter with their own family members.

Many parents were reluctant to be separated from their children, all the more so since up until then Grand Quevilly had suffered little bombing; yet the township was at the mercy of carpet bombing, like that on Sotteville.

Around this time I put Gilbert in touch with Brutelle, section head of the Young Socialists. He worked with us for a while, giving us interesting contacts, distributing our newspapers and pamphlets, but he refused to join the FPJ. There was a crisis in the Young Socialists and in the Socialist Party in general. A body of militants who had remained pacifist or who were simply waiting, refused to get involved in active resistance, namely in military action, meaning the war! Brutelle seemed isolated amongst his friends. He himself was convinced of the need to act and he was effective. One day he took up position at the exit of the Excelsior cinema at Petit Quevilly in order to hand out a big bundle of our tracts. He handed them out hand to hand like leaflets and that day he came close to being arrested. At the end of the summer of 1943, following the visit of Henri Ribière, one of the founders of Libé-Nord,[6] he, together with Raoul Leprettre, set up a branch of Libé-Nord for the département, rallying a number of militant socialists, and he ceased collaborating with us.

In our struggle against relocations to Germany our propaganda was clearly not producing results. In spite of tracts, newspapers and verbal contacts, lots of young people were leaving. How could they do otherwise, being without false papers, ration cards or bolt holes? A number of town hall secretaries or police station clerks provided us with false papers and even official stamps for use in the production of our documents. As for the ration cards, when it came to renewal time, the FTP regularly raided town halls to get ration tickets. Going to ground posed no problem for them as many of those young 'rebels' knew folk in the country or in town who could shelter them. I had kept in touch with Roland who had a reserve supply of safe houses for emergencies. In this way I was able to help a number of young people to avoid the STO (Service de Travail Obligatoire).

In April the threat of calling up teachers became clearer. The school heads in the second school district were ordered to draw up lists of young ladies in their area who had obtained the Brevet Elementaire. There was talk of a list of 250, already drawn up, of those due for relocation to Germany. The authorities seemed to want to delay the due date but it had to happen sooner or later.

I tried to get exempted, using the reputedly effective ruse of 'shrinkage of the mitral heart valve'. It had worked for some of my friends in my year. In vain I consulted two doctors that I knew, other than those already mentioned, to no effect. Rousseau gave me the name of an obliging doctor in Grand Quevilly. I put him in the picture from my angle, without giving him the name of my source. He had a fit. 'Who told you that? You must be mad or what? I have never issued a fake sick note. You are totally misinformed.'

Just like the two others he did not charge me for the consultation.

In my diary for 26 April I wrote about the Katyn story:

'Two weeks ago the Germans announced the discovery near Smolensk of a mass grave containing 12,000 Polish officers. The Polish government in London asked the Red Cross to make an investigation. This enquiry states that

- 300 bodies have been found, 180 identified.
- All killed by a bullet in the back of the head.
- Deaths occurred in 1940.

Moscow raises a formal protest accusing the Germans of perpetrating the massacre.

Here is my personal opinion: given the date of the execution, some months after the end of the campaign against Poland, it cannot be a case of hasty executions of prisoners in the face of a rapid enemy advance. Two hypotheses exist:

1. Moscow offered those officers the choice of joining Soviet ranks. Those who refused were executed at the point of a revolver. Recruitment at gunpoint is not a good method so I go for the second theory.
2. Moscow picked out from the prisoners, former officers of the Russian White army guilty of massacring Communists. An enquiry was held and those found guilty were executed.

There had to be an explanation. There is no reason to execute men like that. Why not others as well?'

At that time I thought and made it abundantly clear even to Roland and Gilbert that Russians were responsible for the massacre. As for the real reasons I was alas far from the truth as confirmed by the recent revelations of Gorbachev.

*Chapter 2*

# Going to Ground

Icontinued to see Renée but for security reasons I never asked her for any service concerning the Resistance. I don't think she would have objected. Our future was really unclear already. The net was tightening. On 18 May almost all my friends had received their call-up to leave for Germany. Mine arrived on 19 May in the form of a travel warrant for Dortmund on Saturday, 22 May. There was clearly no question of my going and a first discussion took place with my parents. My mother, very upset, was in tears, and my father kept repeating, 'You just have to go, just like the others!' They were justifiably afraid of what might happen to me and could already imagine me arrested and shot. I walked out of the room, unable to take it any longer, and went to the German placement office where we had a contact girl in our organization, who provided me with an ID (Ausweis) and blank work certificates.

She changed my allocation to the Paris area. There was in fact a Youth Workshop at Issy-les-Moulineaux which trained young people to be sent to Germany, once they had learned a trade. The course lasted from two to three months and the apprentices were paid the same rate as the workers. The workshop, which came under JOFTA,[1] was managed by the Kellerman centre in Paris. I was housed in the 'Maison du Peuple',[2] requisitioned for this purpose right near the Issy town hall.

The young woman in the placement office let me know that I could send friends of mine to her. I passed that on to all I could get in touch with. For some it was too late, but around twenty were able to take advantage of the offer. The workshop course start was set for Monday, 24 May. This news was a relief for my parents who thought, like me, that before the end of the course a landing would take place.

Fortunately my rendezvous with Gilbert was set before my departure. When I met him he already knew about it and he gave me some new tasks. I was to be active in publicity in the centre so that the greatest number of young people did not leave for Germany. As for safe houses, I was only able to offer them to those who agreed to work for us. Before leaving, Gilbert arranged to meet me the following weekend, with alternative dates in case I could not get leave.

I spent some of Sunday with Réjane and put her in the picture about my clandestine activities and about my departure. I entrusted her with the 588 pages of my diary. She promised to hide it and return it to me at the end of the war and she kept her promise. I could not keep it at home as my mother would have read it if she found it and certainly would have destroyed it.

The youth workshop was a multi-storey building surrounded by welfare housing. The main hall with a boxing ring in the centre had not been adapted. Other rooms on the other hand had been transformed into refectory and dormitories. We numbered at least 150.

The factory where we did our apprenticeship was in a suburb of Issy dominated by high chimneys amid a few remaining green areas. We had the choice of several trade specializations. I chose welding. At the end of the course we were to be sent to Germany to build submarines. We wore the JOFTA uniform, namely big leather boots soled with crampons forged in the workshop which was intended to make them ring out on the road, with baggy trousers, blue overalls, beret and various badges including the 'Francisque'.[3] This outfit was compulsory in the workshop and in town. I quickly realized that it was reminiscent of the LVF[4] and so not well viewed by the Parisians. When we went out in the evening, as we had free time after dinner until curfew, girls avoided us and people in the street gave us a wide berth or gave us false street directions. Some cafés pretended to have run dry so as not to serve us.

At first I changed into civilian kit at the home of Jean's parents some distance from Issy, and then I found a friendly bistro near the workshop which allowed me the same facility. So I came to know the pleasure haunts of Paris. I could get to Pigalle station in twenty minutes without changing metro line.

We were generously paid weekly, receiving twice as much as I earned as a teacher. Life was good. Almost every evening was spent in the major cinemas or night clubs. Some parts of Paris were buzzing at that time. Others on the other hand reeked of fear, misery and hunger. Sometimes the curfew was declared earlier and cinemas were closed because of attacks. All this did not stop me from carrying on my clandestine activities. At the weekend when I got back to Rouen I always had to deliver photos for Gilbert, intended for use in false ID cards. He gave me the finished ones, ration cards, tracts and pamphlets that I discreetly deposited in the effects of their various recipients. On our last course there were some twenty per cent of draft-avoiding youths and I hoped to double that number. Among the trainees were many teacher graduates of the EN, around twenty from Rouen, seminarians from all areas who were given a hard time by some people, a few office workers, some blue-collar workers and even apprentice jockeys! My dealing in false papers began to be known and some pals informed me of the presence of informers in the workshop centre, so I started to take precautions, responding to requests only after I had checked them out and I stopped handing out tracts for the time being.

The training was intense and within a few weeks I was able to weld steel of any thickness, even duralumin, with acceptable results. For my own use I made an aluminium box with compartments in which a dozen eggs could be sent by post. This item was used by my parents for the whole of the war and even afterwards.

Given the uncertainty about my future I made a final trip to Grandcamp to go shell fishing on a day of full spring tide. The Germans had banned fishing on the rocks before Grandcamp for a few months in order to do artillery tests; then, about the time of a spring tide rated 118, the ban was lifted. With my cousins we had a fantastic catch of eighteen lobsters.

To make room for them in the catch baskets, we had to throw back some lesser crabs.

Once a month we were given a leave pass which entitled us to a free rail ticket while in uniform. Otherwise we could travel for a quarter of the normal fare. In order to travel free every week I forged leave passes with the help of correcting fluid. On one trip on the Paris–Cherbourg express, the ticket inspector took a closer look at my pass. I think he must have noticed the slight yellowing of the paper where I had faked the date, but, no doubt influenced by my uniform he said nothing and continued to check other passengers. Perhaps motivated by professional scruples he came back and asked to see my pass again and then, with some hesitation, he said to me that it had been tampered with. I did not deny it, explaining that my family was a long way off and that I was in a Youth Centre, and lacking the means to pay. He charged me the full price and left it at that.

Alas the end of those good times was near. It was after mid-July and the landings we so had hoped for had not happened. I had supplied more than twenty trainees with false papers and ration cards and already some had failed to return from leave. The head of the centre, a demobilised officer and his aide called us together in the main hall and briefed us respectively on the final stages of the course and our imminent departure for Germany. His aide by the name of Lenardi added, 'If some of you don't want to go, take advantage of the next leave without returning, but at least leave the uniforms as the young lads taking your place will need them. Leave them folded on your bed. We will understand.'

Two days after this advice, which left no illusion as to the feelings of our bosses, in the evening on my return, as I was about to change into my uniform at the bistro as usual, the patron warned me that the Gestapo accompanied by soldiers had surrounded the workshop and had taken away everyone inside and set up a trap. I took up position at the subway exit and was able to tip off some of the late arrivals. Then I went to sleep at the house of Jean's parents after dumping the uniform in a trash bin. I later learnt that the director and his aide had managed to get away together with a number of trainees across adjoining roofs, helped by some local residents. It is said that the director was killed in the maquis resistance and, as for his aide, I met up with him later in exceptional circumstances.

Next morning I took the train to Rouen. My return home was marked by a difficult moment. As I packed my bags, my parents, being extremely worried about my future, tried to persuade me to stay (which was impossible after my escape from Issy), or to at least hide at a relative's place. I did not want to share any of my intentions with them. I cut short the leave-taking and left the house as quickly as possible.

In addition to his 7.65mm service revolver, my father had a 6.35mm one which he kept in the drawer of his bedside cabinet. When I tried discreetly to get it, it was not there. He had hidden it, suspecting the worst. I promised them I would write. In fact I sent them two holiday postcards signed Clément, my second name, saying 'Best wishes', both cards posted from a town where I had never set foot.

In anticipation Gilbert had provided me with a ration card and false ID papers. From then on I went under the name of Henry Lenoir. I merged into the clandestine world which in our slang we called the 'Fog'. My destination was Duclair, twenty kilometres from Rouen. On the recommendation of my superior I was to turn up at the place of a certain Engelhard, a horticulturalist who was to organize my lodgings. I set off by bike with my suitcase on the saddlebag rack and I found my contact quickly. He was the local National Front representative and seemed to know everyone in the town. He provisionally placed me outside town limits with the gardener of the Mustad estate. The Mustad family, originally from Norway, owned a factory in Duclair, making horseshoe nails. Some days later, Engelhard found me lodgings with a family in the town.

My room was above a barber shop. I was supposed to be working for the TODT[5] organisation. But my landlady was very discreet and decent and never asked any questions. There were many TODT workers building what were to become V1 launch sites, but we did not know it at the time. These sites brought a flood of workers and technicians. Thus my arrival went unnoticed.

Gilbert came to see me and introduced me to his wife, who liaised with the Duclair section. My new task was to organize the FPJ in the sector. There were about fifteen members in town who knew each other and I was to reorganize them into small cells. Paulette also gave me some contacts known as 'Bases' in surrounding districts. Le Trait, Saint Paul, Saint Pierre de Manneville. She introduced me to the group founder, Rannou, a student in Rouen, and his number two, Legallet, known as 'Mickey', whose mother ran a café near the ferry.

Gilbert let me know that my allocated task was provisional and that he would shortly give me greater responsibility. In the ever likely event of things going badly wrong, he gave me a back-up safe house at the home of the vicar of Monville, Abbé Kérébel.

Paulette was a short energetic authoritarian woman with unpredictable reactions. She suspected police presence everywhere and felt permanently threatened. Shortly after my arrival she was convinced that Rannou was acting for the police. She wanted Mickey and me to 'eliminate' him and we had a hard job making her change her mind. However she seemed to trust me, notwithstanding my father's job. By way of explanation for her ways she told me that she had been denounced and that she had only just escaped being arrested at the right bank railway station, but, endowed with a strength which belied her small stature, she floored the policemen with a kick in the privates and managed to flee.

With Mickey's help I had reorganized the units in Duclair and surroundings but all these youngsters were hungry for something spectacular. So, with the help of Engelhart we found a dump of munitions made up mainly of British anti-tank mines abandoned in a wood a few kilometres from the town. We had stored this in an outbuilding used by the Mustads' gardener. We had planned to use the mines either to blow up the factory, or the electricity transformer supplying the building. This factory was of vital importance to the German army which had a substantial horse-drawn contingent. Moreover the allies had bombed it sometime before.

To find out if the mines were still serviceable I decided to test one of them. They were in the shape of a large cylindrical can like a tin of polish with the big detonator button projecting from it, beneath which were other cans in layers, each containing progressively slower burning charges. There was no risk of one going off in my hands as the detonator spring was blocked by a big copper pin and even a man stepping on it would not have been enough to set it off.

I easily dismantled the smaller cans and set fire to them one by one. As for the detonator, I asked the local blacksmith whom I had got to know for permission to use his workshop which was located next to the ferry loading pier. This area has since been levelled and turned into a parking lot! I secured the detonator in a large vice and give the tit a sharp hammer blow. There was a blue flash and an explosion louder than a rifle shot, which brought the locals out of their houses. The blacksmith bustled me out saying, 'Next time you can do your daft tricks elsewhere!' telling the neighbours that a tyre of his truck had burst while he was pumping it up. I had not imagined that such a small object, no bigger than a pencil, could make so much noise.

There remained the round cans of slow powder, hard and compact, which made up the main body of the mine. I set myself up in a clearing in the Mustad property and set light to it, with some difficulty. At first the stuff burned little by little, giving off black smoke; then as the heat increased, softening the big block of waxy compacted charge, the flames got brighter and the column of smoke rose to about one hundred metres, which was higher than the tallest trees. The gardener arrived, hopping mad, shouting that I would get him shot. He helped me heap grass and freshly cut branches onto the fire to make it look like a brush fire. Indeed the smoke rose less and became whiter.

This experience taught me that the mines recovered were in perfect condition and taught me a lesson in how to handle such items. All the equipment was collected later by Roland and was used by the FTP in various attacks.

Gilbert informed me that the factory sabotage job was not in our brief and was to be carried out by specialists of the FTP. On the other hand, in order to give the younger members in the sector a chance to let off steam, he recommended setting fire to wagons of equipment or to a German depot. He gave us a free hand on condition that we did not use explosives. On hearing the account of my tests he had doubts as to my talents as artificer!

In the news bulletins and tracts of the FPJ intended for young farmers, one key subject was the prevention of exports of wheat to Germany, before any invasion, since we still believed that landings were imminent. At Duclair there was at that time a farm machinery rental business which had several combine harvesters and one of our militants had the idea of setting fire to the hangar where they were stored. From one of my lads I obtained some shotgun cartridge powder and a stick of tinder fungus to ignite it. I filled an empty matchbox with the T powder and trimmed the tinder wick so that it would burn for half an hour before setting off the powder. For the operation, set for Saturday evening, I designated two group leaders, Leconte and Flahaut. They were to light the fuse and hide everything in the straw bales below the hangar, then come to the cinema around intermission time and get themselves noticed. The hangar was to burn during the projection of the A movie, so in that way they would have an alibi.

In fact the hangar burned out and all the combine harvesters were destroyed, but the next day Mickey came to let me know that our two lads had been arrested. What happened was, – they did not want to miss the fire show, so they trimmed the fuse I had prepared for them, allowing only a ten-minute delay. They then took cover in some bushes to watch the fire and only then did they come to the cinema. Unfortunately, in the glow of the fire they were seen, recognized and arrested. They were given prison sentences and one of them, picked up by the Germans, finished the war in Aurigny concentration camp.

Within a few minutes I packed my suitcase, paid my landlady and made off to Monville by bike, after arranging a rendezvous with Mickey for two weeks later in the surrounding woods. I cannot give exact dates for these events since I no longer kept a diary and the press at that time did not report on such attacks.

My stay in Duclair did not last more than two to three weeks and shortly after my arrival an air raid destroyed the shipyards at Le Trait. The wave of bombers passed over the Mustad property and immediately dropped their bombs which I saw falling in clusters. Since this bombing took place on 4 August I estimate my flight to have been around 20 August.

To be sure of finding the abbé in Monville at home I decided not to show up at his place before dusk, so I spent the afternoon in a wood near Pissy-Pôville.

Monville, which is now known as Montville, was at that time not the large dormitory suburb that it has now become. It was a sleepy small town of around 2,000 residents with lots of low houses for workers in the textile industry, which was slowly fading away in that Cailly valley. I had no problem finding the residence of Abbé Kérébel, who lived in a former public school building. He had occupied just half of the staff lodgings; the other half had been occupied by a community of nuns, since disbanded, leaving that part empty.

I rang at the door but another door opened, ajar at first, then slowly wider. The priest explained that as a precautionary measure he never opened the main door so as to give him time to flee in the event of a visit from the 'Gentlemen' from Germany. When I let him know that I had come recommended by Georges (one of Gilbert's code names), his face lit up in a big smile. 'Come in, feel at home, but I wasn't expecting you until early September – for the sake of gossip – but it doesn't matter; you will be my new cousin. The last one left only a week ago and folk may talk.'

The abbot showed me around. Downstairs were the genuine and mock entry doors, the kitchen and larder, and a stairway going to the first floor with two bedrooms, his and mine. One of the windows of my bedroom looked out over the front of the house where I had come in, the other overlooked the playground of the former school, whose class buildings and yard could be seen at the very back. In case of a police alert I could lower myself via this window onto the tin roof of the back kitchen, then vault over the railings to land in the yard, which had a wall with a gate opening onto the street and a side door which enabled one to reach the woods via a series of gardens. I felt safer here than at Duclair.

The bedroom was simply furnished with a wooden bed, wardrobe, bedside table, two chairs and a washstand complete with basin and large jug in the style of Vieux Rouen. After a frugal supper, I fell into a deep sleep. Next morning I was awakened by the sound of a broom banging against the stairs and the abbé's voice saying, 'SSHHH: someone's asleep up there.'

'Someone?' enquired a woman's voice.

'Another cousin.'

'Sir, it's not for me to say, but this "cousin" business, nobody will believe you and you'll end up in trouble....'

Then the sound of voices faded towards the living room but from the tone of voice I could tell that the argument was continuing.

The priest's housekeeper, Madame Ragot, a widow with two children of about 10 years old, who was anxious for the safety of the vicar, took a dim view of the comings and goings of outsiders to his house.

When I came down he introduced me and this good woman very quickly took to me. She confided in me whenever the abbé – 'who would not be bossed around by a woman' – dug his heels in, she would say, 'He's kind, good natured with a heart of gold. He'd do anything to please the children but he's hard headed and no mistake. A real Breton!!! When he sets his mind on something, there's no changing it.'

In fact the abbé did not like women but loved children; especially his housekeeper's which he thought of as his own adopted ones.

He was a square-faced dark-haired good-looking man, ten years older than me. His facial hair was so developed that even after shaving, his chin and cheeks remained swarthy. He was open, uncomplicated and we were on familiar terms[6] from the start. He was not keen on communists whom he considered to be lost sheep, worthy of his prayers, but he hated the Germans through and through, which is why he joined the FN in spite of its communist leanings. For that reason he regretted that our newspapers gave too much propaganda space to the Party.

Next day in Rouen I met Gilbert, who was already aware of the events in Duclair. In those days news about attacks and arrests (which were not covered by the press) spread rapidly by word of mouth in queues or at the workplace. He announced that, in spite of the hesitation of some comrades (still on account of my father's job), he had arranged to have me appointed chief of the FPJ at département level. He had just been appointed regional head (Inter) in charge of seven départements. I was to be directly answerable to him.

He gave me a verbal run-down of the FPJ. The biggest section, Rouen and its suburbs, was the responsibility of Serge, whose real name was Jean Rangée, as I found out later. He introduced me to him some days later. In Rouen there was also a large student branch, created by Georges Touroude, an EN student from the year after mine. We had groups in Le Havre and its suburbs, Elbeuf, Dieppe, Yvetot, La Feuillie, Grand-Couronne, in addition to those in Duclair and Monville. And some bases were endeavoring to set up sub-sections in Yport, Fontaine-le-Dun, Bolbec and Grandes Ventes.

In the next two weeks I made contact, either through Gilbert or Paulette, with the group- and base-leaders. I made a note of these rendezvous, up to three per day, in a small coded diary. For example, 'Thursday 1 pm' was in reality 'Wednesday at 10 am'. The days were plus one and the times were plus three. As for place names they were shifted by one letter of the alphabet, hence Rouen was Q, Quevilly was P, Elbeuf was D, etc. Sometimes I put a name in clear text but in the whole context of the symbols it had no meaning at all. This system proved itself effective in that it was impenetrable to the Gestapo when it fell into their hands.

Gilbert also introduced me to a young lady aged 19 from Monville called Jeanine, acting as a liaison officer. She was the only person who knew my hideout. Her role was crucial in that she was to take my place in rendezvous and, above all, carry material, newspapers, brochures and tracts, with the effect that in case of checks or searches in the town or en route I never had compromising material on me.

As arranged I saw Mickey again in a wood near Duclair. He informed me that there had been no more arrests but the youngsters had cooled down appreciably after the harvester fire affair and that he was holding the fort. I passed him a packet of tracts and newspapers.

For two months I ranged over the whole département, by bike, train or omnibus. The abbé's house was located only a few minutes from the station on the Rouen–Dieppe line; I could be at Rouen right bank station in less than thirty minutes and get connecting trains for anywhere in the département. I was never checked by Germans but I did come under strafing fire.

Early in October, while on my way to Le Havre by the morning diesel train, I suddenly heard the roar of a plane right above our heads. The train immediately juddered to a halt, bringing passengers and luggage to the floor.

Somebody opened the compartment door and, amidst the panic and high-pitched women's screams, I dove down onto the track with my fellow travellers. Sadly there was no platform and the track was somewhat higher than the surrounding field level, so that in falling my hand hit a stone and was injured. The train was at a standstill and passengers continued to jump out of the carriages. The driver and fireman jumped out in turn and rolled into the field. Some seconds later two British planes buzzed low over our heads attacking the train with machine gun and cannon fire, riddling the locomotive with their bullets only to disappear after making a second pass.

Our loco, holed in several places, gave up its steam with a whistle. A number of passengers had hurt themselves in their hurried jumps. One person, who seemed to know what to do, started to group them according to their first-aid needs. Many were just bruised or in shock. My hand was hurting and I thought it was not serious; however the next day, since it had swollen, I went to the surgery of a doctor in Monville who put it in a splint as I had broken a metacarpal bone. Our arrival in Le Havre was delayed as we had to wait for a recovery train to arrive, coming from Rouen.

My main contact apart from Gilbert was Jean Rangée. He was a gifted organizer. Within a few weeks, working from the hospital bursar's office, he had targeted several sections of the administration, with the help of some young people of equal commitment, creating cells of the FPJ in the Public Treasury, the Highways department, the Prefecture, the welfare department and even in the offices of German labour recruitment. His group leaders had been as busy as worker bees creating new colonies in major administrative hubs. On the other hand we made no headway among young factory workers who were mostly organized into sections of the YC (Young Communists). Later they joined forces with the FTP to form the FUJP (United Front of Patriotic Youth), but when I took over the leadership of the movement, it was in its infancy. I think that, for their part, they were reluctant to mix with those white-collar folk whom they wrongly considered to be young bourgeois.

The student branches of the FPJ tried to keep a certain independence. Rangée and I had overcome many obstacles to get them onboard. In the same way, young Christians, coming from the JAC and the JOC (Jeunesse Agricole and Jeunesse Ouvrière Chrétienne),[7] both being banned, and a group of young protestants, and even a section of 'Equipes Nationales' set up on Pétain's initiative, came over to us after discussion.

Paper, being very restricted in supply and not on sale, was not a problem for us as each one of our members could supply us with small quantities from their sources in the civil service. It was the same for stencils and blank documents of all kinds, work permits, passes to forbidden zones and more.

Our newspaper, called *Espoir du jeune Patriote Normand*[8] – *Espoir* for short – increased in circulation, rising to two, three and even five thousand copies for some issues, and it was quickly distributed. Its quality, with the civil service paper, got better. The same was true of tracts of all kinds, especially those against departures to Germany, and others, written in German, destined to undermine the military and encourage them to desert; we dropped these documents at barrack gates.

Rangée had done a simple illustration on a poster in the campaign to collect 500 grams of bread for young people. It was stuck on city lampposts with glue normally issued to town halls. To raise funds we printed victory bonds in values of five and ten francs, overprinted with a capital letter 'V'. Our newspapers of August and September 1943 were all Roneo printed with stencils from the civil service, but it was not easy as we did not have full editorial control of the paper. The stencil was set up for printing and handed to me by Gilbert and was not always in line with the activities we planned. Some articles were deleted and others added and neither Rangée nor I went along with that. I had several serious talks with Roland and Gilbert in which I made it clear to them that, if we were to rally the maximum number of young people, our articles should be drafted in the spirit of our movement; the Communist party had its own paper called *L'Avenir Normand*[9] and the YC had their own called *Avant Garde*. They gave me their word that for the October edition I would have complete control of the stencil make up.

I saw Roland about every ten days to provide him with safe houses that our guys had arranged and also to pass on, whenever necessary, the contacts with potential new members of the FTP. For example, my section leader for La Feuillie passed me three men around 30 years old who had been sleeping in a forester's hut for several days so as to avoid being sent to Germany. I provided them with a decent safe house before passing them on to Roland.

The organizations under Communist control were ring-fenced. This was good for their security but it was difficult for us to pass from one structure to the other, difficult to pass a man on to the FN, and vice versa. In an emergency one had to wait for the next rendezvous. It happened that I lost contact when, because of illness, my opposite number missed the usual meeting and the following rendezvous. I had to go up one level to the comrade who had given me the initial contact details in order to restore the link.

In all these comings and goings I stayed at the abbé's house. We would breakfast together at his place but at midday if I was not absent we ate lunch at his housekeeper's place in town. As for the evening meal, it was a relaxing time. The priest was invited by a number of parishioners who out of politeness could not but extend the dinner invitation to his 'cousin'. We often went to a home where there were four daughters whom we used to tease. The priest was known for his appetite and those evening meals were heavy, too much so for me. On leaving he would say, 'It was like a wedding banquet.'

On the road I mostly ate at midday at black market restaurants paying over the odds. They served burgers and fries or Coq au Vin without the need for ration tickets. To cover my expenses and rent for the priest, Gilbert allocated me 3,000 francs per month which represented double my teacher's pay.

Sometimes I was obliged to stay overnight. In Le Havre my contact, Marcel Julliot, still legally free to be in France, took me to his grandmother's with whom he lived. The good lady with an ever-open door would make up a bed, warning her grandson, 'You'll end up getting arrested with the life you lead. And what'll become of me then? You're all I have. The other day he brought three of them. He's always bringing people home.'

For us 'illegals' it was impossible to go to a hotel as the registrations were checked by the police. In Rouen when I missed the train for Monville I stayed overnight in Champ des Oiseaux street at the home of a pal in my year who had a deferral from STO duty; he was a country teacher, and so his room at home was free. His mother knew that I was in hiding to avoid being sent to Germany for labour service, but nothing more than that. One day as I was getting ready to leave after breakfast she said to me with an air of mystery, 'a gentleman wants to see you.' It was my father, who hugged me with tears in his eyes. In the flurry of my hectic life I had omitted to send them a card since leaving Duclair and they were very worried. My classmates had been indiscreet enough to let it be known that I sometimes slept there and my father had come by for any news of me. By chance he crossed paths with me.

I did not want to get emotional. I told him all was going well, that I had a hideout on a farm and that I would write, and then I made the excuse of having a train to catch in order to slip away as soon as possible. In my hurry I left a satchel containing several blank printed documents, work permits, IDs and others that Rangée had given me. I returned to get it some hours later. On giving it to me my host said to me in a different tone of voice, 'You know Paul, I won't be able to take you in any more. I'm expecting a lady cousin from Le Havre, who has nowhere to live.'

I realised she had opened the satchel and I said so to her. She did not deny it. 'You understand I have a family. It's too risky.'

In addition my father's intrusion had not reassured her. Too many people knew that I stayed overnight at her house. I understood and thanked her for her past hospitality. I hugged her and left.

## Chapter 3

# Turbulent Arrest in Monville

An event took place at the beginning of September which was to have major repercussions. During a working meeting, Rangée let me know that he had a rendezvous in the town hall gardens, with a certain Lefèvre who had given refuge to a parachutist who was hoping to find a network to get him back to England. This contact had been passed on to him by a group leader in Darnétal. I advised him to attend the rendezvous. I myself would be sitting on a bench to weigh up the guy. According to what he had to say I would decide on the follow-up or not to these contacts.

The next day, one hour before the meeting I was to see Touroude to deal with various questions of organization with him, notably the closer monitoring of our student groups. At the end of our conversation I asked him to come with me to the town hall gardens so that he could weigh up this Lefèvre person whose story seemed suspect to me. At the arranged time Rangée arrived followed by Lefèvre. Touroude and I were sitting on a bench appearing to read a newspaper. The two participants passed quite near us several times deep in conversation. Lefèvre, wearing a raincoat, was a young tall blond guy of about our age with slicked hair and an expressionless countenance. After fifteen minutes of discussion he went off in the direction of Rue Orbe and Rangée came to join us.

He explained that Lefèvre had introduced himself as a new member of the Prosper group in Paris, that he had the means to print our posters and newspapers and to provide us with American weapons. In exchange he was looking for a network to pass an American airman that he was protecting, to Spain. The story seemed unlikely to me and I ordered Rangée to cut off all contact with this suspect individual, by not attending the arranged rendez-vous. Since Lefèvre did not have his contact details there was no risk.

Shortly afterwards on September 12 Bucard, leader of the Francistes, accompanied by uniformed militants from the Paris region, was to parade in Rouen before making a speech at the Circus. Rangée asked my permission to organize a counter-demo with his lads, somewhat similar to what we had spontaneously done at the Normandy cinema on the visit of Doriot. I gave my permission on the condition that it should be done on the streets and not at the Circus as our lads could be surrounded in a trap there. We prepared bundles of tracts for the FPJ against departures to Germany, bonds for the 500 grams of bread for young people, and above all for the commemoration of the battle of Valmy which fell on 20 September.

At the location set for the counter-demonstration there were far fewer young folk than anticipated, but some small groups shouted out antagonistic slogans against the chanting of 'Bucard will win' by the uniformed militants. Their stewardship was outnumbered. There were some scuffles during which some veterans who had refused to doff their caps before the flag were pushed to the ground and kicked. Our lads took advantage of this to throw their tracts into the air and melt away. No one was arrested.

The vicar was not inactive. He had set up a small group with a few young people in his JAC group. He did not know anything of its composition but he told me they were willing. Moreover he helped me to restore an old Roneo machine that I had picked up in Rouen from one of our militants. Transporting this device had given me a few problems. I had simply loaded it into a jute sack surrounded by swedes and turnips which made it all the heavier. I had missed the last train for Monville and was unable to turn up at Rue du Champ des Oiseaux, above all with such a burden on my back. I decided to seek refuge at the home of a classmate from my year, recently married, who knew I was in the 'Fog'; I also knew his wife. The couple gave me a cold reception, refusing to take me in for the night, or even take my bag for safekeeping. I found myself on the street shortly before curfew. I was lucky to find refuge for the night with an acquaintance who asked no questions.

This lack of safe house in Rouen was a great nuisance for me and led me to take risks. I told Gilbert about the Roneo incident and he gave me one to be used only in an emergency. After that I was careful to note my last train times and never needed to use the address given to me.

My superior, who was very pleased with the rapid increase in the ranks of the FPJ, asked me to set up a triangular organisation at the top, since I alone could not cover all responsibilities and all liaison duties even with Jeanine's help. Rangée agreed to be a part of it. He would take over the sector of Duclair and Elbeuf, in addition to the area of greater Rouen, and would also run the newspaper. My Dieppe region representative, who I believe also ran a youth hostel, seemed to me to be the best person qualified to be the third man. He assumed responsibility for the northern and central département, where we had numerous bases.

Our first and only meeting took place in a wood near Clères. I briefed our comrades on the département scene as a whole and we debated the future of the movement. I was the only communist; Rangée was a Gaullist and our friend from Dieppe was inclined towards socialism. We fixed a date for the next meeting for 15 October.

Time for allied landings had also gone by so many months of struggle lay ahead of us. If some groups being rather inactive were not unhappy with this delay, others could not understand why their instructors had not taught them any weapons drill. As for weapons, we did not have any, as Roland and Gilbert had confirmed, but we could not tell them that. But in essence they were right. Some of our best elements left us for organisations which had some.

At the beginning of October the abbé introduced me to a 'great friend', Étienne Roche, who had just sold him a second-hand piano. Shortly after that I was perturbed to learn that the vicar had let him in on my activities. It was the cause of our first argument. He swore then to speak to no one else about me. Roche lived with his parents in Anceaumeville near Monville. He travelled a lot either to Rouen or to Paris where, he said, he was working on a film called Mont Renoir. Moreover he lent me the script for a few days. He even offered me a safe house in case of emergency in a chateau where he was a regular guest in the region.

He had introduced his new friend Abbé Kérébel to the Stein-Blankarts, fashionable photographers of the Rue Jeanne d'Arc in Rouen, who held a salon every Monday. The vicar came back delighted with those he had met there: Madame Lion, a language professor at the Rey Institute; Mr Turin, parliamentary assistant to Deputy André Marie; Juliette Billaud, architect; Nicolle Automne, artist; Lemonnier-Leblanc, a lawyer; Canon Delepouve, related by marriage to General De Gaulle and, to everyone's misfortune, a certain Mr Baudry whose father was a farmer at Le Mesnil-Esnard.

I was wary of the abbé's chat and even more so of Roche who recounted to me his life history in chunks when I journeyed with him in the railcar going to Rouen. He was known in Paris before the war in literary circles under the pen-name of Jean de Chavanneau. Then in 1941 he had been a police secretary in Rouen which besides is how he came in contact with the photographers during a routine enquiry. But, being disgusted, as he told me, with the activities of the police under Alie[1] and not being cut out for that sort of work he had joined the office of vegetable oil production staff of Rouen city hall. He often took young people from Monville on visits to Paris and I was convinced he was a homosexual.

Very much aware of the risks I ran from the gossip of the abbé and Roche, I requested a change of safe house from my chief. He directed me to the vicar of Pissy Pôville not far from Monville. Meanwhile the abbé, as ever mesmerized with his new friends, supplied them with food, butter and cream via a young person in his circle whom he called 'my young commissioner'. At the beginning of October, it was via him that the Stein-Blankarts passed a message to the abbé. They asked him to come and see him without fail on Monday, 11 October, as they had something important to communicate.

In the evening of 11 October when the abbé came back to Monville he told me that his friends had warned him to be wary of Roche, a chatterbox who was unreliable, who told them he was hiding a resistance leader. Baudry was present at the meeting, and backed up the photographers, but at the same time he had expressed a wish to see me as, being in the resistance himself, he had a pilot in need of cover.

On hearing this I had a fit. Baudry, on top of the Roche affair, was too much. This time I just had to leave my safe house. Nevertheless I decided to see him again. If I agreed to this visit, 'the young commissioner', in the course of his deliveries, was to place a note from the abbé in the Stein-Blankart's letterbox.

The meeting took place in the afternoon of 12 October at the house of Mme Ragot. Surprise, surprise! The person in question was none other than Lefèvre, the individual that Rangée had stopped seeing after the meeting in the city hall park. He recounted roughly the same story, i.e. he belonged to a group called Prosper and was looking for a network to pass airmen back to Britain. He seemed much taken up with money matters. He asked me if I charged money for false ID papers and if I had a fund set aside to support the STO dodgers. To gain time, as I was no longer in any doubt that he was a Gestapo agent, I suggested a meeting with FTP leaders in front of Bois-Guillaume town hall.

After he left around 4 pm I tore a strip off the abbé, relating the whole episode of the city hall park and I made it clear that we could not stay in Monville. For her part Madame Ragot had checked out the cycle registration plate; it was in the name of André Prieur.

I rapidly crammed some of my things into a suitcase, especially the archives of the movement, and set off for Pissy Pôville, making sure I was not being followed. The parish priest drove me to Mme Duclos – my new landlady. I dumped my load in my room and went back to Monville, ten kilometres away, in order to collect what remained, i.e. paper, a bundle of newspapers and above all the Roneo machine. It was late and I was afraid

I could not get to my new safe house in time for curfew. I decided to wait until first light the next morning. The abbé himself had decided to stay. He did not think the risk was so great, saying he could not 'abandon his parishioners'.

That evening for our last meal together we went to dine at the house of the four girls. I found it hard to mask my unease. The abbé seemed unaware of the threat hanging over us and as usual he dined with gusto and teased the girls. On the way back I tried to convince him but nothing I said could make him change his mind.

I planned to leave early and set my alarm accordingly, but it was not that which woke me but the door bell ringing around seven o'clock. That was not unusual at the priest's house at any hour. I heard a door being opened followed by silence with no voice to be heard. I got up, on the alert. Suddenly there was a knock at my door without the prior sound of footsteps on the stairs. This time I was scared and, pulling on my trousers, I said, 'Is that you, abbé?' There was no answer. I looked out of the window overlooking the front of the house and glimpsed military helmets and dark trench coats. The Gestapo! There were more knocks at the door, which was fortunately locked, and a voice from east of the Rhine said, 'Open up!'

I grabbed a fistful of pamphlets, the rest of my clothes and shoes, and quietly opened the window giving onto the rear of the house while the door was noisily hammered. I jumped out onto the galvanized roof over the back kitchen and landed in the courtyard after dropping two metres and jumping three metres to clear the fence. Unfortunately, being hindered by all the stuff I was carrying I landed on my coccyx and remained semi-paralyzed for a few seconds. I could hear the bedroom door being smashed in and the guttural sounds of the German police. I crept along the fence keeping low to avoid being seen, to get to the door which opened onto the gardens. I was gripped by fear and my spine was terribly painful. I opened this door and saw a German soldier aiming a machine gun. He shouted to warn the others while I closed the door and bolted but he did not open fire. They were doubtless under orders to take me alive. My head cleared and I made my way, limping, to the main gate giving onto the road leading to the cemetery which, when I reached it, began to shake violently. This time my game was up. I slipped my roll of documents under a pile of planks just as the gate collapsed a few metres from me. Two soldiers pinned me to the wall, frisked me and brought me back to the house with blows to my body.

After putting on the 'Massenottes',[2] my guards led me, with my arms behind my back, into the dining room filled with ten or so plain clothes police and SS in uniform. The abbé, whose cassock they had pulled off, was in his trousers. For calling them bastards he received a volley of punches and kicks. For these few moments they paid no attention to me and I took advantage of that to remove my wallet from my back pocket and slip it between the sideboard and the wall. It contained some ration cards, my meeting diary and four photos intended to be attached to false ID papers. Two had been given to me by the section head of La Feuillie and two others I had received from the abbé.[3]

It was my turn for a beating. 'Where's the money? Where's the suitcase?' So they knew that I had left the evening before with a suitcase. The kicks to the kidneys gave me great pain. I must have cracked a vertebra in the fall. I shouted, 'It's upstairs.' I was immediately yanked from the sideboard against which I was leaning and, under a hail of blows from my aggressors, they made me go upstairs into the bedroom whose door had been forced open. They pounced on the suitcase, evidently empty, and angrily yelled with a fresh hail of blows, 'Where's the money? Where are the explosives? Where's the stash?'

In the space of a few seconds the level of terror was notched up. In his disappointment at not finding weapons nor FTP members, a soldier of some rank, indicated by his peaked cap, pounded my face, breaking two teeth, causing a stream of blood from my nose over my shirt and onto the floor. He ordered a soldier to bring a basin of water and sponge my face before the next round. The window had remained open and for a few seconds I had visions of taking the big leap to freedom or death. Sadly, under the force of the blows I had taken, I was no longer capable.

The shouts now came from the ground floor. Down below, the abbé yelled that he knew nothing, that he had nothing to say, and that they were all bastards. The house was not spared; it shook with axe blows as cupboards and wardrobes were smashed. Wallpaper and textiles were torn down, armchairs and mattresses were gutted.

My nose bleed had stopped. The interpreter, called Kubler, gave me a lecture on how it was in my interest to talk, then the French police inspector, Alie, (these two I was later to identify) pushed forward a packet of newspapers, titled *Francs-Tireurs Normans et Picards*, and a draft of a poster for 11 November, items they had just found under a pile of wooden planks where I had thrown them, and he said to me, 'Don't be dumb. Talk! Otherwise they'll beat you up and you'll end up by talking. Use your sense.'

In fact a big ruddy type started to hit me again while the interpreter screamed, 'The leader, where is the ringleader? Where are the explosives? Where's the money?' I fainted. A bucket of water brought me round. I was out of handcuffs. On the landing I could distinguish the old village vicar whom they had fetched and who knew nothing of our activities. He swore he had nothing to do with the affair and that the abbé was genuine clergy. An SS officer pushed the fistful of newspapers under his nose and yelled, 'Fake clergy'. He tried to protest but a powerful blow spun him round into a fall down the stairway.

Suddenly there was jubilation down below. They had found my wallet with the photos, the meetings diary, and ration cards. So the next round of horror began in earnest. A soldier with stripes of rank had pulled a board from the door and hit me again and again, spurred on by the sight of blood pouring from my mouth nose and forehead, yelling, 'Who is the ringleader? Who is the chief?' Just then I realised that my life was at an end and that this big swine was going to kill me with the plank.

Suddenly an idea popped into my head. I started to shout, pointing my finger at something imaginary in the manner of the delirium scene in the film *L'Assommoir* that I had recently seen in a cinema club. I shouted, my eyes bulging. The plank stopped its course in mid-air while half a dozen SS watched me perform my mad act. One of them pitched another bucket of water at me and I cowered in a corner trembling, wild eyed, and pointing at an animal that seemed to be coming to devour me; in the film it is a rat and for a moment I thought I could actually see it and my torturers also looked in its direction.

After some exchange of views they left me in a corner and continued their work of destruction, ripping up floorboards and sounding the walls. From time to time the vicar gave out a groan. The big brute came back with his stick and I began to shake and drool again. This time they seemed to have stopped searching. Anyway they had everything: newspapers, the meeting diary, photos, and ration cards. Some SS started bundling up linen; others filled my suitcase with trinkets, knick knacks, silverware and even clocks. Their leader ordered me to be completely covered in a sheet, after handcuffing me, this time with my hands in front of me. I sensed that they took me down to the ground floor, that we crossed the yard and I was bundled into a truck.

I relaxed while the vehicle travelled, taking me to an unknown destination. I took stock of my situation, as I was tossed about wrapped in my shroud. They had proof of my FPJ activities and my contacts in the Communist Party and the FTP, but they had not found any weapons. By faking madness I had avoided the worst, but for how long? I hoped to be put in an asylum or a hospital, from where I would try to escape, but my act would not stand close scrutiny by an expert.

After a journey of about half an hour, over cobbled streets and tramway lines, the vehicle stopped and I was carried with head lowered before being dumped onto a carpet or a bed. The sheet and rope were removed and I found myself in a sort of cellar on a sofa, surrounded by civilians and military personnel. I stared straight ahead and tried to breathe without moving my chest. One of the men put a mirror in front of my lips, shook me and said in a strong German accent, 'We've got you. Stop fooling around.'

With two hands I pointed to a spot on the floor, to which all eyes turned. This spot seemed to move to a corner where there was nobody and suddenly I yelled, 'The black man!' and I started to shout, as in Monville.

My torturers, having shackled my ankles with Massenottes and tightened those on my wrists, left the cell. I took stock of it, without moving since there was a spy hole in the door where an eye lingered from time to time. It was about five metres square. Besides the sofa there was a slop bucket without a lid, which smelled of urine and a cellar window with two dividing bars opening at floor level onto a small closed yard. I had no idea where I was. I tried to think, but being exhausted with stress, I dozed fitfully, often startled by the click of the spyhole cover. I could pick out the muffled sounds of the street, cars, trucks, and horses. As night fell an NCO came to check the security of my handcuffs, and I fell into a deep sleep.[4]

The next day it was fully daylight when I woke. My head hurt and my face was so swollen that I could see my cheek but worst of all was the sharp pain in the coccyx. I had the impression my lower back was paralysed and my night was a total nightmare. It was brought home to me by the pain of the cuffs biting tightly into my wrists and ankles. The street had come back to life. How good it would have been to be a simple passer-by in the comings and goings.

Emerging when wakening is such a wonderful thing when all is well. If only I could wind back the clock a few days and enjoy the smell of breakfast prepared by the abbé, wafting up to my room. I kicked myself for being so naïve as to get myself arrested so stupidly. In addition to my cheek I could also see my forehead, and the numbness of my back was spreading down to my legs.

In the corridor some French women were chatting about Otto, or Frank…I could hear the movement of bucket and brooms. Doubtless they were cleaning ladies. I painfully pulled myself to the door with the idea of talking to them, but they were possibly scrubbers who would grass on me to the Jerries, so I did nothing and slumped back onto the grubby mattress. I tried to put together a case for my defence which would hold water.

Later in 1947 in my presence in a train from Rouen to Amiens a passenger was recounting to another the Monville saga in his fashion, adding, 'The vicar and the young man fought the Boche right into the church steeple.' At that point I intervened and told the narrator that it had not happened like that.

'But sir,' he replied, 'I am from Monville.'

'That may be so, but the young man was me!'

I could not deny I was FPJ head for the département nor that I was in touch with the FTP but I could give false rendezvous and fake indications. Who had been arrested apart from the abbé and me? Had they identified the youths of Monville whose photos I was carrying?

At midday a guard brought me a plate of lamb with beans. I was extremely hungry, having not eaten for 36 hours. I sampled a few mouthfuls of the beans and ate a slice of lamb from under the others, so as to give the impression I had not eaten. When the soldier came back he was surprised. In German he told me it was good and tried to get me to eat some. I lifted myself up and pointed to something he had not seen before, a sight which I too could not see. I must have been a terrible sight with my beaten-up face and mad look. He picked up the plate and beat a hasty retreat.

In the afternoon I was visited by a doctor who asked me in broken French where I had pain as if he could not see my swollen face. I began my mad act. When he left shaking his head, I was exhausted and wondered if I would really become mad by continuing the farce. For the best part of the afternoon I heard shouts from the floor above and moans from a nearby cell.

Towards 7 pm I picked up the smell of soup brought by the guard. He put it on the bedside table, took off the handcuffs, left the door open and seemed to go upstairs. I sensed it was a trap. In fact he came back a few moments later, but I had not moved and I looked at him blankly. I sensed the onset of a fever and was seized with thirst yet did not want to ask him for anything.

I was dropping of to sleep when two officers, one of whom at least was present at my arrest, burst into my cell. This time I could not stand it any longer and asked for a drink. The brought me a big lemonade bottle filled with chilled water, which I gulped down in one, staring and pointing at the 'Black Man'. One of them, the one present at Monville, looked at me with pity. He had a discussion with the other in German and left with his companion after checking my cuffs.

After an endless feverish night, I was awakened by the chattering cleaners, nattering about Otto. According to their chatter I gathered that at least one of them was sleeping with this Jerry. In the morning the SS brought in new prisoners and I seemed to recognise the voice of Rangée. At midday I ate a little. After the meal the jailer led me to the washroom. In the mirror I could see the full horror of my battered face and my wild eyes. This time I pretended to be afraid of my face. He explained that it was me and tried to calm me down. Those few steps had renewed my coccyx pain but my legs seemed less numb.

In the evening at nightfall two SS men I had never seen before came to fetch me and in spite of the pain it caused me, they made me climb the staircase without any consideration, and pulled me to a door opening onto the street. Then I recognised the place because of the Jeanne d'Arc tower close nearby: I had been locked up in the Gestapo headquarters in Rue du Donjon. I was pushed into a waiting car, while some passers-by pretended not to look and hurried on by with quickening pace.

I was gripped by the cold and my teeth were chattering. The car set off in the direction of Place Cauchoise after crossing Rue Jeanne d'Arc which was as busy as ever. In a few minutes we arrived at Hotel Dieu, which since the occupation had been transformed into a military hospital. Perhaps I would find a way of escaping?

Via corridors and dark archways I was hauled to a small building which seemed calm, dappled in light and accompanied by soft music of an exotic kind which reminded me of the 1937 exhibition. An old German in a white coat, festooned with keys which jangled with his every move, led the way. He opened a small cell and closed it behind me. By feeling my way I came across a soft bed with sheets and blankets.

The room was well heated and I fell asleep quickly in the white sheets. It was my first quiet night since my arrest. The warmth, the soft bed, the renewed tranquillity made me think of my parents who still knew nothing of my fate. I could picture my mother making pancakes, my sister with her nose in her homework and my father whose scolding I now missed, weeding his garden, and for the first time since Monville I cried. I fell asleep with the heaviest of hearts.

As soon as it was light, and my depression had lifted, I rapidly took stock of the place. The window bars were protected by a solid grill and the door to the corridor was closed with a security lock. No chance of escape. In any event how could I find the way out in such a labyrinth of corridors? I was probably in the psychiatric wing. In the room were two small hospital beds, a chair, a bedside table and a chamber pot.

I lay down and closed my eyes to recall the falsified system of noting down my superiors' names and places for rendezvous. Thus when interrogated I could always tell the same story. A short time later a guard brought me a bowl of good coffee and three slices of German bread with jam. Quickly I downed it all, thinking that an empty stomach would not help me, and then two male nurses came in to collect me for a bath. They undressed me and pushed me into hot water. When I got out of the bath, all the walls began to move and I fainted. I came to on my bed as the nurses were slapping my face with cold wet towels. I began to cry again. It was depression time again, the sort where you look for a nail on which to hang a rope. I was seized with panic. Was I really slipping into madness? I could not keep up this farce for much longer. I fell asleep to the sound of piano music coming from the guard room.

At midday they brought me some soup with beef and vegetables, and then I fell asleep until afternoon coffee, served with slices of bread and cheese. Then again I fell into a deep sleep.

The next day must have been Sunday, 17 October, since I could hear the church bells ringing for Mass. In the course of the afternoon a doctor gave me a physical and tested my reflexes with various gadgets. I tried not to have any but I did not think it helped my cause. My blood-stained shirt intrigued him. He questioned me in German and the guards translated my answers. In the evening two Feldgendarmes[5] checked the windows and took my clothes away. Rummaging in the bed frame joints I came across a pencil lead, a nail, a padlock key and a piece of a razor blade. I hid this precious treasure. The razor blade above all seemed like a gift from the gods. It would enable me to slit my wrists if I felt that I could not stand up to torture.

The following day in the afternoon I was visited by two people: one was a Gestapo officer, the other an interpreter. I decided to have done with my madness scenario which would only hasten my execution.

From the outset however the officer made it clear that the treatment received at Monville would not be repeated. He then launched into a long speech of which I recall that I, as an intelligent and idealistic student, was prey to the communists who used us, my friends and me, only to betray us. As a result, our interest, mine especially, was to work with them and help them to unmask the leaders.

I poured out my story, rehearsed during the long hours of solitude, which ran thus: I was ready to help them but I had no names or addresses; I could only give them indications and rendezvous details. Then they pulled out my coded note book, but as the dates and times were shifted they could get nothing from it. To indicate the head of the FPJ, I gave the name of Baudry. By his reaction I gathered that it was he who was responsible for our arrests.

I also informed him that, if he had delayed my arrest until the Saturday, he could have rounded up the regional FTP at my meeting with Baudry in Bois-Guillaume. He replied with a German proverb: 'A bird in a cage is worth two on the roof,' adding, 'You, at least, I have caught!'

He told me that Rangée had been arrested with all the section leaders and that the Rouen FPJ had been dismantled. He finished by saying, 'Think about it. If you want to save your companions, you'll have to work with us. We'll be back to see you.'

I spent a further four days in hospital, eating well, regaining strength, as my face got back into shape. The swellings went down slowly, turning black then brown. I had yellow marks over my body. The base of my spine gave me pain, but the numbness in my legs disappeared.

I kicked myself again and again for returning to Monville for the night. Why did I not heed the advice of Roland and Gilbert? I thought I was better than the Gestapo agents, and through my carelessness I risked my life. The more I thought about it the worse my situation seemed and with that my chances of coming out of it intact.

On Friday the 22nd at midday the nurses brought me my clothes in the state I had left them, dirty and bloodstained, and the Gestapo officer, flanked by his faithful interpreter, came for me, handcuffed me and took me to Bonne Nouvelle jail. On the way they asked me if I had thought it over. I replied that I could not betray my comrades. The senior officer renewed his promise that I would not be beaten again, adding, 'We have other ways of making you talk, and talk you will, you'll see.'

The Bonne Nouvelle prison was not unknown to me. I had often walked by its sinister high silhouette as I went down Jean Rondeaux Boulevard. Moreover, my father, being involved in prison transfer and induction, had taken me there and the gatekeeper had allowed him to show me the yard and buildings. I was even able to glimpse some prisoners with shaven heads in prison uniform and clogs.

On arriving I did not have the same impression as my memory, since the Germans had for some time made their mark on the place. I was searched roughly and all my belongings were impounded in the induction process, including my belt, laces and shoes, and the key and nail that I had found in the hospital, even though I had slipped them into the double turn-up of my trousers. The pencil lead and the piece of razor blade that I had placed in the lining of my jacket were not picked up in the search.

The German key master, big tall and ugly as an ape, with hands like carpet beaters, led me across the garden to the section which the Germans had reserved for their purposes in the wing of the prison running along Jean Rondeaux Avenue. The entrance was independent of the French wing which also included the main gate.

We went into the kitchen where some German soldiers in drill kit were busy (I learned afterwards that they were also prisoners). Once past the kitchens the guard unlocked a door which led us into a sort of large hall or interior yard onto which ground floor cells opened. The cells on the upper two floors opened onto gangways overlooking the yard. Access to them was by a stairway as narrow as a lighthouse stairway, closed at the base by a massive wooden door with a big lock.

The Gorilla (as I nicknamed him) stopped in front of cell 11 on the second floor almost at the end of the passage. He opened the lock of the armoured door with a huge key and a dull sound rang out twice throughout the building. Then he held out to me a mess tin and a blanket and the door closed on me like a tombstone. I entered what, for six months, was to be my universe.

## *Chapter 4*

# **Bonne Nouvelle Prison**

T he cell, which was more like a cellar, measured 3.5 by 2 metres and was lit by a skylight set at the highest point in the ceiling, which was over 3 metres high. This inward opening skylight, protected by two thick bars, enabled me to reckon that the outside wall was almost one metre thick. To the left on entering was a fixed bunk built into the wall with screwed-down boards, covered in a big jute straw-filled sack.

On one side of the door there was a small central heating radiator and on the other, behind an iron trap door closed with a latch, there was a completely rusty slop tin, with sharp edges, smelling of disinfectant, which fitted into a space in the wall. This wall niche was closed off by a thick steel plate. The door had, in addition to the usual spyhole, an opening big enough for a mess tin. This was always closed.

The wall paint, in shades of ochre and brown, long since unpainted, was blistering with saltpetre blisters, flaking and scratched with graffiti. In the early days I spent my time deciphering these and other drawings which were mostly obscene. In them I found first names, dates, and the beginnings of a calendar which I decided to continue. I reckoned it was Friday, 22 October 1943. I got confirmation of it at morning exercise the following day.

The rules were posted up. In particular I read that I was not allowed to use the bunk during daytime and that I was to stand to attention at the end of the cell if the door was opened. About an hour after my arrival one of the guards did his round. I could hear the sound of hobnail boots, then with every pause at a cell door, the short click of the spyhole being opened, then a few more steps until he arrived at mine. After the click I could see the pupil of his eye and that Cyclops-like door set off an anxiety renewed with every round of the guard, which took place without a set pattern every two to three hours.

I deduced that my cell, not receiving any sunlight even if the sky was blue, was north facing. I tried to jump to grab the bars but I was twenty centimetres short of reaching them. There was indeed a solid heavy table and chair on the side opposite the bunk but they were fixed to the wall with a thick chain mortared in place and for this reason I could not move them nearer to the skylight. I lay the chair on its side and by balancing on the chair-back I managed to reach the bars. After a painful hike up, I could make out Jean Rondeaux Avenue, the movement of cars, the guardhouse, the perimeter wall and even the movement of the locomotives shunting in the Orleans railway sidings. Later when I wanted to see outside I used the slop can to hike up with, which proved much easier.

Towards 6 pm there was an unusual movement in the corridor as if a large object was being hauled. I heard the two cells before mine being opened, then, at my door they shouted, 'Mess tin! Coffee!' and two Germans in fatigues pulling a huge urn filled my mess tin with a blackish liquid and handed me two slices of very dark German bread, weighing not more than 200 grams in total, in the centre of which was stuck a knob of butter. It was the evening meal. I found the bread awful and badly baked. I first ate the edges of the slice with the butter and then with what remained I made symbolic chess pieces. This took some time and filled up the rest of my day.

Later at curfew time I could hear muffled voices coming through the central heating pipes, but could not distinguish the words. At one moment someone tapped on a pipe with a metal object and after a short silence I could pick out some words.

'Bastard ! Pile of filth! You'll get it one day! Your time will come.'

It lasted more than fifteen minutes. The message could not be for me, but if not me, who was it intended for?

I spent a fitful night because of the hundreds of fleas that came to feed on the fresh blood and because of the guard's rounds which happened every three hours. The light went on; I heard the click and then after some time the spy hole closed and the light went out. The guard did not switch off without being sure that I still moved, so subsequently I raised an arm which cut the duration of the light.

Around 6.30 was the time for the stirrings of waking up in the prison, the noises of mess tins, coffee urns, the double clatter of bolts and coffee being served. The insipid morning drink was not accompanied by a slice of bread. A short while later I heard the cell door opening and, as I was new, the key guard called out, 'Slop can'. I fetched it out of its cubby hole and found myself on the landing. I saw my neighbour for the first time, like me with slop can in hand. It was a lad of my age, with a thin scared face, looking skinny in his now outsize clothes. He whispered his name, 'G...', telling me he was there for the Barneville cave incident. I only knew about this affair from public rumour and from what Roland had told me: a group of FTP had set up a base in the caves of Barneville; they had been betrayed, and surrounded by SS and Vichy police. After putting up a fight and killing some Germans they had been forced to surrender.

I could not keep up the conversation as the guard came nearer and pushed me aside saying, 'No talking.' We marched off, keeping two metres apart, descending a stairway, and at the bottom we went into a small yard with one small door that I had not seen previously, located near the door to the stairs. In this high-walled yard, doubtless used for exercise, one by one we emptied our slop cans into a drain with a metal grid over it and then rinsed them at a running tap. The guard then threw into them a spoonful of disinfectant powder, giving our cells the smell typical of public toilets and then, still keeping a distance of two metres apart, we went back up to the cells. G... came near me and said, 'D'you think they will shoot me? They promised me they wouldn't since I told them where the cave was.'

He told me his story in dribs and drabs, either when we were going up the stairs or when waiting for the guards to open our cell doors.

He belonged to the Barneville resistance maquis,[1] made up of about ten FTP and one anti-Nazi deserter from the German army. This group had carried numerous derailment actions on military trains. On the morning of 24 August he had taken part with group members in the attack on the sub-office of the town hall of Grand-Quevilly-Extension to steal ration cards. After the operation his comrades left by car to return to their hideout but he, needing to go to Rouen, waited for the number twelve tram at the Bruyères roundabout. He planned to rejoin the maquis later by his own means. But among the tram passengers was a customs officer who had been present during the attack on the sub-office. He telephoned the Sotteville police, who sent an officer to intercept the tram at Saint-Sever station. G, after a struggle was arrested and taken to Sotteville police station. After several hours of interrogation, conducted mainly by Alie, he broke down and told them where the cave was. I asked him if he had talked under torture and he replied that they had put a gun to his head and started a countdown. Not wanting to die he had talked but he refused to take the police to the cave.[2]

All his comrades had been killed or arrested. Most had been grouped in a communal cell adjacent to mine (it must have been number 12) and it was they who called him 'bastard', with other insults, every evening. They banged on his cell door as they passed, opened the spyhole and spat through it saying that he too would 'get it'. He had been sent to Coventry by the other inmates. I was the only one who was ready to listen and speak to him. He kept asking me the same question: 'D'you think they'll shoot me?'

In addition to slopping out, those like me whose cells did not have wash basins would also go down the stairs to wash. We would go through the same routine, waiting first in front of the cells, and then walking two metres apart, carrying towel and toilet bag if we had one, going down the stairway to the washbasins located in a corner of the inner yard. They consisted of a long wide zinc channel over which ran a pipe with holes every half metre. At first I had no soap or toilet accessories. I had to make do with a rub in clear water without drying off.

There were no set positions in the wash facility which meant I was able to get to know my fellow inmates who were in single cells. Among them were members of the FPJ but there I also met the mayor of Monville,[3] arrested in reprisal, who informed me that the vicar had also been arrested, and then released. Two young men from his village were also in prison. They were probably those whose photos I had been carrying. All the prisoners were acquainted with the affair. It had caused a stir, spreading by word of mouth in and around Rouen. By dint of repetition it had assumed legendary proportions.

Midday echoed to the sounds of the soup meal – doors opening, urns trundling in the corridors, the ladle falling back into the heater urn. Later I could judge how thick the soup was just by the sound of it being poured into the mess tins of the cells before mine. But I had not yet reached that degree of perception and the thick soup that I was hoping for, so hungry was I, turned out to be just a thin gruel with badly peeled half-cooked turnip and swede covered by an oily film of water.

I let it cool down a little and ate it with distaste, fishing out the vegetables by hand as I had no spoon, and then drinking the broth. At the bottom of the mess tin lay a mix of about two spoonfuls of potato and a few scraps of fatty meat mixed with bone and grit. Hunger made it seem palatable, but above all it intensified my appetite. To stave that off, I ate my chess pieces and replaced them with pieces of straw pulled from the mattress. I made the pieces one by one, listening out for the noise of the doors.

The first cell below us, number one, was occupied by the guards. One of them slept there at night and it was used during the day by the Gestapo for light interrogation, the harsher ones being done at Rue du Donjon. Numbers 2 and 3 were single cells, number 4 held at least eight prisoners. The same layout held for the first floor, that is 5, 6, and 7 were single cells, 8 was a group unit, and likewise on the second floor, 9, 10 and 11 being singles and 12 a group unit. Given the high number of prisoners passing in front of my cell, there must have been a large group unit in the attic space.[4]

The next day in the wash yard I had the company of two prisoners from the first floor: Leroy, an FTP member, and Sénard from the Barneville cave, both due to be shot. The conversation was short.

Leroy said to me, 'Your case doesn't look too good. Do you want to get out with us?'

'I'd like to know the plan first.'

'We'll give it to you tomorrow and then you must swallow it. It means we'll have to bump off a Fritz.'

'I don't care.'

'Above all not a word to your lousy neighbour.'

My heart was pounding as I went up to my cell and I was already formulating plans for the sequel when I would be on the outside. No question of going back to my district or going home. I intended rather to go to the home of a girlfriend who lived behind the École Normale in a detached house with a garden. I would ask her for a bicycle, some clothes and food, and would leave the next morning towards Petit- and Grand-Couronne via the industrial district, among the morning workers. Then, via Maison Brulée and back roads I would head for La Cambe and Grandcamp. Then when the dust had settled I would come back and try to get in touch with Marie Louise or the cobbler friend from Grand-Quevilly-Extension.

The next morning Leroy slipped a ball of paper into my hand. I immediately put it into my mouth and once I had gone upstairs I unfurled it and read it as soon as things had quietened down. He was to get a square key brought in from the outside to open the steel-plate trap which was on the outer side of the slop-can cubby hole in the wall. On the chosen day he would unlock it leaving it in the closed position. In the night he would merely have to remove the slop can on the inside and push open the outer flap door to come out onto the landing.

Then he was to go and get Sénard and both would wait for the guard to do his round alone as usual. They would knock him out with a plank from the cell bed and take his keys. Then they would come and open my cell door and that of a ground floor prisoner, also due to be shot. With these keys we were to get into the yard by going through the kitchens.

Some tens of metres further on was a wall of about two and a half metres high dividing the staff garden from the rest of the prison, a garden which led to the much higher main outer wall overlooking Jean Rondeaux Avenue. This, although having watch turrets in places, was not guarded or watched. A ladder or a hitch up a doorframe in the wall would enable access to the first wall, and as for the second one, all that was needed was a hand pull up to get onto the rim of it.

The hardest thing for me would be the big jump down to the street since I still suffered with pain in the spine. After reading the draft plan and swallowing it, I hauled myself up to the skylight to check out the existence of this internal wall. It was all correct. In addition there was a post next to the perimeter wall carrying an electricity cable. We could possibly attach a rope made of blankets and use it to slide down into the street.

The following morning I passed on my agreement and comments to Leroy. I pointed out to him that in the kitchen there was a folding ladder, used by the guards to check the prison bars. I reminded him of the risk of retaliation measures against our families. He answered that he had intended to use a rope made of wash towels, to be attached to the post, and on the subject of families he added, 'Me, I've a wife and eight kids, so do me a favour, leave it out if you haven't got the nerve! As for the exact day, you'll get the news during morning wash time.'

I gave my full agreement. I later learnt that he had suggested escape to almost all the single cell detainees, and that I was the only one to accept. The price if we were caught was death, but I reckoned that unless there were allied landings before my trial, which was highly unlikely, I was headed for the firing squad anyway.

During the wait for the big night, I familiarised myself by ear with the routines of the daily prison life, picking out every noise. I could tell which cell was opened, which guard came up the stairs, just by his step. I think I could have heard a pin drop in the corridor. Hunger had a firm grip on me and I ate the remaining chess pieces. In any case I did not think I would be needing them, as my escape was imminent.

A few days later I was called to the meeting hall with the other prisoners. In a room as big as a classroom, small tables with chairs were arranged. Prisoners could sit opposite their families and talk for a few minutes under the watchful eye of German warders. I had the surprise of seeing my sister along with my mother. In the few months since I had seen her she had blossomed into a young lady. My mother, being affected by my arrest, had difficulty hiding her emotion. I was sure she would burst into tears on leaving the room. In the course of the conversation I was able to slip the names of Baudry and Prieur as the traitor responsible for my arrest, information intended for my father. My sister gave me some local news and a greeting from Réjane which warmed my heart. They also told me that following my arrest my father had instantly been transferred and had been attached to the intelligence service of the administration of the camp at Pithiviers. They brought me a parcel but only the clothing was given to me; at least it meant that I would be able to change clothes. I thought of my mother's distress when washing my smelly clothes, stiff with dried blood and stained with flea bites.

Sometimes a guard would take me along with other single cell inmates from my floor to a yard where there was some sand so that we could clean up our rusty mess tins which probably dated back to the Great War. Only when they were scoured to bright metal were we allowed to come back.

Around this time I was allowed showers and for the first time I found myself together with the people from the cave. Most of them, even those sentenced to death, had hopes of being deported to Germany and surviving. To avoid any incident, G was not with us.

'Don't talk to that bastard,' they said to me, 'he's in Coventry.'

On 27 October during morning wash Leroy informed me that it was 'on' for the coming night. The day seemed interminable and I was excited at the thought of how I would be en route for Grandcamp the next day – or dead! As time passed, fear of failure welled up in me. It seemed impossible for the guard to be overcome without yelling.

He did a first round, as every evening, and a second one at about 1 am. With my ear glued to the spyhole cover I listened to the silence of the prison. It was sometimes broken by the noise of a cough, a snore, or a creak; then I thought I heard a squeak and muffled steps, the squeak of a slop trap door needing oiling. Then a new guard came round; after opening the door to the stairs he seemed to hesitate. Had he heard something suspicious? He finally came up. Then there followed high, almost ultra-sound, noises as if a rabbit was being killed, painful to hear, lasting a few seconds but seeming endless. Had my comrades managed to take out the guard? I heard the sound of running, thinking they were coming to fetch me, but alas the noise of the keys went off in the kitchen direction. Through the spy hole I called, 'what about me?'

Then the phone rang in the guard cell. The escapees, no doubt panicked by the noise of the guard's cries, left me along with the condemned man from the ground floor. I hitched myself up to the skylight and could pick out lights coming from the administrative block to our area, which soon rang to the sound of nailed boots and footsteps. I put my slop bucket back in place and slipped under my blanket. The rest of the night was filled with commotion, shouts, blows, and interrogations. A guard came to check my blanket, the trap door, the slop bucket and to search my cell. This rumpus carried on until morning. At the morning wash I learned that the escape had succeeded.

The wounded animal-like squeals of the guard must have alerted the neighbouring block which was the reason for the phone call, which being unanswered gave cause for alarm. I now think that if my two comrades had come to fetch me, those few seconds lost would have been fatal to them as well as to me. I was sure they were still on the wall when the second wave of guards came around and that, without the fog, they would have been caught. Nevertheless at the time I resented being left behind.[5]

I was terribly downcast after so many nights of hope, and to take my mind off it, hearing nothing suspicious, I pulled away the slop bucket and pulled myself up to the skylight ledge to see the city. Suddenly all hell broke loose in my cell in the form of two monsters bursting in on me; it was the gorilla with his big mitts and a big slob with bloodshot eyes whom I had seen in the kitchen on the day I arrived. They kicked and punched me. The gorilla swung his keys on a chain, hitting my already bleeding face with the bunch of metal. Finally I was knocked down and handcuffed hand and foot. They were both in socks which is why I had not heard them coming. I was not the only one to be beaten up, since I heard several prisoners cry out that day. Late in the afternoon a team of French workers came to seal up the outer trap door of my slop bucket recess, as well as those in all other cells. I tried to speak to them, without getting any reply. They were doubtless being watched or were afraid to speak.

After they left, the gorilla came to check out the bars of my cell by banging on them, using the famous ladder which was to have aided the two escapees. And, just to keep me busy, he emptied the contents of my straw mattress on the floor cell. In it he found two books and a picture magazine left by the previous occupant and took them away. I regretted not having done an inventory of this flea sack before he did. In tight handcuffs, I had to stuff all that straw back into the jute bag. By evening I was exhausted and still in pain from the blows.

At curfew time the gorilla came to remove my handcuffs, ordered me to get undressed and made me put my clothes on the landing, leaving me in shirt and underpants, then he put the irons back on my hands and feet so tightly that I could not sleep a wink. In my mind I spent the night cycling back to Calvados.[6]

The next morning another guard took off my manacles and replaced them after I had got dressed, until wash time. When picking up my clothes I noticed little piles of belongings at the doors of all single cells. Thus we all got the same treatment, except that I was the only one with feet in irons.

I learned during ablutions that the gorilla and the other guards were due to go to the Russian front and that the night watch was to be stepped up. It was my turn to have a haircut and shave. There were two prisoners entrusted with this job, a certain Lemoël and a Pole whose French was poor. I got the former who passed me some news in a whisper without lip movement, masked by the scraping sound of the razor over my beard, unheard by the guard who was sitting two metres away. He told me that the escape had only just succeeded, even if it did not go to plan. He told me they had been shopped which is why the guard was on the alert. Leroy and Sénard had waited for him at the top of the stairs, equipped with staves from the plank beds, and the blows the guard received almost killed him, rendering him probably blind. The barber knew I was due to leave with them and that they did not have the time to come and get us, the other prisoner and me.

I did not accept Lemoël's idea that they had been shopped, since in that case the Jerries would have taken the necessary precautions and stepped up the night watch. But nevertheless I was the only one to be in foot irons!

In night after night of insomnia I had visions of the subsequent events to this escape that never was, visions which were never the same. Sometimes I arrived at my aunt's place in La Cambe, sometimes at my cousin's in Grandcamp, always by bicycle, and I pictured the villages I passed through. Another night Leroy and Sénard took me to friends who said, 'Why have you brought us the son of a cop?' then I would imagine taking part in derailment operations or 'cap hunting'[7] and attacks on German detachments. But more often I imagined the pain when I jumped from the wall and I limped across the Boulevard Jean Rondeaux to take refuge in Rue Jacquard in a house with railings around it. I would climb the not-too-high gate and hide in the bushes. I would hardly be able to move, so great was the pain in my back. When daylight came, the shutters would be opened by a pretty young girl. When she noticed me I would whisper with a finger to my lips indicating, 'the Germans are looking for me. Hide me!' She would be living with her mother who could die from any fright so she would hide me in their garage

while I recovered. She would find me food, clothes and a bike. Sometimes she would hug me and at night she would come to me in the garage......
Alas with daylight the sordid walls of my cell reappeared. I could not wait for nightfall when I could pick up my reverie again.

I would also think about hunting down Baudry, tracking him from hideout to hideout. I would wait for him and often I'd kill him, sometimes by strangling but most times with a revolver, after showing him who I was.

We had a new key master who was more human, called Leven, I think, or something similar. He did not handcuff me tightly, for fear of hurting me. Thus sometimes I managed to slip my hands out of the ring of iron. Then one day Lemoël told me while giving me a shave that the handcuffs could be undone by pressing on the spring with a straw. After a few attempts I managed it very well and was thus able to spend better nights. During the day it was too risky, as, since the escape, the guards were doing their rounds in slippers with the effect that we did not hear them until the spy hole opened. Leven however made a point of rattling his keys to announce his arrival.

Seeing me depressed squatting for hours one evening when he was on duty, he asked me if I wanted to talk to a friend. He took off my irons and brought the abbé. We hugged each other. I advised him to load as much as possible on me, to help him get off. He said he suffered terribly from hunger. He thought it was Roche or more likely Prieur who had shopped us, or perhaps both of them. All would become clearer later. He had not been able to resist torture and admitted giving the names of the two young men whose photos had been in my wallet. His visit gave me some comfort. Some days later Leven brought Rangée to see me, which is how I learnt that a part of the FPJ had folded. One of the Monville youngsters whose photo I was carrying and who had been named by the abbé worked in the social security offices in Rouen and had set up a section there. Indeed it was through him that the abbé had been recruited into the FPJ.

Had the Gestapo put two and two together? Had he talked? His section leader was arrested in turn and taken from office to office to finger people.

Through an indiscretion he knew that Serge was employed in the general treasury, but he did not know his real name or the office where he worked. So the SS took him through all of them to end up at that of the bursar of the Hospice where he fingered Rangée. We were a dozen to be arrested, three sector heads among us, plus Rangée and me. The organisation in the Rouen area was leaderless even though numbering more than one hundred, since Rangée was the only link between certain of the contacts. The same was true for me on a département level. As I had done for the abbé, I asked Rangée to pile things on me as much as possible to save his skin.

Every morning G pressured me in order to exchange a few words to be reassured. To me he seemed pitiful, too thin for his clothes, pale and sweating with fear. One morning he was no longer there. The Gestapo had come to fetch him. Through the grape vine and the barber I found out that the SS had kept their word and that he had gone to Germany.

Sénard's father had taken his place in cell ten. Unable to catch the son, the Gestapo took revenge on the mother and father. He was a short fellow who had passed on his piercing eyes to his son. He bravely took on this ordeal, happy in the thought that his son had escaped the firing squad. I think my father would have done the same if circumstances had allowed me to flee with the escapees.

At the beginning of November, the first day I believe, Leven opened my door, saying in his pidgin French, 'Yesterday many my comrades kaput in cinema. Terrorists have throw bombs.' The news spread like a wave of joy through the prison. 'Serve the bastards right' was the universal reaction. The next day, rumour spread that there had been reprisals and the mood gave way to anxiety in the early mornings.[8]

It was the deadliest attack in the Rouen area, as, officially, it killed three and wounded twenty, of whom many died from their wounds afterwards.

Leven was anxious. He told me that several soldiers had been killed by terrorists, that trains carrying soldiers on leave were derailed, and that German cities were being flattened by bombs. I learned that most of his family, including his wife, had perished in the ruins of Cologne. With tears in his eyes he said, 'War...sad. When it all stop?'

At soup time, when there were any leftovers, he unfailingly stopped by my cell to hand me a tinfull, which the other guards never did, preferring to give it to a group cell to avoid opening other doors.

After the attack the atmosphere got heavier and heavier and one day I was awakened by the sound of nailed boots and shoes coming up the stairs before daylight. I heard several doors being opened with shouts of 'Mess tin and blanket!'

My heart was thumping hard but the steps did not stop at my cell door but went on to cell 12. I heard some names called out and the group, together with a number of other inmates, returned passing in front of my cell door.

In the morning when Leven opened my door he said, 'Six of your mates kaput this morning. Bang! Bang! War very sad.' He mimed the shooting gesture. I marked the date on my wall calendar. It was 8 November.

I had not been interrogated since being imprisoned. Thus I was not surprised when on the morning of 11 November I was taken by prison van to Rue du Donjon with other detainees. They took off my foot irons for the occasion. On stepping out of the police cell-van in front of the Gestapo building there was a lull as the SS were talking amongst themselves without paying any attention to us. Passers-by quickened their pace as they neared us and crossed to the other side. I gradually moved a few metres away as they were not watching me, feigning to look at the Jeanne d'Arc tower, and was about to run down Rue Philippe-Auguste towards Verdrel Square hoping with a bit of luck to reach Rue Bons-Enfants where a girl cousin of mine ran a grocery.

I felt weak and hesitated for a few moments. Suddenly an SS man noticed me, rushed up and slapped me in front of a scared group of pedestrians.

I was violently pushed into the building and confronted with the same interrogator as in Hotel Dieu. He launched into a long tirade, translated by an interpreter. 'So Mr Goupil you wanted to give us the slip! Tut, tut, not a good idea! You would not have got very far with your handcuffs. And my men, you know, are crack shots.'

During the ensuing interrogation I repeated the story, still the same one, which I had learned and rehearsed in my cell. I knew the names and addresses of nobody. I just had rendezvous and no more contacts after they had taken place. I spoke freely about all the groups that I knew to have been already arrested, mentioning Rangée, and the abbé, trying to diminish their importance. Suddenly he interrupted me, banging on the table. 'The leaders! Who are the leaders? As you French say, small fry mean nothing to us.'

Faced with my stubbornnesss, after two hours he translated the following deal: 'You enable us to catch the ringleaders or tomorrow your eleven companions will be shot. You have until midnight to think it over and call a guard.'

'What about me?'

'You we will keep; if we shoot you, you won't talk.'

I got angry and called them barbarians. My outburst whipped up the other SS. Soon there were half a dozen around me, while the interpreter translated my words. My officer got angry in turn and replied, shouting, 'And shooting German soldiers in the back as your friends did, derailing leave trains, throwing grenades into a cinema, is that not barbaric? You're just terrorists, TERRORISTS! I was a young student in the Ruhr during the French occupation and believe me, the military police of your country also shot hostages to protect its soldiers…'

Another SS man added his grain of salt with the tale of a resistance fighter against French occupation who had seen all of his family, as far as his cousins, executed in reprisal for an attack. The other Germans expressed their approval.[9]

The officer had me escorted back to the prison van shouting that he would carry out his threat if I did not talk.

I got back to my cell feeling totally downcast and spent the longest night of all my detention. The slightest noise made me jump and I could only think about ways of committing suicide if the SS decided to carry out their threat. I thought that once I was out of handcuffs, the best way would be to hang myself from the window bars, using strips cut from my shirt. I still had the pieces of razor blade with which to open a vein but I considered this method less certain and associated with a suffering which was too prolonged.

Nothing happened and at reveille I went down to ablutions with the inmates of my block. For some of the day I slept squatting at the end of my cell as I was not allowed to sleep on the mattress.

The next morning before daybreak steps rang out to shouts of 'Mess tins and blankets' and some detainees filed past my door. It was not my FPJ friends but a new group from the Barneville cave and some members of Calvados FTP who were put in front of the firing squad.

A week went by then another and the tense atmosphere in the prison relaxed. Parcel distribution, suspended since the escape, began again. Sadly I was only allowed clothing but in those ironed shirts and pullovers I sensed the tender touch of my mother and sister; my caressing hands could feel their tears. I thought of their anguish when they were told of detainees being shot at the firing range which was not far from our house.

I was as ever stressed by the spyhole and the eye watching me and, as if a guard's eye was not enough, a prisoner from cell 12 began regularly to open it when he passed with his companions and I heard him say to another, 'It's a lad due to be shot, 'cos he's got irons on his hands and feet.'

The next day when he opened the spyhole I had put my mouth over the aperture and gobbed. That put an end to his game.

Sometimes Leven was replaced by a young guard with oiled hair, shiny boots, all spick and span, whom I called Dandy. He always had a smug look which got on my nerves. To amuse myself without caring about the consequences, I decided to give him the fright of his life. I managed to climb onto the central heating radiator which was to the left of the door. So when he did his round and looked through the spyhole, all he saw was an empty cell since I was in the blind spot. For a few seconds I could hear his anxious breathing. In his mind's eye he surely pictured himself on the Russian front; he frantically jangled his bunch of keys and while he was unlocking the door I jumped down and stood, facing him. Seeing me calmly standing there, his jaw dropped and he closed the cell door without saying a word. He probably thought he had been seeing things.

Time passed monotonously by, broken up by the usual routines and services. Having a haircut, when I was lucky enough to come across Lemoël, meant I got reassuring news from the front: that Warsaw had been taken and that French units were advancing in the Po valley. These bits of gossip, designed to raise my spirits, fell flat one day. The Germans gave us toilet paper cut to size from their newspapers. I could not translate what was written but one day I chanced to receive pieces cut from a page in French from the *Pariser Zeitung* dating from the day before with a map of the front line showing that it had moved very little in the east and that heavy fighting had taken place in the Vitebsk area. Similarly in Italy the US army was still held up before Rome. This was a fresh blow to my morale, which was already pretty low, and when I saw my barber again I told him the real situation of the war and told him to stop his gossip about the war; but I could see that he had convinced himself of the truth of what he was peddling.

Sénard's father was transferred to another cell and for some days cell 10 was unoccupied. Then at the beginning of December 1943 there was an important arrival and I got a new neighbour called Charles Riva, a short ginger-haired guy of Italian origin with a slight accent who told me he had been arrested in the Paris affair involving the Buckmaster network. At the same time cell 9 was occupied by an older man with thinning hair and glasses, whose case must have been serious since like me he was obliged to have his hands and legs in irons. He was very wary saying neither his name nor the reason for his arrest. To avoid the pain caused by his handcuffs he walked with his palms together, held out in front of him, as if in prayer.

The day after his arrival Leven took me down to cell one where my interrogator was waiting. He immediately showed me a quite large framed professional studio photo which showed a lad of my age whom I recognised. It was Nivromont whom I had met at the home of a classmate, Albert, living in Rue de Bihorel. He was a friend and neighbour whom Albert had introduced to me. On seeing the photo, and since neither he nor Albert had been contacted by the FPJ, I said without thinking, 'It's Nivromont but he has nothing to do with the FPJ.'

My interrogator was jubilant and I realised I had made a grave mistake. For him, Nivromont was the FPJ inter-regional head.

'When did you meet him?'

'At a mutual friend's house, but I repeat that he has nothing to do with our affair.'

'The name and address of the friend ...'

I fell silent then, as having blundered once I did not want to make things worse by involving Albert.

The following day a guard again came to fetch me and I was taken to the guard's canteen near the kitchen. There, in addition to the SS and the interpreters was Nivromont finishing a slice of bread and jam, and he gave me a black look. The interpreter asked me to repeat what I had said the day before.

'This man's name is Nivromont, but he has nothing to do with the FPJ. He is not my chief.'

'I do not recognise this man,' answered Nivromont.

I was then taken back to my cell. I was very bothered by this incident and recounted it to Charles, with whom I got on well. He said to me, 'Since you said that he had nothing to do with your case, they will probably let him go!'

I could not work out how Nivromont's picture had come into the hands of the Gestapo. I was worried about Albert. The key to the mystery was given to me by the balding man in cell 9. The next day, coming up from slopping out chores, he followed me up the stairs, calling me a bastard, a grasser, and other such names, because … Nivromont was his son! I tried to explain but the guard intervened and locked us in our respective cells. Two days later I was able to set out the facts as they happened. I admitted my blunder. He calmed down a bit but told me that now his son would not be released and that if anything happened to him, I was to blame.

This affair was a terrible blow to my morale even if the arrest of Nivromont junior had come after that of his father, a well-known member of the resistance. He had been picked up in Paris where he was a student, but, for the Gestapo, to pin on him the interregional FPJ responsibility was a way of closing an open dossier. A short while later I was summoned to Rue du Donjon. The interpreter translated a document for me in which I attested to Nivromont's inter-département leadership – a document that I refused to sign, continuing to deny that he was involved in my case. The officer in charge of the interrogation said, 'If you don't sign, it will make no difference. Your file will be closed and you will be called before a military court and probably be condemned to death.'

It turned out to be my last summons to the Gestapo and I never appeared before a court. In the days following this matter I slipped into a mood of depression and listlessness. Strange as it seems it was Nivromont senior who tried to lift my spirits. Of course it would have been better for me to have remained silent but he realized that for my part, there had never been any intention of implicating his son.

The twelfth of December was my birthday, my 21st, making me an official adult. I decided to mark the event by giving myself a small concert. I sometimes felt like playing music and, being without an instrument, I would imitate the sound of a violin or trumpet with my mouth, 'playing' well known airs or melodies that I improvised. In full swing and now quite loud, I heard the sound of a guard's footsteps coming nearer. He suddenly opened my cell door and loudly yelled '*Ruhe!*'[10] which made me jump. It was Dandy, hair slick as ever, who was on night watch with another guard. In the face of my blank silence he lingered a few moments and tried to speak to me. I explained by sign language that I had just come of age, being 21. Then he asked me, stabbing his finger at me, 'Warum?'[11] I don't know why but I thought 'Warum' meant 'terrorist', so I replied, 'Nicht terrorist, Nicht Warum.' He tapped his finger against my head signifying I was a sad basket case and then shut the door.

Following the escape and the attack on the Cinédit cinema the visit meeting rooms were closed but families continued to come to the prison gates all the same only to be dispersed with fire hoses. Only after Christmas did they reopen in dribs and drabs, and conversations were only possible through a small grill, so in this way I saw my mother and sister a couple of times. However these conversations gave me more stress than happiness since I blamed myself for causing their misery, and given the situation I was in, I would have preferred to have no family to better be able to keep up my morale.

Around mid-December a German prison inspector visited all the cells. He asked the guards about the irons on hands and feet, and the latter were immediately removed from me and from Nivromont. I had had mine on for thirty-five days. The next day bread and butter rations were increased and the soup was thicker. Alas it was not to last. The horrible rusty mess tin was replaced by an insulated aluminium mess tin, a gift from the Red Cross we were told. We would all have preferred to receive a parcel or a good thick soup.

During those endless winter days Charles and I spent much of our time in communication by tapping on the partition walls, one tap for A, two for B etc. We tapped the walls with our fingers which was enough but could not be detected from the corridor landing. With this system, communication was long and tedious, since to tap 'U' we needed twenty-one taps, so we subsequently evolved a simpler code in which the letters were grouped in boxes of five which limited the number of taps. Thus the letter U, being the first letter of the fifth block, it sufficed to tap five times followed by one tap. In this way we managed to communicate scraps of news and impressions and this became an oasis in the mental wilderness in which we were living.

Sometimes, huddling in my favourite position squatting at the end of my cell, I would spend hours daydreaming about Grandcamp and more besides. I did not feel the need to communicate and did not respond to Charles's call. One day he tapped out a resounding 'Shit!'

One afternoon the guard on duty whom I later nicknamed 'Corporal Clean' decided to make us clean out our cells, doubtless with the aim of keeping us busy. After removing the handcuffs he had a German inmate bring me a bucket, a broom and a floor cloth. I conscientiously wrapped the cloth around the brush and dragged it over the cement floor, rinsing it from time to time. I found the result very satisfying and waited. Half an hour later the guard came back and exploded in curses when he saw the result. He closed the door and came back with his dogsbody bearing two buckets of water, who poured them both over the cement floor and showed me how a cell is cleaned: he rubbed the floor with the broom and then mopped up the water with the floor cloth, which he then wrung out over the bucket. The guard stayed during the whole procedure, punctuating with remarks such as, 'French not know how what is work'. Little by little the dirty water returned to the bucket. It is true that the cell was clean but I was exhausted.

Each time he was on duty he renewed the operation, saying, 'French not clean. Germans clean!'

This cleanliness freak was replaced in the merry-go-round of guard changes by a new character whom I called 'Manta Mouth' because of his mouth which went from ear to ear, and his companion 'Microbe' who was as big as a 12-year-old. For all of them I found a nickname: Gorilla and Dandy, as previously mentioned, 'Hobbly Wobbly' who limped, 'Big Butt', 'Droopy Butt',' Corporal Clean', and others whose names no longer remain in my memory. Only Leven remained unbaptised on account of my respect for him.

Manta Mouth I recognized as a former neighbour of my parents and he recognised me. For several months he had been quartered with a fellow soldier on the first floor of the house opposite ours which had been requisitioned for the purpose. My father had a smattering of German since he had been a prisoner of war and had been in contact with them especially to check if he could still make himself understood. One day I even found them at the table with him enjoying a cup of coffee. It was the only time my mother took him to task, after they had gone, making it clear that she did not want any Bosche in her house. On that day they offered to sell us some butter, an offer which my mother quite bluntly refused. That butter must have been destined for the prison where it was so meanly served to us.

Manta Mouth pulled a notebook and pencil from his pocket and said, 'Write'. I scribbled a short note to my parents to give them some news and to reassure them a little. Above all I asked them for food. After that I did not see him again and he did not pass the note on to my parents. Had he been transferred?

Christmas and the New Year went by for us just like any other day. There were neither parcels nor food extras. It is true that attacks on German officers had been stepped up and the FTP, reorganized after the cave fiasco, were again derailing trains.

One afternoon I was called to the ground floor. There behind a small table a German soldier was opening parcels, aided by two French prisoner-workers. Whereas I was expecting clothing, a huge packet was unwrapped for me containing a pot of butter, white bread, cake, pâté, cheese, sugar, shortbread biscuits and cured sausage. It was all tipped out pell-mell onto a linen cloth, pierced and probed, stirred up by one of the prison workers who, speaking through his teeth like Lemoël, said, 'Your case will be sorted out. You'll probably go to Germany. Your Dad sends his love.'

I went up to my cell, with some difficulty bearing this treasure because of my Massenotte handcuffs. Charles and Nivromont, who had also received parcels, had the same problem. When I got to my cell I took stock of the treasure and sorted it out, eating first only the crumbs of bread and biscuits and lumps of sugar.

I told myself I should divide it up, and that this parcel should last at least two weeks since the bread was sliced into fifteen slices as was the cold sausage. After the breadcrumbs I got stuck into the broken biscuits, eating the ration for that day, and, by way of celebration, the following day's ration also.

Up until then I had managed not to suffer hunger pains, my stomach having got used to a regular routine. I was getting thinner but not weaker and hungry as in the first few days. Faced with this sudden abundance, a wave of gluttony swamped all reason and I devoured slice after slice of bread and cold sausage, and biscuit after biscuit. I could picture Charles doing the same; from time to time he frantically tapped out his expressions of joy on the cell partition. In the evening I was gripped by thirst and, having no more coffee, I had to call a guard to get a mess tin of water. In the night I tackled the butter, which I ate as it was with my fingers, since I was out of bread. I remembered seeing the German soldiers do the same thing at my aunt's place in Saint-Floxel, using cabbage leaves to scrape the bottom of the butter churn. I told myself I was silly but I kept on eating.

And catastrophe struck. In the early morning I was sick and, worse, I got terrible diarrhoea. I felt the waves of colic painfully coming, heralded by rumblings, and I shat the parcel as fast as I had eaten it. I left my slop can out for fear of not getting to it in time during an attack; it stank my cell out. When the guard opened up, I was legless, exhausted, and could not stand up. He pinched his nose, and lectured me in German, suspecting the reasons for my condition. I dragged myself down to the ground floor, fearful of getting the runs again, but I was drained out.

Charles was in no better state than I. He said to me, 'I cleaned up on the parcel but I am as sick as a dog.' Only Nivromont senior was in fine form. He had just nibbled on a few biscuits and had calculated his rations to make the parcel last several weeks. He gave me advice about moderation. Alas it had come too late. The wild gluttony with which I had devoured those items of food had enlarged my stomach and for the next few days I suffered more from hunger than I had when I first arrived in prison. One morning, seeing my distress, Nivromont gave me two small butter pats, telling me to make them last two days, which for me was impossible.

Leven in turn was no more to be seen, on his way, according to the prison grapevine, to the Russian front. Nivromont informed me later that this guard had often had Nivromont's son brought to his cell, had taken out several letters and had rendered lots of services to many people.

One night in February when I was fast asleep, having unlocked my cuffs, the door suddenly opened and two guards burst into my cell and saw that I was no longer restrained. In sleep I must have shown a free arm uncovered which was the reason for their intrusion. During the day my Massenotte cuffs were replaced by a chain with padlock. A few days later Lemoël explained how to open it with a safety pin. He passed one on to me and after some fiddling I managed to do it.

The days were getting longer. I had not been summoned to a military court and I began to be more hopeful. No more did we hear the fateful morning shouts of 'Mess tin and blanket!' On the other hand, German military prisoners, who were as numerous as we were, were executed in batches. One morning there were four. That day the guards looked downcast and ended up by letting one of us in on the details. The group, all from the Kriegsmarine,[12] had been executed for leaving their Ack Ack post to party with some girls.

The German soldiers under prison sentence did not remain inactive in their cells. To the sound of guttural commands they could be heard running in full kit in the inner yards, going to ground, and jumping up with a clatter of mess tins. Sometimes they were just a few but it mostly sounded like the manoeuvres of a whole company, accompanied by the barking NCOs.

At the beginning of March a dawn ray of sunlight shed a pink light on the left side of my skylight, but alas that same morning I learned that two legendary resistance figures, Levillain and Corroy, had been shot. I had not heard the usual to and fro. They were doubtless held in another part of the prison or at the law courts.

Also around this time the Red Cross issued us with a parcel via the guards. It was a package of two or three kilos containing fruit paste, sugar and biscuits. I carefully put everything tidily away and, this time, I made the pleasure stretch to three days, despite the advice of Nivromont who told me to keep it for two weeks. I was not ill but as with the big family parcel I was again hungry for the following days.

One morning I was visited by a German soldier who spoke broken French. It was a priest whose mission was to bring 'the support of religion' to me and my comrades. I replied that, no longer being a believer, I needed nothing but bread. He expressed his regret at having only communion host. He explained that I would be shot one morning or another, and that if I wanted the Lord's grace I had to confess and take communion. I replied that I did not understand how he could wear the German uniform, that of our torturers and executioners. He repeated his standpoint once again, not understanding why I, unlike my comrades, should refuse his services. He seemed sorry, promising to come back with bread, but I never saw him again.

Nivromont and Charles took communion, along with all the other detainees that I knew. Charles gave the justification that in the end it could do no harm and that one could not know what would happen afterwards.

One morning in March I heard the guards dragging a heavy object. My door opened and they threw a prisoner in a bad way into my cell who remained motionless where he fell. He had a gash on one eyebrow and a bruised face. Still on the floor he managed to open an eye and whisper, 'I've nothing to say. No speak!' When he had gathered his wits, he said he was from Elbeuf and told me his name which I have forgotten. A few minutes later a guard brought me a bucket and towel for me to clean him up. In the evening when he was more presentable the guards took him to cell 12.

And so life went on, above all made up of various noises. My ear had become so finely tuned that I could hear the guards moving in their socks in the corridor. I could tell in which cell a slop bucket was pulled out; I could follow the conversations of the detainees who passed by, even on the landing below ours.

I told myself that it had to end one way or another, either in front of a firing squad, or in deportation to Germany, or by invasion and liberation. But when? In a month? or a week? In the spring the white vapour trails of the planes became more numerous, as well as the anti-aircraft fire. Sometimes my small patch of blue sky was a movie screen of aerial combat. Sadly I could no longer make the effort to hitch myself up to the skylight.

I sensed that I was losing my wits. I became inward-looking and no longer lingered on the stairs to exchange a few words with Nivromont or Charles. I went up quickly and only felt happy when I heard the sound of the heavy door closing in on me. I spent hours crouched with my arms around my knees, dreaming of a new life always beginning with my failed escape or in Monville where I had had the chance to avoid arrest. Each time I imagined my escape to Calvados by bike, then came back to be involved in FTP actions, above all to track down Baudry. The idea of taking revenge on that informant brought some comfort to my existence.

At night, having dozed all day, I hardly slept. After removing my chains I hummed tunes in a way that seemed to me quite loud. I tried not to be heard from the outside. I enjoyed intense moments when I produced music for brass band. If only I could remember all those original melodies, harmonies and rhythms which filled my cell!

I also pictured myself going hunting. I walked in the stubble, a hare would bolt out, or a flight of partridge would rise. Bang bang! I would fire and run after the wounded game. Other nights I pictured myself shrimping at Grandcamp. There I would plunge my hands into cracks in the rock, and catch lobsters as I had done on the spring tide when we caught eighteen.

When I came down to earth I found myself squatting, groping under the plank bed which had transformed itself into rocks; I relived at least twenty times the miraculous shrimp catch on the day of the storm. I could see them jumping around me and I stuffed them into the legs of my long underpants that I had knotted at the bottom.

I stopped communicating with Charles, who when he saw me looking haggard he would say, 'Paul, snap out of it; you're going round the bend.'

One of the guards, I know not who, often passed me a lit cigarette via the spyhole on seeing me prostrate on the cell floor. But, as I had known for a long time, it had to come to an end.

## Chapter 5

# From Compiègne to Auschwitz

At the beginning of April the grapevine buzzed with contradictory rumours: for fear of landings we were to be transferred elsewhere, to a prison inland (in central France!); we were to be converted to open prison workers and sent to Germany; we were to be deported into concentration camps. This time Lemoël seemed to be better informed…during the last haircut he told me we were to be sent to a camp in Germany. He had shaved a guard who had already done the journey, and told him that we would be piled into cattle wagons…that once there, we would work in underground armament factories, wearing striped uniforms with a large red triangle on the chest. But Lemoël had fed me so much false information that I no longer believed any of it except the landings which could happen any day soon.

There were more and more signs of it, such as aerial bombardment, dog fights, and anti-aircraft fire. It had become a daily spectacle. Our guards had become nervous as the prison was bursting with detainees held in group cells. One sensed that something was in the offing. If some of my comrades were anxious, I was not since for me anything was better than that solitude, in an antechamber to madness.

On the morning of 11 April there were unusual moves of doors opening, punctuated with shouts. Charles rapped hard on the wall and I replied using our code. 'It's good news for us.'

Later in our worst moments Charles often reminded me of this phrase.

The cell door finally opened. The guard took off my chains and yelled, 'Get everything. You leave!'

I picked up my slender packet of clothing and toilet items, put them in a laundry bag and on the landing I met Charles, and Nivromont who was carrying a big bag of food that he had set aside from his food parcels. The guards drew us up for the meantime in the inner yard and I was able to meet up with the comrades from the group cells who until then had filed past my door anonymously cheering me up with words of encouragement and spiced with rumours. There were also the Boulanger twin brothers who had set up the sizeable Ry-sur-Andelle maquis group in the caves dug in a marl pit which extended as far as under their house which was a few hundred yards from the local Kommandatur. I also saw the Abbé Kérébel who had lost much weight; he introduced me to some young FPJ members that I had not seen before; Néel, de Monville, Burel, Cabot, Castel, and Carouge…

We numbered at least eighty. Our guards took us through a part of the prison we did not know and then it was time to wait for the search and medical.

The Boulangers became the centre of attention for many around who listened as in turn they described the booby traps and devices with which they had riddled their underground resistance hideout. For instance there were loops in which the Germans could be hanged and one of the brothers, Henri, mimed the face of one of the hanged SS so realistically that several of his listeners shouted, 'Let them all die the bastards. Good for you!!!'

Rangée and several other members of the FPJ were not with us. They were no doubt due to be in another convoy. I chatted to some of the younger FPJ that the abbé had taken under his wing. They were some of the minor militants of the group, engaged in distributing tracts, or the *Espoir* newspaper, putting up posters, collecting funds, all of them contributing to the strength of our organisation. Most of them had been denounced by the same person who had caused the Rangée team to be infiltrated by the Gestapo.

The medical visit was just a farce. We paraded naked before an indifferent doctor, exhibiting here a flabby stomach, there an arched back, elsewhere a saggy bottom. Our bodies, ruined by the privations of prison life, bore the marks of their misery in front of the impassive gaze: 'Say 33. Say ah. Cough. Get dressed!'

The last to arrive were the only ones who looked reasonable. I had not seen myself for months and I realised with horror that my skeleton showed via my hip bones sticking out and my prison-bar rib cage.

After this macabre parade we were locked up in the cells of the French block for the night, which were much more comfortable than ours, being equipped with toilet and washbasin. I found myself in a single cell, handcuffed not surprisingly.

Daylight the next day saw us leave by truck for the Rouen north station. A special passenger train had been assembled there. That station had not been used for passenger traffic for several years. On that day it was deserted. No news of our departure had leaked out since there were no family members there at all and the few passers-by in Gambetta Boulevard pretended not to see us. The convoy was made up of old third-class carriages all in wood, with opposing seats for four and a corridor. Each compartment opened onto the track so four detainees chained in pairs were covered by two guards. Chained to me was Raoul Boulanger.

Lemoël who was on the convoy said we were headed for Compiègne but was it more hot air? We went through the market garden district of Lyons road. I recognised the viaduct and the Carville tower, and Darnétal station. We went north towards Serqueux, and Amiens. Were we going directly to Germany? I felt happy to be free from the solitude which little by little was destroying my mind. With Raoul and the two opposite me I talked about anything that came into my head, talking because I was alive and had an existence…I felt as if I was reborn…I was ready for the worst hardship rather than find myself alone again with my shadow. The train plunged through the belt of forests surrounding Rouen where the buds were beginning to burst.

Raoul said to me, 'This is my home patch. If I could jump out I'd be there in an hour!'

We passed close by his patch but with two armed guards there was no question of jumping out. For many of us this departure caused a certain optimism since we did not think that there were conditions worse than those in Rouen prison and most of all we had the conviction we would not be shot. On the other hand those held for minor offences saw their hopes of imminent liberation evaporate. The convoy branched off towards the Paris region after Serqueux but in my euphoria of renewed existence I was so chatty that I did not realise we had arrived in Compiègne.

The Germans unloaded us onto a freight platform and removed our handcuffs. I had been in irons for 168 days. After a ten-minute truck ride we arrived at the Royal-Lieu barracks which were surrounded by barbed wire and transformed into an internment camp. I lost touch with Charles during the administrative formalities but I came across Nivromont who was still clutching his big food bag. Behind him was his son who pretended not to know me.

We were each given a blanket, a mess tin, a spoon, and a metal tag bearing a registration number. I got the number 31 672. Then we were dispersed into rooms in various buildings. I was allocated to a small room in the last hut, number 8 in the camp. The main hall of the building was a theatre and leisure foyer. The room was lined with bunk beds, taking up most of the space leaving little room for access to them with a table and bench in the middle. To make their lives easier, the existing inmates, occupying the top bunks, had installed shelves, hung bags from the ceiling, and set up lines for drying underwear and socks.

On entering, it made me think of the train coming back from Brittany and at the same time of miners' changing rooms. My comrades and I allocated to this room got a cool reception from the incumbents who were not pleased to see the invasion of space vacated by the previous departure.

The room leader found me a place at the lowest level cluttered with boxes, suitcases, bags and packets of all sorts, which the owners had to stow elsewhere. I was amazed at the quantity of stuff that some had. They had set themselves up as if they were going to see out the war there.

The regime of Compiègne was, from the food point of view, much better than that in Bonne Nouvelle since there were two thick soups per day, some prepared directly by the Red Cross. In addition a considerable quantity of parcels arrived at the camp. Every morning the happy recipients went off to the hand-out with a blanket and they could be seen returning bent under the load. They then stored those precious foodstuffs in the masses of baggage cluttering the room. Some, such as the marquis of M… for example, had such big packages that they had to be helped by three companions, one at each corner of the blanket.

The majority of the parcel recipients had formed mess groups and shared their items, and the healthy local home cooking made my mouth water. During meal times I preferred to take a walk, to see prison chums or watch the few football addicts kick a ball around the football pitch on the main barrack parade ground. After a few days the mess group had me bring my mess tin to join in their feast, all the more so as I was a good bridge player and partners in that game were much in demand.

I witnessed some terrible scenes in which scores were settled. One day, a Gestapo agent, dumped by them, was recognised and beaten up. When the guards intervened with dogs to free him from the avenging hands he had one eye put out and multiple wounds. I do not know if he came out alive, but was he really guilty?

Another day I recognised a doctor from Déville, furious, in the middle of a group. He had taken aside an inmate from Rouen prison, accusing him of talking and causing his arrest. 'At my age there's no way I'll get back from this. You should not have pointed to me. All you had to do was say nothing!'

The person addressed tried to justify himself but by the doctor's tone of voice one sensed that he was telling the truth.

Some days later I came across Nivromont deep in conversation with a financier who was owner or editor of a stock market journal called *Les Cahiers de Qunizaine*. This person was very thin and was looking to exchange his bread ration for cigarettes. I pointed out to him that in his condition he was sure to die but he said that he would rather die than not smoke. I did not know that Nivromont was into finance. Both of them were boasting of their recent scoops.

'Zippers, Zippers! That's me.'

'Imitation leather; That's me!'

One would have thought we were anywhere else but on a concentration camp parade ground. In the course of the story I learned that Dr Lecacheux, a député in the département of La Manche, whom I knew, was involved in the imitation leather business and was a company board member.

In my hut I got to know a Parisian fireman, Michel Dubernard. He was tall, well built, energetic and resourceful. He got me food supplements as and when I needed since I had lost more than twenty-five kilos in prison.

I had arrived at Royal-Lieu on 12 April 1944 and right from the next week there was talk of a general roll call and departure for Germany. But the days passed quickly in discussions, card games and reading (there was an excellent library at the camp). On 20 April the previous day's bombing of Rouen was on everyone's lips with the most unlikely rumours spread about the extent of the damage. Michel who some days later had been detailed, with others in our room, to go outside camp on a day job, came back in the evening with a newspaper which gave details which reassured me as to the fate of my family. He, with the other detainees, had been sent to dig up unexploded bombs from Creil station, which had been recently bombed. Some days later other comrades went to do the same job at Porte de la Chapelle in Paris.

Every day I hoped to get a big parcel from my family, all the more so since Rouen lads from my transport had luckily been called to collect.[1] I wandered around the camp a lot, so happy with this semi liberty, to have human contact, and one day I came face to face with Roland. He hesitated at first as if he wanted to ignore me, then he took me aside and said, 'Above all don't let on you know me as nobody knows I was a militant in the Rouen area.'

He told me he had been arrested by chance on a train in the Landes[2] region where he had been transferred at the end of 1943 after the Cinédit attack, with ration cards on him (he did not say at that time that he had been involved). I also knew that he lived in the Cherbourg area, that his name was André Defrance and that he had a son. His wife had also been arrested and he had no news of his family. He explained that there was a clandestine Party group comprising militants and sympathizers and that he would see to it that I was contacted.

On 25 April there was a general roll call and my name was called along with Michel, Roland, the abbé, Charles and younger FPJ members. On the other hand, some veterans in our room who were probably in favour with the camp internal administration were passed over.

The following day in the afternoon it was time to take leave of the few friends remaining and to pack our bags. Only one piece of hand baggage was allowed. The rest was to follow on by truck. Any surplus could be returned to families via the Red Cross. Inspection and search lasted all afternoon. We had to strip and go before a group of SS who meticulously checked and searched clothes and baggage. Once we had dressed we went to camp C where the huts, totally empty of all furniture, were strewn with straw on the floor. I became separated from the abbé and the young lads but joined up again with Michel and Charles.

The next day at about 4 am they gave us some coffee then at dawn we left. We had to return the mugs and they gave us bread rolls and a big starched cold meat sausage. Those who stayed massed along the A compound barbed wire fence to see us off and wish us well. They had a two-week deferral, which was time enough for the Gestapo to fill the huts again.

Going through Compiègne in ranks to get to the station seemed endless. The SS had had all shutters closed along the route and where there were none one could detect figures well back behind drawn curtains. Families who had been informed of our departure stood ten or more metres back in side streets leading off at right angles from ours. The biggest group had gathered around the bridge over the Oise and I could see a baby held up at arm's length by its mother in the hope that its father would be able to see it. After the war some widows confided in me that there they had seen their husbands for the last time.

Then we reached the station[3] with the train and its cattle wagons. The SS quickly made us get into the wagons, a hundred at a time, with whip blows, and the doors were closed. Like the wagons behind and in front of us we were one hundred only and not one hundred and twenty or thirty as some have recounted. It was horrible enough without exaggerating it. We were one hundred with our bags, blankets, coats, sausages and bread, in one wagon, the approximately area of which was seventeen square metres. Air could only enter via a skylight of a few square inches covered with a grid and barbed wire, and from the start there was a rush towards this opening, that is towards air which meant life itself.

There were some more 'adult' persons among us who tried to instil some discipline into the throng. To start with they spread the straw as best they could, then piled things not in use in a corner. They banned urinating in the slop bucket which would have filled up too quickly. This function had to be done in a big tin which after being passed from hand to hand was emptied via the air vent. Then they tried to get everyone seated, which proved impossible, with about twenty comrades remaining standing. Then they tried to organize place changes so that everyone could in turn be next to the vent, which proved unworkable as time went on. Some selfish people had to be pulled away from the vent, and worse still, they used any excuse to block it off completely with their head so as to breathe fresh air.[4]

In the daytime each person slumped as much as possible; a certain order prevailed but at night in the dark, bodies relaxed. Legs intertwining and arms groping for support were nightmarish. Some people lay down in sleep and we had to move tens of limbs to avoid being suffocated or crushed. In this way several were counted dead on arrival.

It seemed as if we were two or three times as numerous at night. Curses, shouts and blows were to be heard with cries of pain as heads, limbs and even genitals were squashed as well as bitten. I felt a hatred with a destructive urge against these foreign bodies and limbs squeezing the life out of me. From this journey I have never lost the fear of being in the metro, or a bus, or in a crowd. In spite of all the misery of my solitary confinement I began to miss my cell and thought that at that time I had spent the best years of my life there!

While we were still in France we wrote short messages to our families which we threw, with a weight attached, onto the track near level crossings or near stations. I wrote one and jammed it into a pen top clip. It did not arrive. Others were luckier than me and managed to contact their families.

At a stop in the middle of nowhere the occupants in the wagon in front of ours, who had started to make a hole in the wall, were obliged to throw knives and saw blades out onto the track. I had noticed that on every second wagon an armed guard occupied the brake-man cabin. Perhaps he had been alerted by the noise or by the shouts of those who did not want to get away, fearing reprisals.

The next day the train stopped at Novéant, which was a simulated station on the border of France and Lorraine, which was now annexed. The door was opened to reveal two Feldgendarmes, helmeted, with chest plates, whips in hand, who were there not to give us water, nor to empty slop buckets, but to count us. In a few seconds with truncheon blows they pushed us into half the wagon space, which forced one hundred into the space of less than ten square metres. Then they calmly passed us one by one into the other half of the wagon, punctuating the process with whip lashes. Once our tormentors stepped down, the door closed on our misery. The craftiest ones took advantage of the confusion to get next to the vent hole. All the organization of taking turns there had to be redone. In this train from hell, with the stench of the slop bucket, the rising heat of a cloudless sky, we went north to Trèves, and Koblenz, feeling parched and scared. Most of us had taken off jackets, pullovers and shirts. Some who were crazed with thirst had already started to lick the wagon bolts on which some moisture had condensed. In reality those bolts were only glistening with the saliva of the previous desperate licker.

Once again night brought the horror of groping tentacles and a long wait at Weimar. Were we going to Buchenwald? Alas the train started again and we had another wait in the station of Apolda. This time the SS had the slop buckets emptied and had buckets of water brought to each wagon, enough for a quarter bucketful per person. The distribution went badly. Some were served twice, and with the water level dropping hands became clumsy, tins were spilled and blows were exchanged under the impassive stare of the sentries. We were slowly turning into animals.

A third day began and town followed town. Some sick ones were placed next to the vent and amid the general lethargy some younger lads took it upon themselves to ventilate the air by waving a big towel, but as nobody took over from them only the monotonous motion of the train and general resignation remained.

In the course of swapping places I found myself next to the old rector of Pont-Aven. He had more and more difficulty breathing but instead of resting he tried to convert our group of atheists. He could not understand how, given the beauty of nature, birds flowers and butterflies, we did not believe in creation. He repeated as in a whisper, 'Who created life, if not God?' We answered him with instances of horror when he could only see beauty, the horror of nature in tooth and claw of which we were an example. 'This nightmare we are living through, is this one of God's works?' He became exhausted and his faithful vicar helped us to get him positioned next to the vent.

At each stop we shouted, 'Wasser bitte', and other wagons echoed our cries. Sometimes German railway workers filled up some tins. In our wagon we were fortunate to have a comrade who had been arrested in shorts and rubber boots when he was in the maquis. Several times his boots were filled up by compassionate hands and then drained to the last cloudy drop.

Crossing Silesia on the fourth day was made terrible by thirst. Some becoming deranged drank their own urine, or rushed to the vent crushing limbs and faces in forcing their passage to it. They had to be hit hard. Michel, Gaston, a friend of his and I gave each other mutual protection from the crush. And the train rolled on and on, ever faster, going through big industrial complexes producing petrol and synthetic rubber, undamaged by war.

Sometimes on returning from fishing I happened to clean out my worm tin and when I opened it after a few days, the worms which had survived, the fittest ones who had been near the air holes, rushed out to escape from the putrid environment of the dead ones at the bottom. When, in the evening of 30 April, the train stopped at Auschwitz freight station and the door opened, there was a rush to the outside world just as for the worms in my can.

We were met by SS troops, armed with machine guns, dogs and Polish Kapos who knew how to handle their rubber coshes.

We had to form up in line, five abreast in the moments which followed. A few deranged ones, one of whom tried to make off with an SS motorcycle, were shot and their bodies were piled next to those who had died in the wagons, being crushed or suffocated – their bodies were dumped on the ground by Poles. The sinister camp of Auschwitz-Birkenau was a good kilometre from the station. The track bringing trains directly into the camp had not been completed at that time.

At the vaulted main gate we turned right then left and followed the camp perimeter almost all the way around with windowless wooden huts on our left[5] separated from the outer patrol path by a swathe of electrified barbed wire and a chain of tall watch towers. As I marched along I recited, like a nursery rhyme, the text of a tract that I had distributed shortly before my arrest which went 'Daniel Casanova died at Auschwitz, Daniel Casanova died at Auschwitz,…'

A few thin shadowy figures in striped clothes came out of huts and watched impassively without any hint of a gesture as we passed. Fear and death emanated from their immobile silhouettes. That impression taught me how to sense the nature of a camp by the posture of the figures, even when seen from afar.

We entered the camp from the back by the Canada entrance after passing near a building hidden in a birch copse from which rose a large rectangular chimney. Later we were to learn that it was the gas chamber and crematoria complex number four.

The SS and their Polish galley slaves piled us into windowless wooden huts similar to those we had seen as we skirted the camp. There were no beds, mattresses, tables, chairs nor floor, just a hard potentially damp dirt base, and still no water. We gathered into little groups centred on common backgrounds, such as prison, region or Compiègne barracks. I was unable to find Charles or the abbé or the young lads of the FPJ. I remained with Michel, Gaston, and their communist companions from the Paris region.

In the night the Kapos began to call out the Compiègne numbers which tallied with a list drawn up in alphabetical order. As the letter L was some way down I tried to sleep, in spite of being parched with thirst. The Poles in the camp, recognizable by the letter P stitched inside a red triangle on the breast of their striped jackets, were dealing in water in exchange for money, rings, and gold signet rings. 'In any case,' they said, 'the SS will take everything from you!'

In the early morning I left the squalid hut for another in a group whose names began with the letter L. On the way our Polish 'guide' explained that the tall chimney was part of a crematorium and that we were all likely to end up there. Some fellow prisoners had already warned us that there was a site where detainees were gassed but nobody believed that tale.

In the new hut we were tattooed and in a few seconds my forearm bore the indelible number 185 899. After this ceremony we were given an ersatz coffee or a hot infusion, then once again our little group changed hut. This time the new Polish 'guide' took us to the sauna complex used for showers and disinfection of clothing. There in a large hall comrades stood naked for hours waiting to be called. Some, already showered, had set up a chain of water cans which they passed to us through the windows. I downed a few litres although it reeked of chlorine and I was not alone in so doing. Those whose names were called out left the hall, naked as before, after placing their clothes and valuables in bags labelled with their names. All other baggage was confiscated and what could not be eaten was shared out.

At small tables in the corridors leading to the showers French–speaking Polish inmates filled out interminable questionnaires about us. During this long wait there were incidents and scuffles, as a result of the stress and fatigue. The Poles behaved towards us in a brutal and humiliating way, accusing us of abandoning them in 1940. During this enrolment procedure we received a soup that most ate out of sticky unclean mess tins with their fingers: there was one tin for six people and no spoon.

When it came to my questioning I was lucky to come across a Pole who knew the areas of Sarthe and Connerré where I was born. He had lived there as a poultry dealer. He revealed to me that the SS were exterminating the Jews en masse by the wagonload in the gas chambers adjoining the crematoria in which the bodies were then burnt. So it was true. Confirmation came from comrades who had seen an SS soldier climb up a ladder and throw something into an opening. They thought it was grenades but in fact it was the gas Zyklon B in granular form. My Polish 'fellow countryman' advised me not to drink the water from the wash basins which carried dysentery and typhoid.

Jammed in that corridor we struggled for air as we waited naked for our turn to have all body hair shaved by the trimmers of the barbers. I fainted and Michel dragged me to the door with the help of a doctor who brought me round. After the shaving process a Pole covered our head and genitals with a sticky petroleum based liquid. Then he pushed us still wet into a corridor swept by an icy draft. There after a rectal search we were handed a quarter of a bread cob loaf and a half slice of cold sausage. Like all my comrades I received a pack of clothes or rather had–been–clothes from a hatch, soiled with suspect stains (dried blood or red lead). Some got items in their packs which were too big or two small, or women's clothes. The same was true of shoes, clogs, or half-slippers and headwear.

Having quickly donned these glad rags, for the first time in days we burst out laughing at the sight of the get-up of our comrades. Clutching our trousers with one hand, our bread and slouch cap in the other, stumbling in our ill-fitting footwear, mocked and harassed by those whom we henceforth called 'Lousy Poles', we returned to our first hut.

At daybreak we again tried to regroup, but for some whose name began with the last letters of the alphabet, the wait lasted thirty hours. Little by little our convoy came together in one of the same two huts. We were allowed to go out and I was able to place them in relation to the whole camp. They were the last two blocks in the Canada sector, close to the perimeter of the infirmary near the path by which we had arrived. We could see the SS in the watch towers moving around and slapping their arms to keep warm.

Through the barbed wire separating us from the medical block I was able to talk to a Frenchman, either a nurse or a doctor, who had approached to get any news. He was the sole survivor of the French non-Jewish deportees of 1942[6] still in Birkenau, the survivors of their group having been transferred to Auschwitz 1, the other camp, and he could not shed any light on the fate of the comrades from Seine Inférieure département who I knew had also left in that convoy. He confirmed the news about gassing. 'Whatever you do don't report sick; if they think it's serious you'll be gassed.'

In the evening there was a roll call (*Appel* in German). We had to line up in rows five abreast and sort out the sick and wounded. One of them suffered from a crushed penis, probably caused in the cattle wagon. With every step he yelped in pain, even though he was supported by two comrades. The next day I visited the area set aside for those poor souls in the second hut, along with Gaston and Michel, looking for a friend. There were about ten of them, prostrate there, agonising, feverish, with pus oozing from their open wounds or boils. I recognised the man with the crushed penis, with his face distorted in pain. We helped the nurses and doctors who were also in their convoy and devotedly tended to them and moved them to one side so that they could benefit from the sun. We returned to our hut with a sense of relief.

In spite of the organisational efforts of some comrades, the soup distribution never passed off without jostling and blows. There was only one mess tin for six and it was not easy to check who had already received a helping. That disgusting tin, sticky with soup, was scraped and licked before changing hands. Some got two or three helpings, and, as the level in the urns went down, the crush intensified and the server abandoned the can, which was grasped by tens of hands, and forced his passage away wielding the ladle as he went. Little by little the social veneer shattered. In those hand-me-down rags, with bald heads, one could no longer tell one from another, apart from close friends. In that sordid anonymity there was theft and worse. Some urinated along the hut walls rather than go to the purpose-made hole outside.

In the morning as we squatted in places still smelling of urine, I woke up with a heavy nosebleed doubtless caused by fatigue. Blood streamed in pulses either through the nose or the mouth. I was gripped with panic; was this the end of the line for me? My pals tried to reassure me, stuffing my nose with a lint strip torn from a dirty handkerchief. From time to time a big clot blocked my throat but little by little the haemorrhage stopped and I calmed down.

That day a convoy of Hungarian Jewish women, many of them young, passed along the path by which we had come, separated from us by the electrified barbed wire. There was a kind of calm and dignity in their march to the sauna or the crematorium. Some carried parcels, others babies. They calmly spoke to their escorts, some of whom attended to children. They were so near that we could have understood them if we had known their language. As we drew nearer to the barbed wire the guard in the nearest watch tower fired a warning burst and we had to return to the shelter of the hut. In contrast to what we had experienced, their guards did not bully them and they seemed to be headed for a haven of peace. The endless convoy raised a cloud of dust and went out of view. Some hours later the chimneys of the crematoria spewed out their sickening smoke.

Meanwhile the Pole from Connerré had come to see me. He talked to me about people I could not have known as I left the area aged one and had never returned. He had left behind a wife and friends. I nodded my head in agreement without speaking for fear of setting off my nosebleed. He told us that the Jewish Hungarian women we had seen passing were all headed for the gas chamber, which was disguised as showers, and thence for the crematorium. It was the third convoy in a matter of days and tens more were due in the coming weeks. He explained that all the work was carried out by prisoners of the Sonderkommando (Special Duty Death Squad) a unit which was rotated every few weeks. To avoid witnesses the previous Sonderkommando was executed in turn.

He was surrounded by a ring of faces, hungry for information. 'What's going to happen to us?'

'You, because you've been tattooed, will be attached to the kommandos (work groups) in the camp. As Arians you may get away with it but we Jews will all go over there!' He pointed in the direction of the crematoria. 'In any event, they'll kill us all before the Russians get here, you'll see!'

He brought me a little food and above all two aspirin tablets, so precious to all of us,[7] worth more than their weight in gold. He also told me that the inmates of the Canada block were given the job of going through the baggage of the new arrivals, and of putting aside anything that was of use to the Germans, such as clothing or objects. The main aim was to look for money, gold or jewellery hidden in the linings or hems of clothes or in heels or soles of shoes or in artificial limbs. As a reward they could keep any food they discovered. This was the reason for the name of this Kommando called

Canada, a promised land. This was confirmed by Charles, who on his way back from the 'sauna', passing close to the sorting centre, recognised the envelopes of our Red Cross parcels, and some suitcases burning on a pile of refuse.

After he left, I took the tablet; the haemorrhage started again in full force and I lost a lot of blood. Was that the day my friends dragged me semi-conscious to another block? I left that sordid place, propped up by them, in lines five abreast, for another sector of the camp near to the main gate. Our barracks were isolated from others by non-electrified barbed wire. Near us was a whole camp containing gipsies with wives and numerous children. We could see them playing and yelling relatively happily in spite of walking in mud.[8]

Our situation in the new blocks had improved. This time we did not sleep on the floor. On either side of a central passage rose brick alcove-like structures with three levels built into each one. I call it a berth between columns, and it housed ten of us in each one. To lie down we had to lie head to foot like sardines in a tin. There were hand basins for washing and, thankfully, latrines.

Those latrines, for the use of that part of the camp, were communal and set up in a barrack building as large as the one in which we lived. We passed along the urinals at the sides; the centre was taken up by an endless line of holes, perhaps forty in a line. I never took the trouble to count them. When they were fully occupied, which was frequently, due to the unhealthy state of the water and the presence of dysentery, we sat back to back in a line of about thirty metres. Those latrines were set up at the end of a row of blocks next to the watch towers, the electrified barbed wire and the path we had taken on our arrival.

Returning from the latrines, sometimes a pal would shout, 'They're still coming. They keep arriving.' Then we would rush out under cover of the block buildings to watch the convoys pass by. Most were made up of women and children but some were of men. They all went quietly to what they thought were showers, happy to be at the end of their journey. How many did I see pass in that way? Perhaps eight or ten. One day two convoys numbered at least one thousand prisoners. If we had been sceptical at the beginning about the real situation, all doubt disappeared after a few days; those convoys were gassed on arrival.

As time passed we gained some confidence in our future, for, as the Pole from Sarthe[9] had said we would not have been tattooed if we were due to be gassed. The prisoners destined for the gas chambers were not sent to be tattooed, nor to the 'sauna', and did not appear[10] in the camp's statistics.

Our aimless camp life more or less became organised, after a fashion, the worst moments being standing in the mud for the roll call. For hours we sometimes had to wait for the order 'Caps off' and 'Caps on' which signified the end of it.

The straw mattresses were alive with fleas. My body had got used to them in Rouen prison but many of my comrades were suffering with them.

With our ill-fitting shoes it was difficult to walk in the mud surrounding our blocks, so we stayed chatting, lying or sitting in our sleeping berths.

Hunger was ever present; some swapped recipes of regional dishes, especially 'Cassoulet'.[11] One of our comrades was nicknamed after it.

Friends grouped together along lines of regional- or prison- or case-history backgrounds. André Defrance introduced me to a Communist Party representative who was supposed to give me some instructions. He seemed sectarian and blinkered to realities so it was difficult to take to him.

In spite of all advice we continued to drink the water from the basin taps since the so-called tea and soup did not quench our thirst. The cans, or rather barrels, used to supply us with water were transported by women who bent under the load between the shafts of the carts and whose shoes amassed clots of mud. This gave them the allure of characters in a slow-motion film walking in an unreal world. Some of them were very good looking, wearing make up, close fitting clothes and leather boots and had the confident gait of the well fed. Their only work was the pleasure of the VIP prisoners such as block leaders and such like.

On Friday, 12 May, we left the camp with no regrets. We will doubtless never know why.[12] A train was waiting for us at Auschwitz freight station and this time we were only sixty to a wagon, which meant we could easily lie down on the straw. The door remained open, guarded by two sentries. It was time to be joyful and sing. That day I met a guy from Le Havre by the name of Vézier. He hummed a tune from that time which stuck in my mind and which, whenever I heard it later, made me think of the time when we left Auschwitz.

.

..

I went back to Birkenau forty years later with some comrades. I followed the route we had taken from Auschwitz freight station as far as the 'sauna' block by the path along the perimeter and the watch towers.

The sauna has remained as I remember it with the big waiting hall, the showers, petroleum sinks, and the hatch where the hand–me–down clothes were thrown out at us. I became aware of how close the number IV crematorium was to us and how pals had indeed been able to witness certain things. Of our block and the Canada area there remained only some hard foundations. All that part of the camp was just one vast field broken up by low walls, and in it on our pilgrimage of 1985 we found rusty cutlery, dental pincers, spectacle frames and other objects discarded by the SS.

I could not precisely locate the block in which we ended our stay; I recognised the latrines, kept still intact for visitors, with its lines of holes. One of the blocks had the same ground plan as ours with its central corridor and its lateral sleeping berths. I slipped into one, wondering how it had been possible to live there, ten in one for a week. Of some wooden huts there remained just a brick chimney pointing its crooked finger to the sky. It all seemed immense to me, out of proportion to the memory I had kept with me.

While we were under the impression that Birkenau was in the middle of a deserted marshland, I was surprised to see tall apartment blocks quite near to the camp. The explanation was given to us by the museum director: in order to avoid the mistakes made at Treblinka, Majdenek and at other extermination camps, the SS had evacuated all towns and villages nearby and demolished them so that there could be no outside witnesses and that the secret of their genocide would be preserved. Now all these places are rebuilt and inhabited again. The white silhouette of the Carpathian Mountains in the distance was as I remembered it.

I seemed to hear cannon rumbling as on the first occasion.

Of the gas chambers and crematoria there remained only a tangle of beams, broken blocks and twisted metal; before evacuating the camp, being under pressure from the advancing Red Army, the SS had blown everything up, hoping in this way to obliterate their crime against humanity.

## Chapter 6

# Buchenwald, from Small Camp to Main Camp

We arrived at Buchenwald two days later, that is to say on 14 May 1944, in the morning. I do not recall the meanderings of that journey, doubtless because we were comfortably stretched out on the straw and we had enough to eat and drink.

When we arrived at the station platform, the Lagerschutz[1] and Kapos had us line up in columns five wide. We took the wide Carachoweg[2] road and had to salute the German stone eagle after passing a curious wooden sign post.[3] On the left it depicted the SS marching to the barracks that we could see screened by trees, and on right, that is in our direction, there were painted figures of a Jew, a monk, and a priest with the inscription, 'Konzentrationslager'.

After passing through the main gate called the 'tower', which bore the inscription in bronze letters 'Jedem das Seine',[4] we went around the parade ground passing near a zoo and a crematorium towards the disinfection buildings.

Hundreds of Frenchmen, gathered en masse along the last stage, tried to recognise anyone among us, seeking someone from his home, a resistance companion, or a relative. Questions came in salvoes:

'Any lads from Eure et Loire?'[5]

'Do you know if X is in your convoy?'

Shouts of joy greeted any such reunions.

It must have been a good camp since all inmates seemed healthy, clean, and decently dressed in well fitting civilian clothes with a cross sewn or painted on their backs. As it was a Sunday the spectators were numerous. Most prisoners were bareheaded with Mohican or 'Street' haircuts.[6]

Suddenly a voice called out to me, 'Hey Paulo is it you? You must be Paul Le Goupil from Rouen EN.' I recognised Yves Boulogne, a third-year student who had inducted me in the freshman days. He had been arrested in 1942 and sentenced by a Vichy court for distributing tracts and, on release from prison, was rearrested by the Gestapo. He told me he would take care of me and that I had to state my profession as 'tailor'.

We went in small groups to begin the same cycle as in the Auschwitz wash house: shaving of all hair, dipping in a bath of disinfectant, head held below the surface by a brute for what seemed an eternity. After once more filling out questionnaires, number 53 354 was allocated to me, this time not in alphabetical order but according to the order we went through. Then I had to put on a fresh set of hand-me-downs. The whole thing passed off in much better circumstances than in Auschwitz, without being yelled at or being hit.

An escort of camp guards (Lagerschutz) led us to the small quarantine camp where we were dispersed into two blocks. That was a holding site before detainees were sent either to the main camp or to what was known in camp jargon as the 'transport' kommando. I was sent to block 57 near the path leading from the main camp to the medical block, in conditions as bad as those in Birkenau. We were still ten to a sleeping quarter, but this time the unit separations were of wood, each comprising four levels of bunks, where we had to lie head to foot. We were subject to violence from block chiefs and their minions. Our joy on changing camp had been short lived.

As for our destination there were numerous rumours. A lot was heard of Dora, the name whispered in fear by everyone. It was an underground factory with a terrible death rate.

In my berth I met up with Vézier whom I nicknamed 'One-eye', as he had a glass eye, and he played the tough guy from Le Havre. Then there was Michel and the pals from the south of France who spent all day swapping mouthwatering recipes. The abbé, Charles, and the young FPJ lads were in the next berth.

Yves had kept his promise and from the very next day he came to the other side of the barbed wire lining the path, preventing any access to the main camp. He gave me some bread and sausage and explained the system of registration, and took my number 53 354 stitched on a patch on my trousers and on my jacket below a red triangle overprinted with a black 'F'. The colour of the badge indicated, as in all camps, the reason for arrest: red was political, green was for a common law offence, black was for sabotage, pink for homosexuals. Everyone in my convoy received the red triangle, regardless. Thus, with time I realised that prisons had been emptied by the Germans. Among us there were quite a number of people arrested for minor offences with no political aspect; trafficking with the Germans, stealing from them, or black marketeering.[7]

If our situation appeared unenviable, it was worse for the convoy of 2,000 Frenchmen that had left Compiègne on 12 May and arrived on the evening of 14 May, since there was no more space and our comrades had to sleep on the ground in one enclosure behind the small camp until large circus-type tents were erected for them.

Our life in block 57 went on monotonously with each day resembling the one before. Towards 4 am the 'Stubendienst'[8] woke those designated for coffee duty and at about 4.30 or 5 am, when the hot liquid arrived, we heard the shout 'Aufstehen'.[9]

Distribution followed quickly. As we slept fully clothed we only had to get up. I was lucky enough to have a red enamelled mess tin that also served as a pillow. Those who had none were served their coffee out of empty tin cans retrieved from the waste dumps.

After drinking the liquid we had to fold the blankets which had to remain in the building, to be counted in each berth by the Stubendienst. At 6 am there came the roll call in the cold and mud in front of the block. It was not very long as it was done per building. Although it was over by 6.30 or 7 am we could not go back into the hut which was being sluiced out copiously by the Stubendienst and his orderlies. The ground resonated to our wooden clogs sounding like tap shoes as we waited to get back into the warm. We were finally allowed to return inside towards 8.30 am after removing the mud from our feet. Anyone who dirtied the floor was in for a hard time. The henchmen were waiting in the doorways. The culprit risked staying outside during the bread hand-out and hence not getting any.

We had a loaf of 1500 grams to share between four or five or sometimes between three as on a Sunday. We also got twenty grams of margarine and sometimes a slice of starchy sausage.

Most people, like me, ate their ration in one go. Those who kept some of it for the evening soon caught on that the best larder was their stomach, so high was the rate of theft.

After blankets had been counted our block leaders led us in groups by sleeping berths to the communal wash blocks of the small camp. From taps poured a continuous flow of water into big terracotta sinks. We had to strip to the waist and scrub ourselves with cake-soap. On returning to the hut the block leader checked our feet personally.

Towards 10 am so-called 'volunteers' were called out and designated for the morning bread chore. There were few takers for it, unlike for the soup duty since there was no hope of leftovers and they had to wait hours for it outside at the kitchen doors. For the soup duty around 11 am came a surge of Russians and Poles. It was doled out from 12.30 to 1 pm. Those who only had a tin can waited for a friend to lend them their mess tin so as not to be losing out as the ladle, when it was not dented or cut down, contained one litre. Those mess tins were so precious that most lucky owners had made holes at the edge and wore them strung across their chests like Feldgendarme breastplates.

The leftovers were not evenly dished out and more often ended up in the room of the block leader. The empty urns were piled in the open to be scraped smooth by those on urn duty. Around 2 pm, each inmate in turn had to wash all the mess tins from his berth.

In the afternoon the comrades from the main camp, on night duty, came down along the barbed wire to see their friends in the small camp. Yves came almost every day with some food for me. It was the only place where we could communicate since at the normal passage higher up near block 47 the ever-vigilant gate wardens, anxious to keep their jobs, prevented all contact.

The big event of the afternoon was the walk to the latrine in the large block designated for this purpose. Urinals without separations lined the outer walls and the middle space was occupied by endless latrines without separations, where two rows of inmates squatted back to back perched on a low cement wall to answer the call of nature. Unlike those in Auschwitz, these latrines had no holes. Wooden bars allowed one to lean back, which stopped the less agile from falling into the two-metre-deep shit pit which echoed from end to end with the sounds of dysentery. Between the latrines and the urinals there was a board walk on each side like the one in Deauville, which was a meeting place. In spite of the smell, anything could be bought and sold in this market place of wonders, even if this was forbidden by internal camp regulations, the hard currency being cigarettes or bread rolls. And there were also gangs of thieves, mostly Slavs from the small camp; they shared out their spoils, scores were settled and a person would disappear into the shit pit.

We could also go and see our friends in the invalid block or get news of friends in the small medical block. The main thing was to be back at the hut by 6 pm, after which some stayed in the sleeping quarter chatting; others hung around near the wire in the hope of being recognised and helped by inmates in the main camp. The curfew was sounded by a whistle at around 9 pm. Lights went out except for a small lamp left lit at each end of the block.

As warned by Yves as soon as I arrived, I stated my profession as tailor. He later explained that all intellectuals, teachers, or white-collar workers were systematically sent on quarry or tunnelling work kommandos. He hoped to get me into his kommando which was the best in the camp, since there were advantages in taking care of the clothes of the camp staff hierarchy; in addition the work was seated and sheltered. He added, 'Above all keep it to yourself, don't even tell your friends that I am looking after you.'

In block 57 theft was on the increase and a piece of bread left out of sight for a few seconds was sure to disappear. And yet in our quarters we were only Frenchmen. Later, in the kommandos, Russians and Poles were accused, but among ourselves how could that be? Anger was simmering and two or three days after our arrival a comrade thought he had a thief. It was the Pole who had shaved us and given us haircuts in Rouen. The poor man who spoke French badly was unable to defend himself. First he received several blows from the rubber cosh of the block leader, who then hauled him onto a stool and made him hold a brick in each hand, arms outstretched. Some who considered the punishment too lenient slapped him whenever his arms dropped a little. A crowd had gathered and suddenly it turned nasty. Someone shouted that he had been an informer in Rouen prison and that he had spilled the beans on an escape attempt plan. Another thought he knew him in the same role in Lyons prison and a wave of bald heads surrounded him and attacked him in spite of the brave intervention of some comrades who were looking for justice. All the accumulated hatred for Poles, thieves and informers was focussed on a scapegoat. He was just still alive and someone said, 'Finish him off.' He was dragged to the door and drowned in a rain water butt. He remained there in the mud until the arrival of a cart collecting the dead, a vehicle with two shafts pulled by two inmates, used to pick up the dead thrown out at the doors of the huts.

One morning the abbé came to see me with a young FPJ member to tell me that Nivromont junior was putting it about that I had denounced him to the Gestapo in order to spare the lives of real miscreants. I explained the circumstances of that sad event and I went to see Nivromont senior. The final explanation between father, son and me took place. The son had a fixed look, was very weak, and I sensed he was fixated on making me the cause of all his trouble, in the belief that without my involuntary gaff he would have been freed. The next day he had to be hospitalised with meningitis and after some days hovering between life and death he fortunately pulled through.[10]

We received several injections, which were vaccines against various diseases, carried out by nurses in the medical block (Revier). The same needle was used, being simply wiped with cotton. Some comrades hid, believing that they were being injected with a sickness or were being sterilised. The quarantine period for new arrivals was made shorter and as early as 20 May there were rumours that we would be leaving.

I went to see some folk from Rouen in the sick bay, among them Dr Crutel, who was a deputy from Rouen, crouching among the wounded who could not work. As I was looking for anyone who might know my family in the départements of Manche, Calvados or Eure et Loire, he directed me towards a certain Davignon who had only one arm and who had lived in Montlandon, a village near Illiers. He knew several people, notably the Sédillots who managed the farm called Grand'Barre in Illiers, whose son had been shot by the Boche. He was happy to talk about his area, the shopkeepers of Illiers where he did the local market and sold his chickens. He received parcels and several times he invited me to share his crispy bread or bread with butter and cake that his wife had made. He was much older than me and his kind round face lit up when I went to see him and chat about his area. In his Perche accent he used to say, 'You'll come and see me in Montlandon; we'll have a big party and dance to your accordion.'

He had a padlocked wooden locker that he slipped under his bed and in which he stored his parcels. Whenever he laboriously slid it out and opened it, with his one arm, I observed a ring of faces covetously staring down from three levels of bunks, ready to devour the contents of the box. He would shout, 'It's not for you; I've already had to chip in to the common pot. And some of you have helped themselves!'

Envoys from the secret underground network in the main camp tried to find out the reasons for one's arrest, so as to ultimately get such and such a person moved into the main camp. The Communist Party and the Front National had set themselves up with group leaders. Mine was the same as in Auschwitz, a moaning blinkered type who above all concerned himself with his pals from the Paris region. I related this to Defrance who said I had to trust the Party and that in the main camp the comrades would take care of us. I did not mention Yves to him.

I noticed the antics of a deportee from Déville, whom I had known in the Rouen prison. I overheard his conversation with one of the 'envoys'. He passed himself off as an important leader in the FN. He was one of those who moved up to the main camp and, after liberation, he made out that he had doubtless been mistaken for somebody else and he did not know why he had stayed in the main camp.

I was one of the first if not the first to be called and transferred to Yves's block, block 40, one week after my arrival. It caused a stir in our little community. Grumpy, my group head took me to one side and spoke to me in these words: 'It's not right what you've done, you may have taken the place of a more important comrade than you! The Party won't forget this.'

Hoping to join me soon Defrance and Charles were both pleased for me but I felt awkward vis à vis the abbé and the young lads from the FPJ. I noted their numbers to try to get them moved but I felt like a general abandoning his troops and this dampened my joy. I confided this to Yves who told me, 'What I did for you cannot be done for anyone else, all the more since I've got problems of my own.'

The internal camp organisation, doubtless alerted by Grumpy, accused him of short circuiting procedure. He had gone to see Willy, the head of Arbeitstatistik,[11] a German prisoner that he knew, to get me out of my convoy group and into his block. His precipitous action probably saved my life as I had lost weight and was anaemic, and I would not have survived in a hard kommando.

Some days later, Michel and Gaston, who had met up with their friends from the Paris region, came over to the main camp in turn, but on 25 May, Charles, the abbé, the young FPJ lads and Defrance left for Flossenburg. Defrance, whom I saw in Cherbourg after the war, was still bitter about it since he was, at the time of his arrest, the military delegate for the whole of the south west, under direct command of Ouzoulias, and he was in charge of the Cinédit attack, the most violent of all Normandy resistance actions.[12]

According to the statistics published by Paul Durand[13] resulting from a serious study done in Arolsen by Arnoult, out of the 1,682 deportees of our convoy arriving in Buchenwald on 14 May 1944, 700 left for Flossenberg, 200 for Dora, 500 were attached to various outside camp kommandos and 282 remained in Buchenwald.[14] Furthermore among the latter were the invalided, in the sick block, among them Nivromont's son (his father going to Dora). It is not known exactly how the groups were composed. I only know that from the département of Seine-Inférieure, out of the eighty prisoners only a few from Le Havre and three from Rouen went up to the main camp, whereas the proportion of militant trade unionists, communists and FTP from the Paris region who were moved into the main camp was much greater. Future researchers with access to the Arolsen[15] files will be able to be much more accurate.

Buchenwald, like all other concentration camps, was entirely administered by the detainees with a pyramid hierarchy, comprising, from the top down, Lagerälteste, Kapos, Stubendienst, Vorarbeiter, Lagerschutz etc. This organisation allowed the SS to manage a town–size population of detainees with just a few hundred soldiers. The SS came only rarely to inspect the camp, limiting their intervention to giving out orders to this army of administrators and staff who were all the more docile as they desired to keep their status and the perks that went with it.

The real 'lords' of the camp were not, as some maintain, people like Marcel Paul, Colonel Manhès or other party or resistance group leaders. It was the staff of the Arbeitsstatistik section who had control over all the detainee files. Indeed the SS was not concerned with knowing who was on the lists of those due to leave the camp. They simply told the Kapo Willy that they needed 200, 500, or 1,000 'Stuck'[16] for Dora or another kommando detail. Willy then drew up a list drawn from the new arrivals in the small camp, and if that was not sufficient he would top up with those from the main camp. Those concerned received the order to report to the tower. If they knew someone higher up or if they belonged to an organisation they would contact them rapidly; the latter would alert one of their comrades working in the worker statistics section who would juggle the files, striking out the name of the recalcitrant and replace it with another.

Niether Marcel Paul nor any other leader knew who took whose place. The hand of man became the hand of the devil instead of the hand of fate. The number of departures did not change; no life was spared by this juggling, but one life was replaced by another.

Marcel Paul in the preface to Pierre Durand's book frankly details the system in place already prior to his arrival stating that less well protected foreigners took the place of Frenchmen; but as I previously indicated, only researchers having access to the archives will be able to establish who replaced whom.

Before the arrival of Marcel Paul, the French community, lacking a prominent communist to head it, was poorly represented in the international committee which was led by German communists. My compatriots, having a bad reputation and being considered generally as disreputable traffickers and riff-raff, constituted the major component of out-of-camp kommandos for work in underground sites like Dora. Marcel Paul was able to rectify this situation, giving our community its rightful status, thus avoiding the massive transport of Frenchmen on the worst kommandos. Of course there were slip-ups, settling of scores, Frenchmen who were substituted for other Frenchmen, but generally the facts speak for themselves. Before the arrival of Marcel Paul, more than half of the convoys, sometimes as much as two thirds, were transported to Dora; after 14 May this number dropped significantly.[17]

Marcel Paul has been described by some as a 'Kapo' in the 'Arbeitsstatistik' responsible for parcels. Some claim to have seen him inspect the camp dressed in white and with a smart white peak cap and gold shoulder braid, like Goering. All that is nonsense and discredits those who have spread such untruths. Furthermore, why is he subject to a hateful and false campaign while things happened in the same way in all the other camps? This is born out by a reading of Michelet's book.[18] Marcel Paul was the leader of the French communist community after the assasination of General Delestrain by the SS in Dachau, a camp dominated by German catholic inmates. In it he writes of the difficulties he had saving a personal communist friend from a transport detail, and of the reproaches he then had to endure!

Block 40 was a construction in concrete, divided into four wings, two on the ground floor and two on the first floor accessed via an external staircase. I was allocated to wing B on the lower right where Yves was also billeted. In this part of the block there were very few Frenchmen; Yugoslavs and Czechs made up close communities; there were numerous Germans and some important figures, such as Soudan, an ex-Belgian government minister. Due to the fact that a certain number of Germans in our wing worked in the kitchens, or held positions in the camp, we received benefits: some mornings we had a supplementary serving of white soup, usually reserved for those in the sick bay. I had a bunk to myself and a cupboard with shelves in which I could store personal items or food. The block chief was a very strict character[19], interned as a German student since 1933, who granted no favours to anyone. He valued cleanliness, order and discipline. Yves had warned me about all that. Above all, at the beginning, the Stubendienst[20] gave me a thorough inspection after the ablutions and I was only allowed into the block after he uttered the customary 'Gut'. Only once did he make me return to the washbasins to remove a small mark at the back of my foot, which I had not seen.

Each independent wing of the block was divided into separate parts. The entry lobby gave onto washrooms where water cascaded umbrella-fashion into two large circular basins. In this room were also collective latrine cabins with individual seats, urinals along a wall and sinks for washing mess tins and cleaning boot soles. There were scraping irons fixed to the ground used to remove mud from clogs. From the corridor one passed into the common room where there were chests with shelves, several large tables and benches where each person had his own place even if it was impossible for all to be seated at the same time. My soup tin, my bread and margarine rations were fourteenth on the right side of the first table on the left on entering. If anyone, for reasons of working hours, was late, his ration stayed there all day if need be and no one touched it. On our bench seat places we piled our clothes in the evening before lights out.

From this room, in which it was not easy to move around, so close together were the tables and benches, we passed into the dormitory where there were rows of three-storey single bunk beds. Mine was at the end of the room on the right, second level. The Stubendienst made sure that all blankets were pulled tight and that nothing littered them. They were so close together that one had to move sideways and it was not easy to get up to the second level. Later in more difficult times, they were used by two detainees: one worker on the dayshift (Tagesschicht) and one worker on nightshift (Nachtschicht), alternating occupancy.

This organisation, this cleanliness and discipline made a great change from the bays and rotting boxes I had squatted in before. Moreover here no one had more clout than another and there was never an argument. The Stubendienst intervened at the slightest lapse.

During the next few days I stayed in the block, carrying out chores as I had not been detailed for a specific job. Yves tried to get me attached to the tailor service which contained for the most part notable inmates and in which places were coveted. He did not succeed and at the beginning of June I was allocated permanently to hall 4 at Mibau, a factory to which I will refer later.

We were not allowed to write to our family for a period of several months but Yves very generously gave me the use of his return letter rights so that I could inform my folk of my arrival in Buchenwald. It was dangerous for him to write directly to my parents so he used a ruse. He got me to write a letter in German which he signed as was the procedure, intended for one of their neighbours, asking him to greet the

Renard family* and requesting a parcel. The answer came in the form of a postcard posted in Germany from the son of the family working there:

'Today I received a letter from Rouen posted on 27 June. The Renard family is well and in good health. I will ask at the post office if I can send you something. If so I'll do so immediately. Best wishes. Bye.'

Alas the post office must have said no, or the parcel was confiscated, since nothing came from that quarter. Later I finally received authorisation to write to my parents and I received one parcel sent from Pithiviers.

Yves was in cahoots with some friends in the tailor kommando. It was a big ring which had received plenty of parcels and Yves often allowed me to have his bread as he had enough to eat from his mess group friends.[21] He often would only take his margarine and sometimes his soup. Several detainees at my table, some of them German, also gave me their rations for the same reason. It happened that on some days I would get two or tree rations of bread and a few mess tins of soup. I quickly got my strength back and recovered my weight from pre-Bonne Nouvelle prison days. Yves also got me an impeccable serge blue civilian suit with a cross of St Andrew in a lighter colour on the back. Because the camp administration supplied us with a change of underwear each week, we were respectably clean.

I had moved up to the main camp during its least disreputable period, for which it earned the label 'sanatorium' in the eyes of some people. Unfortunately it did not last and those who experienced it could not forget the previous days when the SS let their dogs loose on the inmates and were liable to beat someone to death on the slightest pretext. Yves, André Marie (former deputy of the département of Seine Inférieure) and several other Rouen men showed me their legs, still red from the scars of dog bites.

In those summer months I lived through the least depressing moments of my deportation, and as in other camps all that mattered was the present. Those few summer months allowed me to build up some strength and get

---

* This was a coded reference to Paul's family name, Le Goupil, which is a popular term meaning 'fox'.

back into a state of health to be able to confront fresh trials in the best possible condition.

Yves tried to get me into his mess clique, but amongst the French in the camp who enjoyed plentiful supplies, social class groupings had developed and, with a few exceptions, the big parcel mess-group kept to themselves. But Yves, acting alone, enabled me to enjoy some luxuries.

The Czech and Yugoslav communities shared their packages globally and sometimes one could see on their tables rows of bread slices with quarters of sliced sausage, cubes of fruit gum or butter and other garnishes. It was shared out to the nearest mouthful. My compatriots did not have this sense of solidarity and they were reluctant to give to the common cause because of individualism or selfishness. Davignon thought it was tantamount to theft, but he complied for fear of being put on a transport list. If I had received big parcels would I have been more willing to share than the others? With friends yes, but with everyone?

I could not keep much stock of bread in my locker since the Stubendienst regularly looked in the cupboards and took away any food that was likely to go bad, thus from time to time I took a small bagful of chunks of bread down to the small camp. This helped old man Davignon, whose parcels had become scarce, doubtless pillaged.

He told me of the arrival of some youngsters from the Illiers area. There was the son of the music director, the son of the pharmacist-assistant and others that I cannot remember. I had accompanied my grandpa to their parents' houses when he went to read their electricity meters. In the group was a certain Pipret, whose wife, who was the mistress of a policeman, had caused the arrest of a significant number of FTP members. Sadly they all left after a few days on a transport to underground work and not one of them returned.

As in the small camp the block came to life around 4 am with the departure of those on coffee duty. A short while later the common room resounded to the unique cavernous resonance of the urns being dumped heavily onto the floor and at 4.30 am the Studendienst would shout out '*Aufstehen*'.[22] We tumbled out of bed, tried to pull on our clothes laid out the benches, and looked for our clogs. Then came the big rush to the washbasins followed by the serving of the hot liquid which was downed quickly since at 5 am everybody had to be lined up in front of the block to go up to the parade ground. '*Ausrichten*'[23] was the command.

At 5.30 am the kommandos formed up, always in the same place, and the Kapos counted their men with guttural palaver. At 6 am the tower loudspeaker sounded the order to leave camp. First through the gate went the camp brass band in red trousers, blue braided jackets and berets,[24] playing a march, often the Eagle march, then they took up a position to the right of the tower and played on. The kommando groups then began their march in step, 'Links rechts, links rechts!', saluting as we passed under the archway. The order never changed; first went the Gustav and Mibau factory details hall by hall, then the Earthworks kommando, the Eisenbahn (railway) and the out-of-camp kommandos.

Exiting camp took place quickly. Then we went along the Carachoweg and had to salute the stone eagle which was at the roadside. Next we reached the main crossroads leading to the station, to the factories or to the barracks where the painted wooden signpost stood. Towards 6.30 am we formed up in groups in front of hall number 4 and we were counted once again. As soon as the nightshift came out around 6.45 am we entered the workshop and took up position at our machines. At the sound of a siren at 7 am we started work which was non-stop until 5.30 pm with a thirty-minute break at midday.

In hall 4 we mainly made parts for the gyroscopes of the V1 rockets. Two large presses churned out what were called cores; they consisted of two rings machined half flat made from castings from powdered metal with methyl alcohol. These half pieces were tested by a team I was in which tested their flux permeability ranging from forty to fifty.[25] The tester then marked the result on the flat side with a special pencil and then matched the half rings, combining for example 46.5 with 47.5 or 46 with 48 to obtain a homogenous batch with average value 47. Then the rings went to a workshop where each ring was wrapped in paper before passing to a coil-winding machine which wound electric wire around each ring with the number of windings corresponding to its density, forming the gyroscope coils. All these parts were assembled in V1s in the Dora underground workshops.

These cores arrived stacked in large crates at our small quality control workshop, which was separated from the rest of the hall by a glass screen. There were only half a dozen technicians, of whom only two or three were skilled in the trade. For the first crates I made an effort to correctly mark the results but the two Frenchmen in charge of the workshop told me I had got it all wrong. They took a crate and without passing the cores in the test machine they marked them with anything at all between 45 and 55. It made things go faster and gained us some free time. For inspection purposes there were always a few correctly tested crates within arm's reach of the German foreman, who came to check them from time to time.

We had seats, which was a bonus, since workers in most of the other shops had to stand.

It was not advisable to move around in the hall nor linger too long in the toilets as an SS soldier called 'Wineroot'[26] traced the malingerers and dished out at least twenty-five strokes on the backside. If necessary he would lift the toilet seats to see if there were any stools and if not he hit out. He passed through the workshops sniffing deeply, hoping to pick up a trace of tobacco smoke and punish the offender.

To pass the time, especially if we were on night shift, we would slip in turn into an empty horizontal locker designed to hold the crates of cores, and our comrades would close it up. In the event of a check, or the arrival of Wineroot, one had to move smartly to get out. Several times one of us remained stuck inside during an inspection and it was a close shave.

In the hall I came across several friends from my convoy, among them Serge, a metal worker from the Paris region who worked on the press, and Michel from another workshop.

On the way back in the evening we would cross paths with the night shift and after saluting the eagle statue and the tower, we entered camp in reverse order to the morning departure, as ever accompanied by the sound of the brass band which came in last after the final kommando. After dismissal there was a rush to the blocks to try to get hot soup before roll call, but sadly it was often too late. The order was '*Antreten*'.[27] It was 6 or 6.30 pm. We had to go out and line up in fives in front of the building and march off behind block 39 which was aligned behind block 38. The fifty blocks were placed in three rows all precisely aligned. The first roll call took place around 7 pm. It was often not accurate and the Stubendienst would go back inside to see if anyone was still sleeping. Then the SS would restart their count. Meanwhile the soup continued to cool down and the detainees would begin to wander around, sit down, or play 'Hot Hand'.[28] At 8 pm came a fresh count, this time corrected, otherwise checks continued for hours. When the loudspeaker gave the all clear '*Das stimmt! Fertig!*'[29] there followed the rush to finish the cold soup and bread which made up the only meal of the day.

While we ate, the block loudspeaker gave out news and communiqués in German, followed by the numbers and crackling calls for block leaders to go to the tower. Towards 9 pm or later, if the roll call had been delayed, a whistle announced the curfew and it was lights out until the next morning.

Shortly after my start at the factory the block radio announced the news of the Normandy landings. On that day I was on the night shift, so I was in the sleeping quarter. Shouts of joy woke those who were asleep. Since I knew Normandy well, many of the German inmates came to see me in the following days to get information. From memory I drew a map of Lower Normandy, locating the Pointe du Hoc, Bayeux, Carentan, Périers, Tilly, Caumont l'Éventé and the famous Marcouf battery, whose names peppered the news reports every day. I became viewed as a sort of expert on hand to be consulted as soon as a new place name was quoted.

My thoughts were with the members of my family and I missed not being able to live this great moment in history with them. I did not know at that time that some were in mourning and that a naval shell had obliterated my cousin's farm in Grandcamp.

Our joy faded quickly with the stabilisation of the Normandy front. Parcels arrived but were more and more pilfered. I received one from Pithiviers with its dry biscuits crushed, some crumbs of bread and some tobacco. There remained still a fine pair of ankle boots in leather, one split kilo-pack of sugar and some fruit paste. Yet indirectly I was happy to get news of my family in this way. I tried the shoes on and they pinched. They were too fine for a simple prisoner and might have caused some resentment. I decided to exchange them for some food even though this was against the unwritten laws of the camp. They netted me the value of two or three good meals.

One day there was a problem in the top job 'tailor' kommando. André Marie had been called to the tower. He came back wearing a new set of the striped prison garb with orders to leave for Dora. Was it a mistake, a warning or a settling of scores? He alone could have explained but he remained ever silent in the matter. It turned out to be just a false alarm. With the intervention of Marcel Paul, the deputy of Seine Inférieur département returned to his place in the tailor section. This showed the precarious nature of our situation in the main camp, the importance of keeping a low profile, and staying 'in' with the inmates in positions of administrative power in the camp.

In Buchenwald there were already three graduates of the Rouen École Normale: one comrade from Le Havre, Basile, Yves and me. Within a few days two more from my year arrived: Lelièvre, called Suber, and Brutelle, whom I previously mentioned. Yves pointed the latter out to Marcel Paul via a French Stubendienst in block 40, Lucien Chapelain, suggesting he could help. But he was already in contact with Thomas who was a socialist deputy from the north, being well connected on the committee of French interests, who took charge of his case and got him transferred to the main camp.

I much preferred the night shift as I managed to spend some of the night in the cubby hole. I was not too tired and a few hours sleep were enough to get me on my feet. I was able to wander around the camp all afternoon. Often in good weather I went down to the small wood opposite the sick bay, passing by the 'Pouf'[30] and the small camp to take a nap and chat with a number of characters who came to make contact, lawyers, assistant préfets, soldiers, teachers. It was a select worldly group where everyone could rediscover civilised good manners. Introductions would sound thus:—

—'May I introduce B of the Institut Paseur?'
—'Mr X, sub-préfet of ...'
—'Mr Z, journalist from ...', etc.

We chatted about whatever came up, as if we were sitting on the terrace of the Café Victor.

I went down to the small camp to meet up with Forcinal, Crutel, Davignon and other acquaintances. In exchange for a gift the gate-keepers let me pass. One day Davignon told me how while in the depths of his sleeping berth he had overheard the deliberations of a sort of commission attached to a jury which decided which inmate be put on the transport lists, either because he did not wash, or had stolen a piece of bread, or refused to contribute to the common food fund. His friendly face took on a downcast air, as if it was he who was destined to be put on a transport detail. 'The poor lads who get put on work transport just because they don't chip in to the general pot, or 'cos they don't wash!'

He repeated this story several times after the war. I believe him all the more since several genuine accounts of the camp after liberation refer to it.[31]

In block 40 a group of artists and poets flourished and when parties were organised in the cinema we joined in to create a revue. I recall a remake of Mistinguette and Maurice Chevalier with the song *Paris, c'est ma grand'ville* in which I had a small part.[32] I must admit my disappointment as a Frenchman that some performances such as the Russian ones were far better than ours. Those folk had an innate sense of dance, rhythm and music. They threw themselves into their performances and made us forget the camp.

We were also able to attend cinema shows with very biased original language films without subtitles, such as *The Swiss Jew* or *Ivar Kreuger*. From time to time there were deliveries of beer at the canteen[33] which we had to pay for in camp paper money, funny-money used only for that purpose, being a few marks given to the factory workers. That was a day for celebration even if the beer was mediocre and alcohol free.

As for the brothel, which we passed by to reach the small wood, its clientele was mostly Germans who had posts of responsibility such as block seniors, Kapos, Stubendienst and the like. The women rarely showed their heads above the fence. Feminine presence was felt above all by their voices, the sound of which we had not heard since Auschwitz; those ladies seemed to have fun sometimes and they laughed hysterically.

The clandestine committee had entrusted me with the organisation of the chess tournament. Faced with too many players I needed to eliminate the losers from the draw in two rounds leaving a grand finale. In spite of that we still did not have a winner because of the limited number of chess sets. No French contestants, me included, were remaining, only Germans and Russians.

The 24th of August 1944 seemed like any other day. I was on dayshift and I was grading the cores by flux number when an alarm sounded in the factory. It made the on–off noise of an old car horn backed up with a visual signal, i.e. three big lamps went on and off in sync with the siren sound. In order to evacuate the factory we lined up and went down towards the station and the woods beyond, guarded by the SS and staff members.

For a week the alerts had increased and the SS had decided not to leave us in the factory as had happened previously. Many tales have been told on this subject, namely that the SS had been warned about bombing raids by leaflets dropped and being informed by this method believed that if they

(*Above*) The author, centre row, far right, on an outing with fellow students.

(*Right*) The author, often a one-man band.

Shrine to Hitler on his 52nd birthday, in the inner courtyard of the EN.

German soldiers training for invasion at Grandcamp, 1940.

A German poster of Rouen.

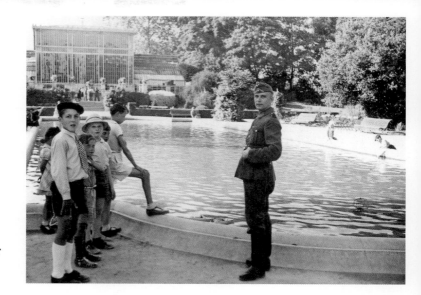

A German soldier poses in Rouen's botanical garden.

Occupiers relaxing in the Mustad château. (*Photo courtesy of Albert Valet*)

Celebration of Hitler's 52nd birthday, in Duclair. (*Photo courtesy of Albert Valet*)

(*Left*) Abbé Kérébel.

(*Below left*) The Kérébel house plan, sketched by the author.

(*Below right*) SS and Gestapo HQ, Rue du Donjon.

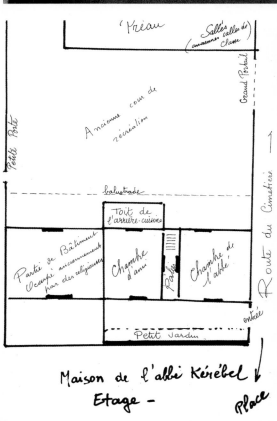

The author's sketch of his cell in Bonne Nouvelle, view towards the door.

1 paillasse
et 1 ou 2 couvertures

Sol ciment

Cellule vue de la porte

Bat flanc scellé , 1 Table et 1 chaise chaînées
de telle sorte qu'on ne puisse pas les pousser vers
l'imposte.

Dimension. plafond H. 4 m
au sol    1,70    X    3,20

The author's sketch of his cell in Bonne Nouvelle, view towards the window.

Compiègne, sketch of the hut interior.

Compiègne, sketch of food being brought from the kitchen.

Auschwitz, the Final Solution.

Buchenwald, the main gate.

Buchenwald canteen ticket, for Junkers Halberstadt out-of-camp workers.

Buchenwald, internal money token.

## Häftlings-Personal-Karte

Haft.-Nr.: 53.354

-Name: Le Goupil
ame: Paul,
am: 12.12.22 n: Conneré
d: led. Kinder: keine
nort: Petit Querilly
se: Dp.Seine Inf.
ion: r.k. Staatsang.Frankreich
nort d. Angehörigen: Vater:
René Le G.,
Petit Querilly,w.o.
ewiesen am: 30.4.44.
: BDS Paris (Liste)
.: Auschwitz
d: Polit.Franz.
trafen: keine

Überstellt
am: 14.5.44. an KL.
Buchenwald
am: an KL.
am: an KL.
am: an KL.
am: an KL.
am: an KL.

Entlassung:
am: durch KL.:
mit Verfügung v.:

Personen - Beschreibung:
Grösse: 175 cm
Gestalt: schlank
Gesicht: längl.
Augen: grün
Nase: l.eingeb.
Mund: nrom.
Ohren: norm.
Zähne: 7 f.
Haare: braun
Sprache: franz.

Bes. Kennzeichen: keine

Charakt.-Eigenschaften:

Sicherheit b. Einsatz:

I.T.S. FOTO Nr. 697

Körperliche Verfassung:

16.988

### Strafen im Lager:
Grund: Art:

XL 43-500.000

The author's Buchenwald ID card.

Buchenwald main camp wash facility.

(*Above*) Sleeping quarters reconstruction at Buchenwald.

(*Left*) Junkers wings being built at Halbersatdt. (*Bundesarchiv*)

Langenstein prisoners, September 1944. Photo taken by a guard.

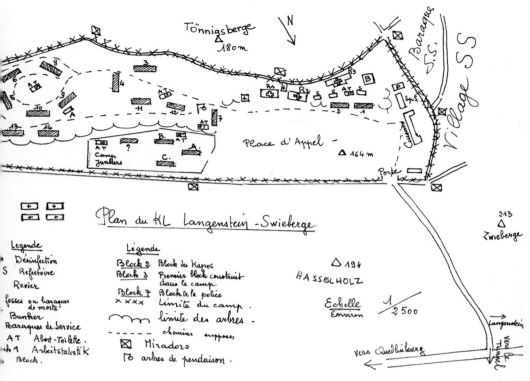

Plan du KL Langenstein - Swieberge

Tönnigsberge
△ 180m

N

Baraque S.S.

Village SS

Place d'Appel -    △ 164 m

Camp Junkers

213
△
Zwieberge

△ 194
HASSELHOLZ

Echelle Environ   1/2500

vers Quedlinbourg

Langenstein
vers le Tunnel

### Légende

Désinfection
S   Refectoire
Revier
fosses ou baraques de morts
Bunker
Baraques de Service
AT   Abort-Toilette.
ck 1   Arbeitstatistik
Block

### Légende

Block 3   Block des Kapos
Block 3   Premier block construit dans le camp
Block 7   Block de la police
x x x   Limite du camp.
~~~~   limite des arbres -
- - - - -   chemins supposés
⊠   Miradors
T8   arbres de pendaison.

(*Above*) The author's plan of Langenstein.

(*Left*) Langenstein prisoners, photographed by American liberators.

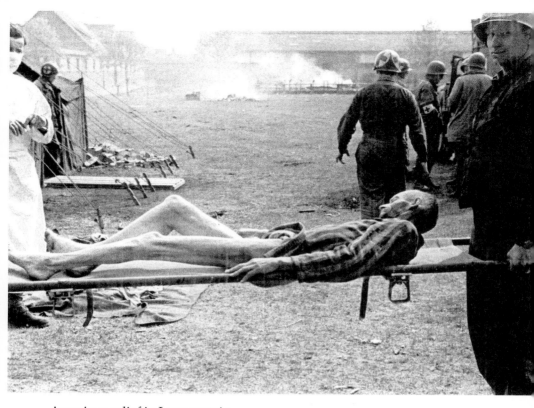

American relief in Langenstein.

A Langenstein prisoner. American photo.

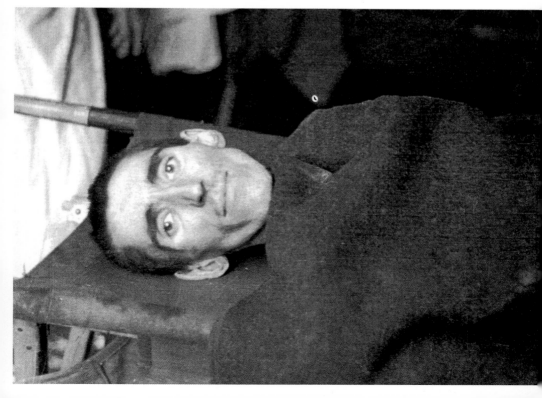

(*Above left*) Michel Rodriguez poses in his camp uniform after the war.

(*Above right*) Paul, seated, plays the accordion for Yves Boulogne, his Buchenwald guardian angel, newly-wed in August 1945.

(*Below*) Könnern, the Saale viaduct.

le  26 Février 19
Le Président
Départemental :

(*Above left*) Mühlbeck, one of the many monuments on the route of the death march.

(*Above right*) The author's deportee card.

(*Below*) The author's certificate of delousing in Dessau, by the Americans.

MILITARY GOVERNMENT
Dessau, Germany

C E R T I F I C A T E

i s    is to certify that the body and luggage of  *Le Goupil Paul*
dusted with DDT at the Displaced Personnel station at Dessau on
25/5/45        1945.

JOSEPH R JEHL
Capt MC USA

The author on his Triumph motorbike.

The author revisiting
Auschwitz.

The author, camera
in hand, revisiting
Mühlbeck.

The author, fourth from right, revisits Langenstein railway station.

The author receives the rank of Officier de la Légion d'Honneur, 13 May 2017.

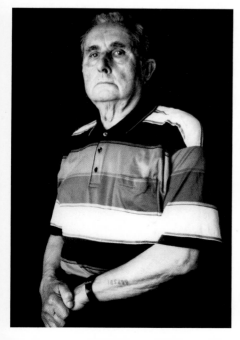

The author, Cherbourg, July 2002, from *Down to Earth. (Courtesy of Martin Morgan)*

left us in the factory the city of Weimar would be flattened. There is no documentary evidence for this. The alert was, as ever, a holiday for us. We stretched out on the ground in clearings in the forest, waiting for the end, surrounded by a cordon of SS. The previous one had lasted more than two hours and I fell asleep.

This time the heavies seemed headed towards Berlin. One of them released white smoke which heralded bad news, something I had already seen as a sign preceding bomb drops over Rouen area. Suddenly the air was filled with the typical screaming noise, a sound engendering fear. Anyone who has not heard this noise falling on them from the sky cannot imagine the stomach wrenching fear that is beyond control, the fear dormant in our primitive spirit when faced with a natural danger.

I threw myself down at the foot of a tree and was quickly covered by other bodies who tried to bury themselves in the ground like me. The ground trembled for a few minutes, followed by a quiet broken by the moans of human shapes wandering about in a cloud of dust. While we were getting up the air was rent yet again and we plunged into our pile at the foot of the tree. This time the impacts were nearer to us and I clearly heard the rat-tat-tat of automatic weapons and other arms. The cloud coming from the station and the factory had thickened. I thought I had come through unscathed when suddenly a shower of fire fell on us in the form of small hexagonal magnesium incendiary bombs which gave off blinding light and thick smoke. Two metres from us a comrade was burning alive from a direct hit to his back. Burning branches fell on our pile of bodies, paralyzed with fear. The smoke was so thick that one could only sense shadowy figures running about in the light of the fire 'display'. I extracted and raised myself to lean against a tree to offer less of a target to those darts of death. Close by a Russian was screaming as his leg burned away. Then one by one the fires went out and the crackling and hissing of the flames gave way to a wave of moaning from a chorus of hundreds of wounded. I was suddenly overcome with joy to be there intact, in one piece, and I could have danced amid those hundreds of mutilated and burned bodies. Once more luck had been on my side.

Many comrades were in shock, motionless, dazed and quivering; one of them, sitting on a tree stump, was dusting down his pants.

The cloud of smoke and dust slowly dispersed and I was able to take stock of the damage. The factory was flattened and continued to burn; the SS barracks were open to the sky, and many hundreds of my comrades lay burning, bodies split open, gravely mutilated and in agony.[34]

Transport for the wounded to the sick bay was quickly organized with make-do methods such as wooden panels retrieved from the station, stretchers made from branches or human chair lifts. In this way I transported my first wounded, who had both legs burnt, all the way along the road. At the sick bay he was laid, alongside hundreds of others awaiting first aid under the trees. Some of them lay there for twenty-four hours. The communal help chain had been set in motion and the last of the wounded were regrouped by evening in the cinema and the brothel, both converted into hospital annexes. I found time to dash to block 40 which fortunately had not been hit. Only some huts in the kitchen area, a few paces from our block, had been destroyed. Nearby the huge oak tree under which Goethe is supposed to have meditated[35] was burning. It was to be cut down a few days later amidst general rejoicing; it symbolized German strength which, according to legend, would die with it. Yves had been looking for me everywhere since the bombing. He had received reassurances from my workmates but when he came across me as I returned to the block he hugged me with great emotion and began to weep. I cannot say whether in reversed circumstances my feelings would have been equal to his since the things I had endured until then, above all the solitary confinement, had encased me in a shell of coldness and indifference. I made an effort to think neither of the past nor of my family. As we had no future I made no plans, except the desire to kill Baudry if ever I were to get back. Only the present and the next day counted. Each day snatched from uncertainty brought me nearer to my goal. 'But what goal?' I said to myself. 'Where will I be next month? And for Christmas? And in a year? Will there be a next month for me? Or a Christmas, or another birthday?'

The next morning I was detailed to transport the dead bodies to the crematorium with hastily improvised wooden stretchers. The bodies lay stiff as they were killed, among the trees and still smoking tree stumps, sitting or bent double, their torsos bearing the mark of death. Many stomachs, rent open by the magnesium heat, smelt foul and were covered in flies. Fortunately I did not recognise any of my friends among them. In the gyro workshop kommando only one man from Tours had to have his arm amputated. When I went to see him in the sick bay, he told me that the bomb had struck the ground a few centimetres from his arm, as he lay, but that the pain had been so great and sudden that he was unable to move. Those little hexagonal bombs, a few centimetres wide and pencil shaped had a lightweight metal extension acting as a fin. In some places they fell three or four per square metre. The complete load of that third wave had scattered over the wood where we were grouped whereas the first two had been well on target on the factory, the SS barracks and the garage.

In bringing back our dead we had to negotiate the bomb craters on the Carachoweg road. The stone eagle had been destroyed as well as some of the huts and buildings along the road leading to the tower, including the camp kommandant's house. To our right an immense pile of shoes brought from Auschwitz to be repaired was still burning and was to burn for weeks afterwards.

The next days were chaotic. Our Mibau kommandos had no more reason to exist and we were detailed to clear up the factory and barracks, as well as to salvage machines undamaged by the bombing. It rapidly became a matter of sending us on outside details, since the destruction of the factory had wiped out 8,000 jobs.

The bombing and its effects had dampened our joy at seeing Paris and Rouen liberated. We all hoped that the Americans would not halt at the

Rhine, and the wildest rumours spread in the camp, none of which were confirmed by the German communiqués. Sadly we had to face the facts, namely that the SS beast had dug in along the Siegfried line and would not be easy to dislodge.

After the liberation of France the flow of parcels quickly dried up. The different messes had to manage the shortages and on the table of block 40 no piece of bread or soup tin remains were left over after a meal. I received a Red Cross parcel that I shared with Yves and Davignon, then the International delegation decided with the agreement of the French that the whole camp should share in the parcels sent to the French. For some days they were tipped into the soup in which biscuits and fruit paste chunks could be found. This measure was dimly viewed by the French who thought it was a waste of good food and that the remaining parcels should be better dispatched.

The work in the clean-up kommandos was hard since under Kapos and SS supervision we had to move machines, steel beams, and sheet metal together with deportees of all nationalities, who did their best to save their energy. I learned how to handle a spade or pickaxe only when the Kapo was watching me, and how to hunch the shoulders a few centimetres when, together, we carried a heavy load such as a rail for example. Everybody did the same and we reached our destination, bent over, knees failing, and on the point of collapse.

On return to the block, Yves raised my spirits but 'the good old days' were over. No more parcels arrived and hunger began to haunt the French along with the threat of being transported to the unknown. In September, along with many comrades from the Mibau factory I faced a commission of slave dealers. I declared myself as an electro-technician in order to be selected for a factory kommando, in the event of an outside work allocation, such as Schönebeck which had a better reputation. The commission members, overweight and overfed industrialists, could be heard tut-tutting as my file already showed 'teacher-tailor', but I gave some details of work at Mibau and they seemed to be interested. Then, like my companions I had to show my teeth, legs, and take a few steps like an animal at auction in front of potential buyers. I heard no more about it and for a few days I returned to the clean-up kommandos doing uninteresting site work and clearance. Yves had assured me that I would not be put on a transport kommando but I no longer had an allocated job and one morning I was called to the tower with comrades from the block. Like them I knew my registration number by heart in German. It was one of the first things to learn in a camp even if, like me, one had no gift for languages; not to respond to it immediately was asking for trouble.

Sadly for me I had to exchange my blue serge suit for a new striped uniform with a cape and cap. I had informed Yves at his workplace. As I was greeting the numerous Frenchmen who were due to leave with me (there were a few tattooed ones, Vézier, Serge, Michel, Caillet and many others), I was surprised to hear my number called again with orders to return to the block. Yves had stepped in and on my return to the wing he embraced me, warning me to be wary of the kommando postings, even the good ones as I would be liable to be transferred to others, since I would no longer be 'protected'. As I returned to the block someone else was going up to take my place as the SS were only interested in the number detailed to leave. I returned to my bed but later that evening my number crackled out again from the loudspeaker and the Stubendienst came to fetch me.

Yves was upset and told me with a hug that he would block my departure. I asked him not to intervene. Someone at that moment must have been returning to his block and was not necessarily the person who had replaced me. Block places were preciously held and those who held them fought hard to keep them. I was getting tired of this ding-dong between the tower and the block. I was glad to be off on a factory kommando with a number of pals. If I stayed for a few more days I risked being sent on a transport to an underground site such as Dora, Laura, B2 and S3 with their sinister codenames.

The next morning after the departure of the local kommandos, our group (of perhaps 200–300) was assembled. Near me I recognised the tall Hugo

Lenardi, assistant head of JOFTA in Issy-les-Moulineaux, who had been arrested a short while after the events of August 1943 that I have already mentioned. He was in discussion with one of his comrades from block 43 who was accusing him of leaving with a pair of shoes which the latter had lent him. Hugo was indeed wearing some fine leather shoes such as we had in the JOFTA. The kommando set off for the tower and the discussion was cut short. For the last time we went through the gate, saluting, and we made our way via Carachoweg road towards the station. The transport conditions were the same as during our return from Auschwitz, that is, fifty persons per wagon. It was 12 September 1944.

I returned to Buchenwald forty years later as a visitor. I found the site of block 40, of which only the floor remained. The crematorium is still there ready for use with its sinister chimney pointing skyward. The small camp has been reclaimed by nature and in that impenetrable thicket I was not able to recognise anything. On the other hand the station still has its platform, and amidst the ruins of the factory reclaimed by trees and bushes I found hall 4 among the bomb craters where hundreds of gyro cores were dissolving with corrosion into rusty remnants scattered among the bushes. I ate in a self-service cafeteria which had been an SS barracks. Some relics are kept in a museum installed in the former shower block, among them the painted Carachoweg road sign, and human skin decorated with pretty tattoos, tanned and transformed into book covers and lampshades. Alas the Nazis were not innovators in this domain since at the time of the French revolution it was chic to have books covered in the skin of aristocrats[36] just as, at that time, human fat was also traded.[37] As for the camps themselves they were invented before 1900 with the advent of barbed wire. The British had the questionable distinction of setting them up in South Africa at the time of the Boer Wars, naming them at the time 'Reconcentration camps'. Before then prisoners squatted or died on islands or on disused hulks. During the war the Nazis merely added the innovation of the gas chambers as instruments of genocide.

## Chapter 7

# Halberstadt and its Junkers Factory

Our train often stopped to allow convoys of war material and troops to pass heading for the western front, and after travelling for more than two days in good circumstances since we had food, water, and space, it stopped at the picturesque station of Langenstein which seemed to be our destination. We went through the village to reach the camp which made a poor impression on us. The inmates walked slowly as if stuck in the mud, their silhouettes similar to those who used to hang around the sick block in Buchenwald small camp. Not a single one gestured to us or tried to make contact. The SS had us line up in a sort of covered yard to the right of the entrance while we waited for orders. Our morale slipped as the time went by.

Suddenly the convoy leader had us fall in again and we went back along the station road. There had been a mistake and we were in the wrong place. We were glad to be leaving that sinister place. The pace quickened and there were no slackers. The train had remained in the station and we reoccupied our places in the wagons. After a fifteen-minute journey we got off at a small station in Halberstadt, probably Spiegelberge, this time for good.[1]

The camp was on the outskirts of town near the Quedlinburg road, near a railway line serving that industrial zone. It comprised only four huts surrounded by non-electrified wire, with a roll call yard at its centre. We were received by the few inmates present, mostly from the camp called Saxo. The others were at work in the Junkers factory which was a few hundred yards away near the railway line. The atmosphere seemed very different from Langenstein. We seemed to have drawn a good kommando detail.

As of the next morning we were led to the big workshop where the wings of Junkers 88s were made. The civilian management allocated us to teams consisting of German workers, either non-conscripts or draft dodgers, volunteer or requisitioned foreign workers, and PoWs most of them being Italian. All staff were managed by German foremen. The huge factory hall had been bombed shortly before our arrival and had been crudely patched up with odd sheets of metal.

Several lines worked simultaneously and each produced a wing every four hours. Later the factory management gave out a food supplement to workers who could produce a wing in three hours, and once this was demonstrated, a few days later all teams had to conform to this standard without a food supplement. However at midday the firm dished out a thick and copious extra soup ration for everyone.

Each two-man team had a wing section to fit, always the same work. I was teamed with a Belgian volunteer worker who had come to Germany to earn some money. He held the compressed air gun, equipped with a flat impacting ring, and I held the stop block, or vice versa, and we had to do 350 rivets in three hours. There was no way we could sabotage things as German civilian inspectors checked the work at every stage. Any rivet head incorrectly fitted was removed with a drill and another was fitted. That delayed us and as the line inexorably moved on, if we had not finished we blocked the flow to the next team, namely some dour Russians who yelled and cursed until we enabled them to take over. If all went well however and if no refit was necessary, that gave us a few minutes break between wings, time enough to go to the toilet. In this way the twelve-hour shift passed quickly

Towards 6 pm we returned to camp along the railway line. On the way everyone collected a few lumps of coal to bring back to the block, picked up from a huge pile which continually smoked and smouldered in spite of often being doused by firemen. Our guards let us do it, being old locals without any meanness. It meant we could decently heat the blocks and cope with temperatures which fell that winter to minus twenty degrees.

We worked alternating weeks on day and night shifts and as the work never stopped, with few exceptions such as Christmas for example, that gave us a rest of 24 hours every two weeks and a day of double shift also every two weeks. Once we even had to work for thirty hours – I cannot recall why – but the lines had to stop as the workers fell asleep on the wing trestles.

Fortunately for our rest there were more and more frequent air raid warnings. During the daytime the guards took us outside town along the Quedlinburg road. There we could watch the hares bolt in the fields, and the numerous aerial dog fights since there was a fighter base between Halberstadt and Langenstein. Several times we saw planes shot down and one day a pilot whose parachute had not opened fell like a stone into a field a few hundred metres from us.

At night we were shut in the factory with all power cut off while the civilians went down into the shelters. Luckily we were never bombed. The night alerts were better for us as we could sleep. Unfortunately the heating plant was cut off along with the power and via the gaps in all the badly patched metal sheeting the cold came inside, and after a thirty-minute raid we were freezing. During one of those long night bombing raids, together with a friend from northern France who had tailoring skills, we took down a brown camouflage curtain made of thick material about ten metres long which served no useful purpose as the windows had been replaced by metal sheets. We cut it in two and wrapped it around our bodies to get it out of the factory. The next step was to fashion two thick waistcoats that we wore next to our skin to keep us warm en route or during the alerts. Fortunately this theft went unnoticed, since it would have meant being hanged for sabotage.

Straight after our arrival the camp kommandant asked us for a translator. A comrade called Georges Drouvin, alias Jo, stepped forward. More of him later… Under the guise of various professions he had mostly lived off women. A well built former amateur boxing champion with a Clark Gable look, he spoke several languages, among them Italian, German, and Russian.

The kommandant also requested a nurse for the factory. Among us was a pharmacist from Lyon who should have got the job, but, when the request was called out during roll call, he was slow coming forward. He was beaten to it by the tall Hugo Lenardi who stepped forward to the kommandant mumbling in half-baked German and giving his number. Thus he earned the medic armband. But in the camps where the plum jobs were worth gold, the winner was the one who had the cheek to go for it. In the factory he had a vast treatment room. His services were limited to dressing a few minor cuts, since when faced with complications he was wise enough to send them to the hospital. He treated small wounds with the finesse of a manicurist handling gauze, and crepe bandage with tweezers as a professional would have done. Some of the German civilians, impressed with his confident manner, even asked him for advice for those among them needing treatment. To a foreman who described his wife's sickness, he answered that it was probably a prostate problem! When we were on night shift and there was an air raid warning, we asked him for shelter in his room which was the only place left with electricity and where we could keep warm. Sometimes we were twenty or so sleeping on the floor. From his window we could see the fires raging in Magdeburg, Braunschweig, Halle and even Berlin. The night Magdeburg was flattened the ground shook as if in an earthquake and we felt as if it was right near us although the town was more than fifty kilometres away. Since Hugo felt bad about sneaking the medic job from Joubert, he managed to get him appointed as his associate by persuading them that he needed a day medic. In this way they covered the day and night duties.

One afternoon when we were returning from Quedlinburg road after an alert, we came across a group of footballers speaking French on their way to the stadium and I was surprised to recognise Gilles Simon, an EN student from Boulogne. He had been called up with the 1940 class year, taken prisoner and transferred into free outside-camp work; free, that is, as they were unescorted. I shouted 'Gilles, Gilles!' as loud as I could to attract his attention but one of our escort guards threatened me with the butt of his rifle to shut me up and Gilles, deep in conversation with a pal, passed by me without hearing me. That evening I was in a black mood thinking about the missed conversation opportunity. If he had seen me he would have let my family know and perhaps get some grub sent to me via civilians and who knows what else... ideas raced through my head... he could perhaps find me a hideout in the event of an escape.[2]

My team mate, the Flemish Belgian, a plump volunteer worker, downed several sandwiches in front of me without offering me a single morsel. Sometimes he belched or farted, which I had long ceased to do, and then slapped his belly with a satisfied air. I resolved to get my revenge and one night during an alert I broke into his padlocked locker in the darkness and ate his sandwiches made for the night. After the air raid when he came back from the shelter he shouted out accusing the 'zebras' as he called us of stealing his food. He alerted the authorities but they did not organise a search knowing full well that the food had been eaten. They asked him to take his sandwiches to a safe place which he subsequently did.

The food, even with the factory supplement, was insufficient but we could do deals with the factory civilian employees. My team mate several times lent me some marks on the understanding that I would repay double the amount in French money after the war (he is still waiting for it). With this money I had packets of Belotin brought in from the outside. It was a mixture of low grade cereal and substitute animal feed, freely available, which we fashioned into pancakes placed on the stove of the hut. When they cooked they dried and fell onto the floor, but if we wanted to eat them we had to be more watchful than the ever-present thieves. We enjoyed them with the same relish as if they equalled the best French patisserie in peacetime.

One of the blocks had a wall separating it from the potato store, and during the winter a Russian team without being noticed had managed to make a hole big enough to put an arm through. This emerged at the base of the potato pile and trading in them quickly thrived in the camp. Michel managed to get four weighing about half a kilo each, in exchange for I know not what, and gave me one. I savoured it to the last morsel and the taste of it stayed with me for several days. It was the only one I was to receive since, as the pile of potatoes was being mined from below, it collapsed and the theft was discovered but not the thieves. As a punishment the kommandant banned potatoes from the soup for several days.

In this small kommando where the French group all knew each other – we were perhaps fifty or so – I met up again with Vézier, Serge, Pierrou, and Willard, and I made new friends, among them Richard who was practically a neighbour of mine, since he lived on Boulevard du 14 Juillet in Sotteville near the Trianon cinema. He had been arrested for having hidden his rifle in the staircase, only to be denounced by his wife who had a lover and wanted to get rid of her husband. Then there was Caillet who ran a bistro in Harfleur, and many more besides. I bonded above all with another Michel, Michel Rodriguez; I will call him Rodriguez to avoid confusion with Michel Dubernard.

As Christmas drew nearer the French received a certain number of Red Cross parcels and we of table 16 decided to put some of it into a common pot in celebration of Christmas. In some there were tinned peas, sardines, noodles, chocolates, fruit paste and tobacco. Rodriguez, being head of our table, took charge of the cooking. He prepared a meal with the menu, which he kept:

> Jardinière de Munich
> Croquettes chleuch braisés
> Gâteaux sans soucis barbelés
> Belotin halberstadesque
> Boisson: bière maison Borngole
> Vin pour cent[3]

Hugo decorated the table with a small fir tree and composed a quatrain in honour of our chief:

I'm sure he expects many compliments
Gloating on his chair, highly content
Tell him he cooks well, him, t'will please
Our table companion, our pal Rodriguese!

On Christmas day the factory gave us the day off. All the mess tables had prepared a special meal, and then there was entertainment. The Russians put on a song and dance routine which was much appreciated. One of their singers had a deep velvety bass voice. He was accompanied by a small band of balalaikas. Where did they come from? I could not say, nor whence the chromatic accordion came, brought in by Hugo. He played it quite well. I took over for more than an hour, getting back my fingering and my favourite tunes. There was also some boxing. Joe had managed to find two pairs of gloves and easily won three fights, one of them against Hugo.

That day we were happy and we felt optimistic about the future. We thought we would end the war in this small kommando from which the Americans would come and liberate us without difficulty. Alas, the worst was to come.

From the first week in January there was a lack of raw material in the factory and, more seriously, wings began to pile up at the end of the assembly hall and along the railway platform. It was whispered that the assembly factory had been destroyed. What could be done with wings without fuselages? One production line stopped on 14 January. Five of our table pals, Michel among them, were part of a substantial group of about one hundred, which left on foot for the other camp, Langenstein, which had made such a forlorn impression on us, on the other side of the mountain.

At the end of February the temperature fell to minus 20°C for several days. We ploughed our way through one foot of snow and our feet suffered terribly, wrapped Russian-style in rags around wooden-soled clogs which slipped off our feet.

Lice swarmed on us in contrast to what happened at Buchenwald, since we no longer received a change of clothes from the main camp. We washed our shirts and underpants after delousing them by hand and scratching out the clusters of eggs which were incrusted in the seams. To speed things up we passed a match flame over the places where the eggs were most densely clustered and we heard them crackling as they burst in groups. By way of experiment I hung my shirt outside when the thermometer showed minus 17°. When I pulled it in the next morning, stiff as it was, I thought I would find the fleas dead. Not at all! In the heat of the stove they thawed out and crawled about as normal. As for the eggs they crackled as usual when squeezed under the fingernail.

Good or bad news came in waves blowing hot or cold on our hopes of liberation. In the east the breakthroughs in the eastern front heralded the imminent arrival of the Russians. In the west the Ardennes offensive gave us a shock like a cold shower. Our happy guards toasted this victory which led them to hope that the Americans would be pushed back to the sea. Several of us brought back issues of the *Petit Echo de Nancy* – a collaborationist newspaper handed around among the volunteer workers in the factory and it made a demoralising read.

Food became ever harder to come by. The 1.5 kilo loaf had to do for four or five rations, then five or six. On some days there was no margarine. On the other hand some comrades and I received a parcel from the Red Cross in Switzerland containing sugar, pasta, figs, lentils, dried apricots and tobacco. Rodriguez even had two of them and for a week our table was exceptional, since we shared the contents.

At the beginning of February the camp kommandant decided to implement a general disinfection to stop the flea invasion. We killed hundreds of them during our rest periods. One day I killed 230. The guards took us in groups to a workers' camp a few hundred metres from ours where there was an autoclave. We had to wait naked for several hours to get our clothes back. This session had only a temporary effect since, a few days later the infernal dance of the fleas started again.

The work in the factory was down to a minimum. There was no more night shift and we all were back in the block hanging around getting in each other's way, especially in the evening. For this reason the medic job was axed and it was Hugo who kept his. Rumours of a departure for the other side of the mountain flew thick and fast.

One morning I was designated, along with other detainees called by number, to go and work outside camp. Accompanied by sentries we went through some of the suburbs in the direction of the hills. There in a large hall numerous civilian and prisoner workers of all nationalities were digging out a sloping gallery. Powerful steam-driven windlasses were hauling up small wagons full of dirt and stones which we had to push to the exit. I do not know what happened to them after that since another team took them over. That was a mammoth task since, once outside, they had to be brought back empty. There were two tracks, one up and one down, with very little space between them. All this was accompanied by shouts and blows. By the midday break I was exhausted and down in spirits, all the more so since none of my pals had been detailed to this job. What is more, unlike in the factory work there was no supplementary soup ration.

During the break, without anything to eat I wandered on site and tried to get some information as to the purpose of the job from a group of French ex-PoWs who had volunteered to become free workers. They seemed embarrassed by my presence and conversation as if any contact with me would not look good for them. Indeed a sentry shouted to me to return to my detainee group. Nevertheless I found out that we were digging out a shelter for the town's VIPs.

In the afternoon I was bushed, and my fellow prisoners, a Russian and a Pole, cursed me for my lack of effort. Suddenly I stumbled on a track sleeper, and, losing my balance, I moved sideways. The cart coming in the other direction hit my right elbow. I felt a sharp pain and remained motionless. The Russian called a foreman who had me replaced immediately as the wagon chain could not be held up. He led me with my arm hanging down to a corner where there were already two with injuries, one to the foot, and the other to the knee. No one gave us any treatment and on the return journey to the camp we trailed at the back. I wedged my forearm between two buttons of my cape but my elbow caused me more and more pain. I had to endure the roll call which was luckily a short one. In that small kommando it never lasted more than thirty minutes.

My mates had come back from the factory and Joubert had set about making me a splint with sticks of wood to immobilise my arm when a German prisoner no older than 25, wearing an armband, told us to wait. A few moments later he came back with pre-plastered bandage and a kind of wire mesh support. He no doubt worked in the small camp infirmary. Hugo and Joubert were medics only at the factory. Like a professional he adapted the plaster cast to protect my hand from accidental knocks and after wetting the bandages he wrapped them along my forearm at an angle of about 120 degrees. He got me a sling to support everything and a sick note of a specified duration. I thanked him warmly. He came to see me in the following days to check on his work.

I stayed in the hut in the warm, playing bridge or reading. We had managed to obtain via civilians some card packs and some books. Jo had also got hold of *Captain Conan* by Roger Vercel and I read it three times.

This was not to last long as, on the morning of 22 February after roll call, about half the kommando, that is 200 inmates, had to form up and leave to go to the other camp over the hill. In spite of my handicap I was to be in the convoy with the majority of my pals. Only Hugo had managed to stay behind in his cushy number. It was with regret that we left the small kommando group to join the one in Langenstein which had made such a poor impression on us. By way of reassurance we talked ourselves into believing that the situation there had improved. We crossed heathland along a snow-covered path which led directly to the camp located some kilometres away.

*

**

Forty years later I returned to Halberstadt. Our camp had disappeared. On about the same spot was a huge grain silo. The railway line was still in the same place and I could visualise the wings stacked up along it. I did not recognise the factory buildings which had been rebuilt a little to the rear of ours which were completely destroyed in the bombing raid of 8 April 1945 which flattened the town centre and caused 2,000 casualties.

## Chapter 8

# Langenstein Zwieberge and its Tunnels

O n arrival the SS allocated us to a small camp called Junkers, consisting of three huts where we were delighted to meet up with our pals who left in January. Tired and thin looking, they already showed the signs of the hard labour in the tunnel. Above all there was Michel who, completely dispirited, seemed to have lost the spark of life. He said to me, 'It's hell, a penal colony. We'll all die unless they arrive soon.'

He told me about the work in the airless tunnel with heavy pneumatic drills, wagons to push, cement mixers to fill, rails to carry, choking in dust, beaten by the SS and by civilians. Seeing my arm in plaster he managed to smile and said, 'You've got your excused-duty chit. Hang on to it as long as you can.'

I then realised that the young German had done me proud in plastering my arm and that perhaps he had saved my life.

The Junkers camp enclave attached to the immense parade ground represented only a small part of the whole, perhaps one tenth. About twenty blocks were scattered on the slopes of a wooded hill.

The valley floor, once a field, now a mud bath, made up the parade ground and bordering it on one side was the Junkers camp and on the other were the kitchen and SS administration buildings. The place was called Zwieberge (two mountains) which was the name of the hill overlooking the camp. It was in the foothills of the Hartz Mountains leading to the large plain which extends from Halberstadt to the valley of the Elbe. When we arrived, the main camp held 5,000 inmates and the small one 500. The whole camp was surrounded by watchtowers open to the wind and by an electrified fence, illuminated all night. This kommando, known in the cryptic Buchenwald terminology as B2, or Malachit,[1] was intended to excavate a system of underground galleries under the hill between us and Halberstadt in order to set up new Junkers factories to produce jet engines and V3 pilotless aircraft. Our kommando, composed of aircraft 'specialists', was supposed to install the machines and start weapon production in a tunnel which theoretically was ready. Unfortunately it was not and our mates worked in it alongside their pals from the main camp excavating and building the galleries in terrible conditions similar to those in Dora in the early days, and to those in all tunnel kommando tasks in their construction phase. Our pals in the main camp were convinced and remain so to this day that we enjoyed better treatment than theirs, that our food was more generous and our work was easier. Alas none of that was true. The only advantage was occasionally to have shorter roll calls since we were less numerous. On the other hand we had no beds or mattresses and slept on the floor rolled up in our blankets.

As I was fortunate to have never gone down into the tunnel with its eleven[2] kilometres of side shafts in which my companions wore themselves out, I can only describe it via the accounts that they gave when they came back, haggard, gasping for the air they craved during those long hours underground. Sometimes they did not have the strength to eat their soup and just threw themselves to the ground wrapping themselves up in their blankets. Their hardier pals fed spoonfuls into their mouths as if they were babies.

Unlike the blocks in which I had lived until then, the Junkers kommando blocks had closed sleeping quarters with walls and doors opening onto a central corridor. The first one on the left on entering was reserved for the Stubendienst. As soon as he arrived in January, Jo with his interpreter armband was designated Stubendienst. Per room we numbered twenty to thirty, that is as many as could be accommodated lying down, and there were about ten such sleeping quarters. The blankets were folded and stacked to allow the floor to be swept and without tables or chairs the room was gloomily empty.

Even if I cannot describe life in the tunnels, I was well placed to observe camp life. At 3.30 am things began to stir and the block came to life. Volunteer teams (all of whom received extra rations) went off to fetch the coffee from the kitchens and towards 4 am the Stubedienst knocked on the doors and shook those who were slow to rise. Some went to ablutions after drinking their coffee. The wash basins were near the fence separating us from the main camp. It was a sort of shed open on three sides, like a school yard shelter. It was swept by a chill wind and few comrades stripped to the waist. I know that for me it was a skimped job. I merely wet my face. I preferred to be grubby rather than get bronchitis. Around 4.30 am it was time for a roll call by block for those in the small camp. It did not take longer than in Halberstadt as we numbered about 500 dispersed in three barracks. All that took place under the glare of searchlights, amid shouting, pushing, with the mud sticking to our clogs.

Then came the dispersion into kommandos. When dismissed from roll call, those without medical exemptions rushed onto the open ground in the hope of getting into an out-of-camp work detail, but sadly the Russians and Poles who were in the better work parties ejected them by dint of fist and foot if needed and only the tunnel details were left. Then one by one the complete teams passed through the gate, escorted by the SS, Kapos, and foremen.

The squares of exempted detainees remained in odd groups and then followed the second act of the drama: Kapos and SS checked all the medical sick notes and, to make up the worst kommandos, they picked out the fittest of the sick in spite of protests, aided by truncheons. One had to know how to display one's wounds, raise trouser legs to show legs swollen with oedema, or cough one's lungs out. I always positioned myself in the first row with my plaster stuck out in front of me and in the six weeks spent at Zwieberg I was not once drafted for work.

When all the teams had left fully manned we went back to the blocks. We had to sweep the sleeping quarters and corridors before the return of the night shift which had just been relieved by the day shift. Those comrades verging on collapse threw themselves down on their blankets totally exhausted and, after downing their coffee, they slept in spite of various noises, comings and goings, doors slamming and Jo's shouting.

Towards midday the excused-duty inmates had the chore of getting the soup, accompanied by the Stubendienst. The urns were heavy and it took two of us to carry them. There were no wooden stretchers, just side handles, which called for a firm grip and marching in step. We did twenty paces very quickly, even running, and then put down the urn. Then after a few moments of rest, on a signal we forced ourselves free of the mud and set off on the next dash. The distance from kitchen to block seemed endless. Since then I have revisited the site and realise that it was no more than three hundred metres. The mud made it seem longer. The urns were always full to the brim and from the swaying caused whenever we got out of step, a little of the soup spilled out onto the ground. We were always followed by half a dozen men at death's door who picked up bits of carrot or turnip.

These four or five containers were locked in an empty quarter before distribution. I rarely went on this duty since with my arm in plaster I could not change hands, nor side, which made the trip painfully hard for my partner and for me. Fetching the bread contained on my back in a blanket forming a knapsack was less of a problem.

These duties entitled us to an extra soup ration or a very generous helping. To do this the Stubendienst would lower and raise the ladle slowly so as to fill it with thicker soup. There were many knacks in dishing it out. Depending on how often one clashed with the Stubendienst, one got a full or half-full ladle, a thicker or thinner helping, and this was true of all camps. Jo had a way of just moving the ladle at the top of the urn, giving the impression of stirring the base; he would tap the sides and just stirred the liquid. The recipient would end up with a mess tin of liquid in which floated some carrots and turnip. If he scraped down to the bottom he would bring up potatoes and small bits of meat.

Later, as the excused inmates grew weaker, we went in fours to get the urns so as to work in relays, because towards the end we did not have the strength to get the urns unstuck from the mud.

The lads in the main camp had to go up via a slippery muddy path to get back to their blocks and for them it was a Herculean task whereas for us we were lucky to have to cross flat ground.

The night shift and the excused-duty inmates could eat as soon as it arrived. The others could eat only after roll call around 6 or 7 pm.

Jo did not cut the bread but handed it out per sleeping quarter according to the number of occupants. A room of twenty-two men would receive five and a half loaves on the basis of one loaf per four men. We cut them into shares and got whatever came up, like the luck of the 'Galette des Rois'.[3]

In our quarter it went off relatively well but elsewhere there were ruses and tricks for getting the biggest piece, such as stealing or even hiding dead comrades until the following roll call so as to receive and eat the dead man's ration! Some comrades fashioned home-made scales to ensure a fairer share-out, which made the distribution interminable. The margarine pats on the other hand were pre-cut into sticks of twenty grams, so the hand-out was never a problem.

Shortly after our arrival I had to go to the sick bay to get my exemption chit renewed. At the appointed time the muddy paths to the blocks were lined with the sick, some limping, some supported by their stronger comrades, and a queue formed at the sick bay entrance, lengthening as more arrived non-stop. All the camp ailments were on display there: the runs, swellings, boils, wounds, coughs spitting blood. After a long wait in the mud and cold I was attended to by a Polish doctor who gave me a one-week extension without any questions. The main issue for me was to get the exemption extended as long as possible to avoid the tunnel work detail.

For the next renewal I carefully washed my plaster and scratched off the stains on it to make it seem more recent, and from another doctor I got an extension of ten days which took me to mid-March.

From civilians working in the tunnel, who were reliable comrades, we learned that Cologne had fallen to the allies who had crossed the Rhine. Even though the Russian front had faltered on the Oder, this news lifted our spirits. We had to hang on but some sadly could not; they died in the sick bay, struck down by dysentery.

One day a pal from another block informed me that Michel was asking for me. I had not seen him for a few days. I found him lying on the floor, the bones of his large frame visible under his blanket. His swollen face seemed almost normal. He said to me, 'You can have my bread and soup. I'm done for. Take my things, give them to my parents.'

Among them were a small address book with the names of people to inform, a cigarette holder and an aluminium box he had made in Halberstadt. I tried to get him to swallow his soup and raise his spirits. It was useless. He had given up the struggle and decided to fade away. In spirit he had already departed and whatever I said to him was to no avail. When I went to his block the next day he was no longer there, having been taken by the death–duty detail to a small hut; it had been erected at one corner of the parade ground and was locked to prevent a recurrence of cannibalism cases.

Some days later at the exempt-duties roll call I was detailed by an SS guard to join the corpse collection team. In the following days four of us under his escort went with a blanket into the huts of both camps to pick up those who had died during the night. We carried two in a blanket and went down to the morgue hut. The SS opened the door and we threw them onto a pile which gave off a terrible smell since the corpses at the bottom were already decomposing, purple and mouldy. A thick liquid oozed from the pile and leaked under the door.

In a flash, as the SS closed the door I immediately recognised the face of Michel with his eyes open, and two other youngsters from our block, one called 'Petit Patissier', so nicknamed for the cake recipes he passed on to us to take his mind off his hunger and stress. I was overcome with nausea and vomited a wave of bile. The sight of them discolouring haunted me for several days.

Those young people, rounded up from the villages in eastern France, had arrived by the hundred directly to the camps in their civilian clothes. They had had no mental preparation, no apprenticeship in misery via a stay in prison. They had been dealt a terrible shock which had killed most of them in less than three weeks.

As the Quedlinburg crematorium where the bodies were sent could not take such a quantity[4] of dead, large pits were excavated on a mound behind the camp boundary about 100 metres from our blocks. We did not know the purpose of them until one evening when the kommando came back, the SS ordered the workers and excused-duty inmates (my arm in a sling did not excuse me from the task), after the roll call, to take the bodies up to the common grave pits. Four inmates took two bodies in a wooden box to be emptied into the pit. A line of them brought the empty boxes down to be refilled. During one of these sadly repeated tasks I slipped and fell into the pit onto the corpses. I had to walk on the mattress of soft flesh in order to get out and for several days I experienced bouts of nausea which made me throw up my soup, which was yet so precious.

The morgue hut was never completely empty as the bodies at the bottom were too decomposed to be moved without disintegrating, making the undertaker's task all the more odious. The nauseous liquid spread widely beyond the limits of the hut and the smell reached the first huts, carried on the wind. During this duty I went into all the main huts and I realised that in some the medically unfit outnumbered the fit. One of the blocks holding mostly Jews evacuated from Auschwitz laid out at least ten corpses every morning.

In the small compound there were also huts of Jews, most of them Hungarian. Jo had real problems with them when serving the soup. One day they seized the urn before it was empty to get at the scrapings which were not intended for them that day.[5] To fight them off Jo hit out with the ladle which broke and the urn toppled over. He replaced the ladle with an empty pea tin can fitted on the end of the original ladle handle but all the huts complained because it did not hold a litre and Jo had to get another utensil.

In the passing weeks the leftovers became scarcer, especially since the urns passed via Jo's sleeping quarter before being distributed. Part of the soup issue became the currency for various trafficking in things such as tobacco, the contents of Red Cross parcels and clothes. I witnessed individuals coming to his room from the main camp bringing wrapped packets and leaving with mess tins of select soup helpings. Sometimes there were feasts and an agreeable smell of fried food wafted under the door. One day I even saw a young man with whorish make-up leave his quarter. There were several in the camp who prostituted themselves, one of them in our block whom we nicknamed 'the little pansy' being much sought after by the Kapos or others of higher status in the main camp. Like many riff-raff he never had difficulty obtaining a sick note and never went into the tunnel.[6]

Among the 'excused-duty' there were many who had been arrested for black marketing or dealing with Germans. How they obtained real or fake chits, I never found out. I got to know them by playing bridge with some of them, occasionally professional players. One of them, aged about 40, maintained he had never worked, living entirely off his card winnings. He explained some of the racing rackets that I later saw flourish in horse race betting. He was banned from casinos and plied his talents in gambling dens. He handled cards like a magician, could draw an ace at will and played the Three Card Trick. I had noted his address to meet him after liberation as I was fascinated by his personality but when I turned up they told me he had never lived there. He had simply given me a false address.

Another, called Bernard, was a gold dealer who trafficked gold bars into Switzerland for whoever could pay well, be they German or French.

In one of the bridge games I got to know Charles Porte who was recovering from an illness. He was a former police commissioner in Chartres who had known Jean Moulin. He had been ordered by London to investigate the Caluire affair. He believed that Moulin had been betrayed by Didot[7] with a view to a view to eliminating him, as being a suspected communist infiltrator.[8]

Among the long or short term excused-duty inmates there were many French deportees who should have been wearing the green triangle rather than the red.[9] Everything could be bought in the camp and the sick note was, like medicine, the most valued commodity. Rodriguez, whom I now call Michel, since alas the other had died, was wasting away working in the tunnel. He needed a chit to keep going. He confided in Jo, who got him a note for ten days in exchange for his gold tooth cap.

I noted that Jo had put on weight. Sometimes he looked vague and sounded like someone who had had a drink. He had gone off the soup, which had dropped off in quality as time passed and contained more and more peelings. He confided in me that he could not eat it any longer. When he was in his room before dishing it out he fished out the pieces of potato and fried them in a pan in several portions of margarine and which itself had a story worth telling.

That pan had been made by one of our pals, whom we will call X, in Halberstadt. He had sold or lent it to Jo in exchange for some food. I had noticed that he, being always hungry and on the look out for food, went into Jo's place and came out with some soup or a piece of bread. One day he knocked or rather scraped on Jo's door, opened by an exasperated Jo, saying he was fed up with hearing about the pan, that once and for all he had bought it and paid for it, and he slammed the door in X's face. The latter insisted and began to knock again. Jo, furious, came out wearing his boxing gloves and landed a couple of blows before starting to take X back to his billet, calling him a 'lousy bag of bones, walking dead'. One unfortunate blow to the nose started a bleed in front of all the French who had come out to watch. Jo, immediately deflated, realised the aggravation he was in for as a result of his action. He took X back into his room to clean him up and gave him a mess tin of soup. Shortly after that, he invited several of the witnesses to the pitiful scene, me included, to come and eat in his room. He was clearly worried that complaints could be made about him to the camp international committee and that the Lageralteste (camp seniors) would dismiss him from his job.[10]

On the initiative of Serge and Lefaure the Communist organisation structure had been re-established in the small camp and had managed via contacts in the main camp to have the Stubendienst and leader of block A replaced by Party chums, B and C. They were hard core militants who had been arrested in 1940, since when they had experienced Vichy prisons, camps in North Africa and German prisons. They had been put in charge of block A to make it a model to counteract the corruption of Jo's block C. Serge had got me transferred there with a number of pals, himself included. I was not pleased with it as I preferred the company of my friends in my block even if there were some low-life types in it. After this relocation I spent more time with Michel and my old pals than with those in my new sleeping quarters.

I remained in the old mess team with them and we shared the few Red Cross parcels which arrived.[11] One of mine and two of Michel's contained chickpeas and couscous flour amongst other things. We decided to make a big do of it, not knowing what the future held for us. Jo, in return for being invited, took charge of cooking the semolina flour. He had managed to get all the necessary ingredients. However when it came from his room the couscous had reduced and there were some complaints from pals who would have preferred a bigger share of steamed semolina, rather than a smaller amount, however well cooked. His meal nevertheless made an excellent impression on me that I can remember forty-five years later.

One morning in mid-March there was no dismissal after roll call, but a general search. Two blocks were emptied of occupants, even the dying and the Stubendienst. Kapos and SS searched the blocks from top to bottom. They soon emerged with axes and saws with which we cut up tree branches for firewood, as well as all kinds of tools and materials. It seemed they were looking for some dynamite which was missing from the tunnels. Then one by one we had to undress in the cold and leave our non-regulation clothes such as pullovers or jacket liners made out of cement bags. I regretted having to abandon my warm waistcoat made from the Halberstadt factory curtain and I began to shiver. The next day my temperature was over forty degrees. Joubert diagnosed pneumonia. In no way did I want to be transferred to the sick bay among those with tuberculosis or diarrhoea. Being already excused I was able to stay in the block. Serge went to fetch Jo who was the only person who could obtain medicine. A few hours later he came back with sulphonamide tablets. I was delirious for three days, not even aware that my pals dragged me out for the roll calls. All I could think about was my house in Rue Edgar Quintets, my little bedroom, my parents and my sister, Illiers and Grandcamp. I told myself that I had to fight for my life to get back to all that again and to tell the story of the hell I was living through. Above all I thought of the traitor Baudry wandering around somewhere in my mind, and whom I had to kill. Gradually this idea shut out all others, giving me the strength to pull out of it.

As my excused-duty chit had run out I freshened up my plaster which, in spite of my efforts, was showing cracks and getting frayed at the edges. I went up to the sick bay, coughing, spitting and ever thinner. There too the situation had worsened. There were not enough plasters for small dressings. Open boils and festering wounds were everywhere on those emaciated bodies on which only the eyes showed signs of life. Some of the sick could not even moan and lay there trembling, huddled under their blankets used as capes.

My turn came after a long wait and this time I was seen by a French doctor who was under no illusions about the age of my plaster. He warned me that by remaining in that state my arm would wither, being already thinner than the other one. He agreed to give me a chit but said I had to have the plaster removed. I asked him to do nothing with it as I risked being sent on a bad kommando after the roll call of the excused-duty people. He left it on but gave me only five days more. I was terrified at the thought of the approaching moment when I would have to lose it and go to work with an atrophied arm. After returning to the block, I managed to pull my arm out of the plaster then and put it back into its tomb. At night alone I tried hard to exercise it by lifting bigger and bigger stones.

It was a relief not to have the itching caused by the fleas which were hiding under the plaster. In Zwieberge the flea invasion was much worse than in Halberstadt due to the degenerating state of health. In one afternoon I killed 470 of them, and almost as many the following morning. I recall this number as it was a record. With their blood sucking, especially under the plaster, small flakes of skin had disappeared, at first lentil- and then pea-sized. I called them 'flea spas' as I was sure that even if I had just deloused myself, another colony had taken their place at the watering hole.[12]

Once when I was looking at the body of a comrade who had died some hours before, lying on the floor wrapped in his blanket, I observed a caravan of fleas making its way across the floor, leaving the cold body in search of warm bed and board. Many of the sick no longer had the energy to delouse themselves, allowing the vermin to feed on them at will, and since our bodies were in contact on the floor at night, one man's fleas became another's. What could we do? The dying could not be forced to delouse themselves.

For the next medical I once again freshened up my plaster, but sadly the edges were crumbling more and more and I only got an extension of three days from a Polish medic. However it was towards the end of March and the eastern front was on the move: the Allies had crossed the Rhine and were advancing across the German plains. For the first time the armies were spreading faster than the rumours.

In my new block, the two French representatives, B and C, like Jo were called on by mysterious visitors from the main camp. The less soup extras we received, the more they paraded in their new well cut suits, and the more choice food they ate. Serge had a stormy exchange with them but it made no difference and I really regretted leaving the other block, all the more so as my old pals gave me the cold shoulder, thinking I was enjoying extra rations while still being in their food sharing group. After the couscous parcels no more arrived and the numbers of the sick notes gradually went up. Some of them, namely those with dysentery, had to be transferred to the sick bay for their last days of life.

One morning from the window of block 6 of the main camp I witnessed the hanging of five escapees who had been recaptured. This event was not public, but every window with a view of the hanging tree was crammed with faces. I positioned myself there at the moment when the prisoners were rolling some empty drums, arranging them under the branches from which already hung five ropes; then came the higher-ranking SS in their peaked caps followed by the five condemned men, hands tied behind their backs, under military escort. They climbed onto the inverted urns, aided by inmates, and then the SS executioner passed the rope over their heads after checking the solidity of the knots. The charge was read out to them, probably by the local Gestapo chief. For us it played out without sound as if in a silent movie and the only sound to be heard was our breathing and suppressed coughing. On the signal of the officer in charge the SS flipped over the drums and the bodies swung after some quivering, except one whose feet touched the ground, who gesticulated like a puppet trying to escape from death. The officer gave an order and an inmate pulled at his body to finish him off.

The small group went back down to the SS barracks, the inmates rolling the drums, and the SS chatting with heated gestures, one of them imitating the jerky movements of the puppet-like hanged man. There was a moment of silence heavy with emotion and then someone said, 'The bastards! They'll pay for that one day. Anyone who makes it back must remember this.'

My main concern was to get food and renew my medical chit. The soup got thinner and more watery, and the porters who had the right to clean the empty urns no longer had that pay-off as there remained nothing stuck to the inside of the urns. The loaf of 1.5 kilos was more often than not divided into six or eight shares instead of the usual four or five. It became harder and harder for me to get an extra tinfull for the chore of carrying the corpses; the reason given was that everyone had to be served first. In reality the dealing in soup and bread among the inmate administrators and the SS at all levels forced the Stubendienst to reduce our rations. The ladles were less full, dented or cut down in size or replaced by ¾ litre tin cans with handles. Even though I was not working I quickly lost weight but I was privileged in comparison with my pals who went into the tunnels. Some, especially the strongest, turned into skeletons, their faces ashen, their eyes sunk into their sockets, and often I did not recognise them when I had not seen them for some days.

At the end of March I attended the sick bay for the last chance of a sick note. On duty that day was a French medic or doctor who without question gave me another week. By chance since my arrival I had never been examined by the same staff. I went back to the block humming a song, since in spite of the insufficient food that sick note would enable me to keep going until the arrival of the Americans who were pushing towards the Elbe.

From the early days of April we could hear the distant rumble of artillery in the evening. Was it from the ack-ack or from cannon fire at the front?

Our guards seemed very uneasy and the wildest rumours buzzed on all sides. We heard talk of evacuation, camp destruction, and plans to bottle us up in the tunnel and blow it up.

On Saturday, 7 April, after morning roll call there was no departure on work kommando and we went back into the huts. The grapevine announced the liberation of Buchenwald and the arrival of the Americans in Magdeburg on the Elbe. Most of the comrades, happy not to go into the tunnel, rolled up in their blankets to sleep, but a few were so excited in expectation of the unknown that Serge asked me to tell a story to occupy their minds. Among the small number of French books available in the camp, in addition to *Le Capitaine Conan* there was a simplified version of Einstein's theory of relativity that I had read and re-read during my long hours of idleness. I chose this for my subject and did a scientific exposé of space time in which maths was replaced by imagery. I realised then that I had a talent, hidden until then, for narration, as I was listened to by about fifteen attentive inmates whom I distracted for a while in this way from the prevailing anxiety. We decided to renew the experience if we were to be off duty for some days. But on the next day, 8 April, events overtook us quickly. First came a terrible air raid on Halberstadt and an enormous column of smoke rose behind the hill that hid the city from view. Then horse-drawn carts were brought to the kitchens and loaded with bread loaves. Were they intended for the evacuation convoys that were rumoured, or were they supplies for Halberstadt, the centre of which had been destroyed?

The next morning, 9 April, the Stubendienst confirmed that the camp was to be evacuated, leaving only the sick unable to walk. Should we go, with the chance of escape, or being shot, or stay and await the arrival of the Americans with the threat of the destruction of the camp by the SS? Jo advised us to go. After consulting with some others I went along with the majority view and decided to leave with Serge, Michel and the pals. I slipped off my plaster and hung it on the block wall like an empty cocoon, before going to roll call.

It was no ordinary roll call, as our guards, assisted by the administrative Kapos, were drawing us up in lists by number, of those who were to leave or stay. At the end of this roll call we were pleasantly surprised to see our old comrades from the Halberstadt kommando who swelled the numbers of our invalids since their kommando like ours was ready to move out. We heard that the bombing of the previous day which had destroyed the town centre, had killed thousands of civilians, but, although the Junkers factory had been destroyed, the camp remained unscathed and our pals were safe. On the road to us they had come across anti-tank traps being built. According to them Magdeburg and Braunschweig had been taken and the arrival of the Americans was only hours away.

The huts buzzed with preparation for a major departure. Without being ordered, everyone rolled and tied up his blanket and filled his kit bag with his most precious objects: notebooks or address books, lists of recipes, boxes, some made in Halberstadt. The hunt was on for civilian clothes and a gang of Russians forcibly removed the pants off an unfortunate Hungarian in the Jews' hut; he doubtless had paid for it with his bread ration. Nobody answered his cries for help.

After soup there was a special roll call for the camp administrative inmates, hut leaders, Kapos, foremen, Stubendienst, Lagerschutz. They all quickly assembled, well dressed. Jo, squeezed in to his smart blue suit, now ill-fitting since he was now over-weight, in patent leather shoes and scarf, seemed dressed up for a gala evening. We watched them from a distance, as they stood to attention, listening to an address from the kommandant.

When he came back, Jo told us that he had thanked them for their cooperation in the efficient running of the camp, then he authorised them to remove their numbers, since they were henceforth freed. However, since the able-bodied inmates were due to leave that evening in groups of 500, they were to accompany them to their destination. He had concluded with a pessimistic prognosis for the future of Germany.

Jo gave Michel bread and jam to be shared among those leaving the hovels, while on the parade ground gangs with clubs attacked isolated individuals with their bags or in civilian clothes. I clung to mine containing my mess tin, a notebook and pencil for further notes, plus the belongings of Michel Dubernard to give to his parents, and a piece of bread received from Jo.

Late in the afternoon was time for the final roll call and leave-taking from the pals who had decided to stay. I took a look at my plaster hanging on the wall, wishing I could take it with me as a souvenir. It had enabled me to face the road in very much better shape than many others, and was worth putting in a glass display dome on my return.

I was placed in column number one with the inmates from the Junkers camp. The five others had formed up, each like ours of 500 inmates, each one backed up by a horse-drawn cart of supplies camouflaged with branches. We set off escorted by numerous soldiers armed with rifles and sub-machine guns.

In the twilight glow our column headed along the dirt road around the camp away from the village of Langenstein and the tunnel. We went off towards the unknown in the east and soon the watchtowers and the mound of the mass grave disappeared behind a slope.

\*

\*\*

When I returned to Langenstein forty years later I took the same road again and nothing had changed, but the camp was no longer there. Only a few vestiges were still visible, respectfully maintained by the museum staff and schoolchildren; posts, scraps of barbed wire, watchtowers. The hanging tree had been coated in resin, and a few sections of wall, that is to say remnants of the wash block and the sick bay that had survived the ravages of time, dotted the boundary with the wood. Of the wooden huts not a trace could be seen. They had been sold to local farmers after the war for use as stables or chicken sheds. Their location could be inferred from the less dense vegetation in the wood. We were unable to find any trace of the small Junkers camp on the huge roll call square which had become a grassed open space, also once having been a cattle meadow and a potato field.

The mass graves and camp entrance are commemorated by fine creations of local artists. As for the tunnel, we were told that for more than forty years, once stripped of anything useful such as cable, machines, rails and scrap metal, it had been abandoned and walled up to prevent accidents. Now since the fall of the regime and state of East Germany, we have learned that it had been used by the Soviet army then by the East German Republic which had invested several billion marks to refurbish 6.5 kilometres of galleries. The

Bundeswehr[13] has taken over the site to stock weapons and munitions from former East Germany and the Stasi,[14] which are to be destroyed in coming years. Following that it could be used as a depot for German air force spares or as an underground currency vault like Fort Knox in the USA. Bank notes of former East Germany have already been stored there.

On the site a small museum has collected some objects, souvenirs and photos. We hope that Germany reunited will preserve this homage to the 7,000 dead in the camp, of whom 700 were French, and that cows will not repossess the roll call parade ground.

## Chapter 9

# The Road to Hell[1]

On the evening of 9 April 1945 we marched to the east; we were 3,000 divided into six columns[2] moving at a mere two or three kilometres an hour on that dirt road. Some comrades were ordered to help the horse pull the supply cart in difficult passages such as slopes and rutted surfaces. By nightfall we were on the road from Blankenburg to Quedlinburg and Westerhausen and we quickened the pace a little towards Quedlinburg. The roads were full of troops who were retreating eastwards like us. There were foot soldiers, horse-drawn vehicles and military ambulances. This sight raised our spirits, recalling the debacle of the French army, but this time the roles were reversed. Since our column hindered the troop movement, the kommandant made us turn south into the suburbs of the town, endlessly meandering through its cobbled streets, often repassing the same spot. Towards 3 am we were parked in a large hangar near an airfield, now non-existent, in Rieder. In the morning the SS did a roll call, the only one on the evacuation route. Fourteen inmates were missing, three of them French. Among them was Colonel Valantin.[3] Michel handed out the rest of the food given by Jo, bread and jam. Then our guards had us line up in fives and gave the outside person a loaf to share out; this was rapidly done for fear of a raid by the Russians and Poles who outnumbered us by far. Fortunately it went off without incident. In the afternoon there was an allied air raid on the adjoining airfield, scoring direct hits.

On 10 April at dusk the column reformed and we again headed east via country roads and villages. Some comrades planned to escape but we were escorted every four or five metres on both sides by soldiers, ever ready to shoot, and it was not yet very dark. We hesitated to make a dash and all sorts of reasons were put forward to delay the venture, such as …the terrain was not favourable, …it was not dark enough, …it would be better to wait for the end of the leg when the guards would be tired etc. The fact is we were afraid of launching off into the unknown. Suddenly a shot rang out just behind us followed by the moans of a wounded man and the sound of a second man keeping him quiet. I found out it was Nossik, a Pole who had tried to escape. He had been hit in the thigh and then finished off.[4] That death dampened our urge to escape.

Towards midnight there was, for the first time since our departure, a glow on the horizon like that of a distant storm, followed by the characteristic rumble of artillery. The front was getting nearer. Perhaps it would reach us? So why escape?

The glow was sometimes to one side, sometimes behind us as we followed the twists in the road. We joined up with a wide paved road along which were fleeing disorganised troops, some without vehicles or weapons. Then came the town of Ballenstedt and once again we took to much quieter country roads. When we reached Ermsleben around 3 am the artillery was silent. The SS parked us at the entrance to a sports stadium between the cemetery wall and a big potato silo. The sports field was already full with the columns which had preceded us.[5]

We had no shelter. We rolled up in our blankets to sleep against the wall. The spectacle the next morning was grotesque. The stadium was in a hollow, three to four metres deep, probably based on the site of a former quarry. It swarmed with almost 3,000 lousy ragged escapees from hell. Some fires were lit, I know not with what, heating mess tins of potatoes 'organised'[6] from the nearby silo. There was no roll call since all the columns were mixed up, with the SS merely guarding the cemetery wall and the sports field boundary. Our supply cart, absent during the night, had returned to us with the administrative staff and we received one loaf between six with no margarine.

Jo came to take leave of us, bringing a loaf of bread to divide up. He, along with the other camp administrative inmates, was allowed to leave the column. Our former Stubendienst as well as B … and C… got the same treatment, without coming to see us, likewise the Kapos and block elders.[7] They were all decently dressed in civilian suits paid for with our soup and bread.

Towards 6 pm the columns reformed in a sort of merged fashion. Some like ours had grown with the addition of Frenchmen from the main camp. Others had shrunk. As the march began again, the artillery rumbled in the north and south-east. Were we about to be surrounded? Faced with this threat our guards stepped up the pace. Many of the minor roads were stone paved and our clogs drummed on the ground like the sound of horses' hooves. Village followed village endlessly. On the winding road we sometimes had the illusion of walking towards the artillery fire. In the middle of the night we arrived near a huge barn where several columns had already settled, occupying the interior. As there was no more space they parked us in the yard.[8]

Early in the morning of 12 April we were given a loaf between three with a pat of margarine. Some comrades munched grains of wheat found on the ground. The farmer thought he was doing us a good turn when he emptied a bag of carrots for us in the yard. A violent fight ensued which was ended by blows from the guards' rifle butts. It smouldered on later, sometimes for one carrot, like chickens in a pen chasing the one chicken with a worm in its beak. Several bodies lay there with cracked heads, until we left. All day long we saw troops passing, under duress but this time armed and under command. On the railway line which blocked the horizon no trains passed. Dusk once again meant it was time for us to leave.

We left that barn in Wiederstedt to the sound of artillery and after going through Sandersleben where troops were hurriedly setting up defensive positions we continued our monotonous march along the small stone paved country roads. We were supposed to cross the Saale, an important river before the Americans took the bridges and among us prisoners the word spread to slow the column's progress as much as possible. Voices shouted out

'Pause! Pause!' which was taken up by others in turn. Rifle butts silenced them but others took up the protest, 'Pause! Pause!' The SS, losing patience and seeking to make an example, killed a tall blond prisoner (I believe he was Dutch), who refused to be quiet. Several shots at the rear of the column quickened the pace. We called out friends' names one by one and closed ranks to be able to render assistance to each other if necessary. Finally the bridge appeared against the glow of artillery fire. It was a concrete arched bridge and was being mined by a German engineer corps. Quite near to our left the flashes and rumbling of artillery fire meant that the battle was near, but alas we crossed before the arrival of the Americans.

On the other side, the town of Konnern was swarming with troops in disorder. It was as active as in daytime, but at two in the morning. After another hour's march the order was given to stop in a former sand pit near the village of Kirchedlau. I rolled up in a blanket on a bed of twigs, totally exhausted. We had just covered thirty kilometres at a faster pace than at any time previously. The next morning, 13 April, we were still harried, but some comrades, instead of sleeping on had got up to gather some herbs to make a brew. The place favoured us by offering plenty of dried brushwood.

Towards 11 am a louder rumble led us to conclude that the bridge had just blown. Then little by little the artillery fire sounds became more distinct. Instead of a rumble we could identify each shot. According to experts the battle was four to five kilometres away. Then suddenly around 4 pm the SS told us to form up. We had to put out the fires and empty our mess tins of 'soup'. As we set off our guards handed a loaf to the end man to be shared among six, without margarine; we had to cut it up and eat on the march.

A few hundred metres after leaving the sand quarry, drama struck. A cluster of American tank shells landed on us. In the ensuing confusion the column broke up and some groups rushed for a line of bushes some tens of metres away, but the SS were vigilant and fired over our heads to get everyone back in line. Two comrades were injured: my friend Richard by a small shrapnel wound to the thigh, and Herbert, from the Eure département, who was much more badly injured and was given the coup de grâce by the SS.[9]

Richard could keep pace with the column, slightly limping. His wound did not seem too serious since after a few kilometres he was walking normally. Cannon fire rumbled on but there were no more hits on our column, the Americans probably realising their target error. About 10 pm there was a pause at the roadside near a rapeseed field. Everyone gathered clumps of the plants and stuffed them into their bags. As we ate it we sounded like a herd of cows munching a meadow of grass. Guards let it happen on the nearside but dealt rifle butt blows to anyone who ventured too far. We set off into the darkness our bellies full of grass. The road signs showed that we were still eight to ten kilometres from the town of Kothen which we left to the north. Around midnight the SS parked us in a hollow at the intersection of two country roads, in which was a pond, near the village of Hinsdorf.

Battle recommenced a few kilometres away on the morning of 14 April. We could see the smoke from exploding shells and our infernal march began at 8 am. Richard found it difficult to get going as his wound was painful and he leaned on me for a few kilometres. Around 10 am the SS stopped us at a small camp of French PoWs where the kitchen staff dished up a half litre of thick sweet soup. They encouraged us to keep going as they thought the Americans would be there in the course of the day.[10]

Quite near, the battle rumbled on along the Berlin–Leipzig autobahn on our northern flank and then in front of us. The kommandant, now uncertain, interrupted the march several times, sending parties out to reconnoitre upcoming villages. Liberation was taking place close at hand and we were full of hope. Suddenly we came across the autobahn, the prize of the on-going battle. Less than one kilometre away vehicles were burning and groups of fleeing civilians pointed out something in the direction of the smoke to the kommandant. He then ordered us onto an almost impassable dirt road and parked us in a field surrounded by thick hedges. We waited for orders, the supply wagon and the other columns. They arrived in dribs and drabs followed by the supply wagons. We were given a loaf between six with a pat of margarine and then our guards straight away led us onto the autobahn on which the Americans were probably progressing towards the village of Rieder.

Many corpses from a preceding column lay scattered on the central reservation and in the fields, most likely shot during a mass escape attempt. The terrible march continued towards the tall chimney visible in the distance, belching out brown and yellow smoke.

For endless kilometres we had to march through the huge industrial complex of Bitterfeld, following lines of huge smoking tubes, sometimes arching over us like futurist triumphal arches. The smell of sulphur smoke intensified our thirst. At the site of a pump, converged on by previous inmates, there lay several dead, their heads beaten in and with their mess tins in their hands. We thought we were going to stop on the outskirts of the town but the march continued through the woods after crossing the Mulde. We reached the small village of Krina towards midnight. We were parked between a field of asparagus and a football ground. A number of our comrades had disappeared, escaped or been killed, and our column had shrunk to half its size.

On Sunday, 15 April, we were awakened by shouts and shots. The SS had recaptured half a dozen escapees and they shot them in front of us in the asparagus field to show us what would happen in the event of recapture, then they gave out one loaf between six of us. We could no longer hear artillery and our morale slumped after the hopes of the previous day raised by the proximity of the American forces.

Towards midday we set off again for a short leg which took us to Sollichäu at around 6 pm in a wood near a lumber mill. The stretch was short but littered with bodies because the long leg of the previous day, almost 35 kilometres, had dealt such a shock to the weaker ones that they were shot from the outset. I had to support Richard almost all the way and I was exhausted. His leg had considerably swollen since the previous day. I could have asked the comrades for help but many of them were struggling to keep up and the fitter ones were already taking care of their friends who were in the same bad way as Richard. I tried to raise his spirits but he knew that at the current pace he would not last long. For those few days the noise of close battle had kept him going since he expected to see American tanks break through at every bend in the road. When the artillery fire had ceased to sound he felt that the game was up.

In the evening I met 'Kid Francis',[11] a former boxing champion, in the clearing where the SS had parked us. He was at the end of his tether, hardly able to breathe. His large frame was reduced to skin and bone. He carried his press book, weighing a few kilos, in his bag; it contained the articles and photos featuring him. He opened it to show me and for a few moments that seemed to fortify him. In one photo he paraded in a smoking jacket in an open-top car surrounded by pretty women.

During the leg which took us to Sollichäu I had noticed bags and blankets thrown by the wayside by those poor fellows who lacked the strength to carry the slightest thing. I saw one prisoner take of his coat then jacket before collapsing into the roadside ditch to wait for the coup de grâce. The nights at that time of year were still chilly and often brought white frost by dawn; on that leg the hunt was on for blankets by those who had discarded them or who had been robbed of them. A crack of noise in the dark and sometimes a chase resulted in a blanket lost. I just managed to save mine by having the strength to hang on to it, but Richard, too exhausted to chase the aggressor, found himself without cover. I pulled him against me, so much did he shake with fever. His thigh had swollen even more. His shrapnel should have been removed which meant having a minimum of surgical instruments, at the very least a good knife!

On Monday, 16 April, we left at 8 am. Getting up was very laborious and about fifteen prisoners, unable to stand, were finished off with a bullet to the head.[12] The column, down to less than 200 men, started out on a road strewn with stiffened corpses.[13] Towards midday there was a pause in a wood for the hand-out of a loaf of bread for six of us. The afternoon passed kilometre after kilometre, wood, village and heath in succession. Shots at the rear made the head of the column step up the pace in spite of calls of 'Langsam, langsam!'[14] moaned by those at the rear who could no longer keep up. We asked for stops, then for drink, but nothing slowed the relentless harassed pace. Richard with a stiff leg swollen to twice its size, hobbled in a jerky fashion and his arm pulled ever harder on me. Several times I had to drag him forward from the rear of the flock. With every step he grunted in pain as if he was planting his leg like a post in the ground.

As we went through one village, Trossin I believe, German women wept as we passed and some had placed buckets of water along the roadside but the SS kicked them over before we could get to them.

Finally, around 6 pm we crossed the Elbe on a boat bridge in the direction of the town of Prettin close by. Just outside the suburbs companies of teenagers around 14 to 16 years old, enrolled in the Volkssturm, were laying out defensive chicanes and Panzerfaust[15] weapon emplacements as if they were playing schoolyard games. On entering the town we took the Torgau road for two kilometres, then a dirt road to the river, far from any habitation and stopped in a marshy field beside a pond bordering a small wood of pine saplings. By parking us thus next to a pond the guards solved the water problem. It was for sure a vector for dysentery, but no matter how green or fetid we drank copiously since we had just covered thirty kilometres without a drink. This time we had reached our limit and if we had been forced to leave in the morning, half the column would have remained on the spot.

Fortunately, on Tuesday, 17 April, there was no order to leave, nor on 18 April. The battle seemed to have stopped and we stayed there drinking the pond water and eating the buds on the pine trees. We had been joined by two or three other columns and we numbered three to four hundred. The meadow grass was rapidly consumed, cooked in so-called 'soups'. Some looked for water snails and we ate them raw. The daily ration was down to one loaf for eight men. The first day I made a soup for Richard and me out of clover leaf and pine buds. I only tried it once. It was a lot of work and gave us no nourishment. Serge and several other pals were of the same mind but others, a wine grower from Burgundy and a hefty metal worker, fussed about looking for clover, firewood and pine cones. They were executed on the last leg.

Since we had stopped walking I had an almost constant cramp in my right leg. I found it difficult to get up and was afraid of not being able to leave. I continued to look after Richard who was almost motionless. His thigh was becoming gangrenous and smelt bad. Only a rapid amputation could have saved him. He had the will to live and clung to every rumour that spread in the encampment, such as, 'The SS are awaiting orders from Berlin to re-cross the Elbe and hand us over to the Americans.'

On 18 April the SS gave out a loaf between six men without margarine, an event which until then had passed off well; the end man cut the cob and everyone took his share as it came, but that day we were attacked by a gang of thieves as soon as the pieces were shared out. My bread was snatched by a Russian and a Pole before I could get a bite out of it and as I ran after one of the aggressors, the other took my bag from behind. It held no food but contained some souvenirs including the things that Dubernard had given me for his family, including his address book.

Attacks took place all around the meadow and I was not the only Frenchman to be robbed. The others had quickly swallowed their ration to avoid the pillage and so there was no more sharing; some men, Serge included, went for two days without eating. Fortunately for me, Richard, shaking with fever and having lost all appetite, gave me his share.

We prepared ourselves for the hand-out the next day; four of the fittest pals defended the share-out with sticks but it did not prevent the attack. Richard's share was stolen and he refused to take a piece of mine. The three days in Prettin put an end to the solidarity that had bound us together up until then. None of us were minded to save some food for those who had been robbed. Lefaure, attacked and robbed and unable to get anything from the others, summed up the situation thus: 'In other words it's every man for himself!'

On 19 April the SS quickly assembled the columns together for a departure shortly after an American air raid in the Torgau area from where big columns of black smoke rose. With the sound of artillery which had recommenced in the north-west, the SS set about 'weeding out' in the camp. Richard found the strength to stand up and clung to me. My cramp miraculously evaporated when I heard the shots. Gouzy, a comrade from northern France, helped me to drag my companion through Prettin. He could no longer move his sick leg and hobbled moaning in agony on the other. Even though we were supporting him on both sides he could not go on. He begged us to leave him. This fellow prisoner friend seemed to be the last line of defence between death and me after the loss of Dubernard and I clung to him as he did to me.

Gouzy who spoke German had a bold idea. He got an interview with the kommandant and asked him not to have Richard shot since he was war wounded. The argument was accepted. The kommandant answered that if the inhabitants of a house on the road were willing to take him in, he would be left there alive. Gouzy and Richard accompanied by a guard made their way to an isolated farm to our left. I was not allowed to go with them. A few moments later my comrade from the north came back, very upset, and told me that my friend had been executed in front of the house,[16] since the residents had refused to take him in. During this leg of the march I could feel the grip of his clenched fingers on my arm and, for many years I would wake up with a start feeling a pain in my arm as if he were still there at my side clinging on for dear life. But we had to keep marching and the arm of Serge, who was tiring, replaced Richard's on mine by the end of that stage.

The green water of the pond had caused serious diarrhoea among many of us. Those who could not hold it positioned themselves at the head of the column, stopped, dropped their pants at the roadside and made their way back to the front before the arrival of the SS who pitilessly 'cleaned up' those who remained squatting by executing them. Some preferred to fill their pants, which stuck to them giving off a pestilential stink. When they weakened nobody wanted to assist them and they disappeared, in spite of their pleas, in the cauldron of the march.

Around midnight we reached Jessen, twenty kilometres further on. After turning right at the entrance to the village the SS parked us in a pine wood on the Scheinitz road. Two other columns joined us in the night. We were down to no more than 200 in all.

It was 20 April 1945 and the Russians had just broken through on the Oder eighty kilometres away. The distant and continuous rumbling got nearer, shaking the ground. The bread hand-out passed off worse than ever since the inadequate bread supply meant that the last in line went empty-handed. This led to a general mob, one half of the column attacking the other. This time the attackers included Frenchmen. I received a crust, torn rather than cut off; I forced myself to swallow it in lumps. With fist and club we fought like animals. Some ate two shares, others none. My last piece was stolen by two deranged attackers, one of them French I regret to say. Serge and several comrades had got nothing and no one came to their aid.

The SS forbade all fires and remorselessly knocked over mess tins in which pine buds were cooking. There seemed to be fewer sentries around our bivouac and some small groups managed to escape. As in Prettin we had to fight off blanket thieves at night. I could not save mine and Serge gave me cover under his.

Towards 4 am on 21 April before daybreak, a siren warning of a tank attack began to wail in Jessen signalling the arrival of the Russians. Our guards quickly struck camp, executing those unable to raise themselves. Shots rang out in every clearing of the wood. Some bodies were given more than one coup de grâce.[17]

The remainder of our column, now down to less than one hundred, reached the village of Arndorf after going through a wood and negotiating an abandoned checkpoint. There was a lot of activity there. Civilians were helping the youths of the Volkssturm to build chicanes blocking the road to the north, through which our supply wagon only just managed to pass. On this paved road we were met by waves of refugees on foot or pushing all sorts of vehicles, among them several four-wheeled carts. Curiously we seemed to be headed for the front.

Suddenly a large open-topped car carrying two ruddy, thick-lipped officers lounging in the back seat overtook the refugee convoy at speed and forced us to cram against the roadside. As the car passed by us one of the officers stood up and emptied his revolver magazine firing in our direction. No one was injured except a guard whose shoe (and doubtless foot) was pierced by a bullet. His mates came to his aid but anger was vented on us, who in their eyes were responsible for the incident and a volley of rifle blows fell on those nearest.

As we left the village I stepped aside to pick up a big dandelion, without noticing an SS guard nearby. At the instant I was pulling on the flower to pick it, he crushed my hand under his nailed boot and pushed me back into the ranks with rifle butt blows to my ribs. I had a cut thumb which bled badly. I made a bandage for it from a torn piece of my shirt.

To avoid that choked road the kommandant had us turn off to the left and we plunged into a conifer wood along a sandy path where it was hard to put one foot in front of the other. The supply wagon got bogged down and our guards ordered the fittest of us to help the horse in difficult passages. As the wood grew denser a group of Russians tried to flee en masse, but most were shot before they could reach cover. We progressed slowly through the wood, growing weaker with each step. At last we came onto the paved road leading to Seyda. Before starting on it the SS allowed a pause in a clearing, ostensibly to enable a bread issue. After a few minutes the sentries left their posts to confer with the column leader. Were they going to leave us there? Some believed so and a small group slipped into the woods without any reaction from the guards. Serge smelled a trap and told us to stay. Perhaps ten minutes later, when the SS took up escort position and gave the order to march with the bread issue, we came across groups of civilians with hunting rifles, coming from the village. They were starting the hunt for fugitives.[18]

A heavy soaking rain began to fall, fortunately for the first time since we had left Zwieberge. During the stop I had retrieved a blanket which was lined with a waxed cloth, abandoned by an escapee, and I spread it around my shoulders and marched on. Those who still had their blankets did the same but they became heavier as they soaked up the rain adding to the discomfort of the march. We reached the parish of Seyda leaving a number of bodies, among them Boussion who was executed at the village name signpost on the boundary. The artillery continued to rumble and between Seyda and Zhana, the next town, the SS stepped up the pace again. Some of our comrades had used the semi-liberty of the stop in the wood to find sticks and the macabre rhythm of them hammering on the paved road, mingling with the shuffling of the clogs, the groans and death rattle of those nearing their end, were sounds which haunted my sleepless nights for a long time.

Some stragglers, breathing their last, tried to hang on to the fittest and we constantly had to fend off the clutches of their hands pulling us with them towards death. In the cattle wagon taking us to Auschwitz I believed I had sunk to the very depths of horror but it was not comparable to that despairing march towards extinction. From time to time a shot at the rear whipped the rear element to catch up with the front, accelerating the hellish staccato of their sticks. We reached Zhana around mid afternoon, and began a long descent down a wooded road in the direction of Wittenberg and the Elbe.

In the forest through which we passed the attitude of the guards changed. On this section of the route, which was uninhabited, they encouraged those who wanted to leave and little groups plunged into the woods, amazingly without being shot! Thus little groups left, including Fauvel, Gaben and many others. Serge, Vézier, Michel and a number of Frenchmen including me decided to stay. The rumours about the Elbe with the Americans waiting for us on its opposite bank revived and went through our minds. Furthermore we had not had our bread ration and thought we would be more likely to starve to death in that inhospitable forest whereas our chances of survival would be greater farther on in the open country.

Occasionally we could detect a railway line to our left, and then there were some houses on the edge of the forest. The first one to try to escape in that direction was shot down and the 'dance macabre' began again. The march hastened, advancing in panic, tripping on the feet and sticks of those in front of us. Suddenly a Pole near me threw off his blanket then his coat and jacket. Open mouthed, he was gasping for air, his arms crossed, and motionless like a man overboard drowning as the boat sailed on. Suddenly at the rear of the column he fell without a shot.

Farther on when we reached the residential suburbs of Wittenberg, a living skeleton stepped onto the driveway leading to a house, walking like a robot. Two children were playing on the steps and the SS could not open fire without injuring them. The children began to scream, women came out and the poor man held out his arms to them but the SS guard who had approached and changed his angle of fire shot him before he could reach the first steps. As I moved on with the column I did not see the rest. I could hear the children yelling and weeping, the insults of the women and the sound of the coup de grâce.

The Frenchmen, mostly from the small camp, had regrouped. We were about ten and helped each other.

It had stopped raining and I had folded my blanket. I continued to help Serge who now regretted not having left with the others. Around 7 pm near the signpost outside the town the SS gave us one loaf between eight and with a pat of margarine. This time everyone got a share and the hand-out passed off without incident as no one had the strength left to attack another. After a short pause the guards, aided by rifle butts, got us to stand up. Beyond the railway station we could see the Elbe and a bridge which seemed intact but we left towards the west towards the town centre via Mittelstrasse, one of its its main avenues. Imagine a column of seventy deportees in rags, dirt-faced, sunken-eyed, hobbling, moaning, and leaning on one another going down the main street of a big city, such as Rue Jeanne d'Arc in Rouen! This is what happened in Wittenberg on the evening of 21 April 1945.

At the beginning of the avenue some plane trees had been wired with explosives and Panzerfaust teams were getting ready. Further on, groups of civilians in their Sunday best, some hand in hand with children, paused, transfixed on the pavement watching our ragged horde of ghosts in disbelief. As we passed a classy hotel-restaurant the chef wearing his hat and his staff came out to watch. Suddenly a prisoner at the rear stopped and sat on the edge of the pavement. Did he think that the SS would not dare to shoot him in the city centre? One shot put an end to his illusions. Shouts could be heard from the groups of spectators and fists were raised in our direction or towards the SS. Children screamed, the onlookers retreated in fear into the hotel and the pedestrians faded away. The nearer we came to the town centre the more ruined it was, still smoking in places, while rescue teams were working on clearance. And we pressed on like a hunting party, with our clogs and sticks striking the road of that damned town. It was nearly the end, the last minutes and the last few kilometres. Serge leaned more and more heavily on my arm but I had made up my mind not to leave him even if it meant carrying him on my back. After the town centre and the industrial district, the ruins were more dispersed.[19]

Darkness was almost upon us and we were still in the town. I thought of the suburbs of Rouen with its long avenues going through Déville and Maromme. We had covered more than six kilometres since the station and were not yet in the countryside. Serge and I, despite all our efforts, were always at the back but could one say there was a front and rear since there were only about fifty of us left?

A Frenchman of about 40 years old tried to cling onto one of us. He begged us one by one, saying he had four children and did not want to die. Suddenly he clutched at us and unbalanced us. I had difficulty getting his grip off us before he dragged us down. Some metres further a 'street cleaner'[20] pushed him with the barrel of his machine pistol, making him stumble and fall. He placed his foot on his chest and put a bullet in his brain in spite of cries for mercy. For a long time his voice came back in my dreams, reproaching me for abandoning him, but I, or we, could not have done any more. We were at the end, the last metres to go to reach the frontier of death, or life.

As we went through the town our guards were more numerous, acquiring killers, who, to hasten the elimination of the column, pushed the weaker ones to make them fall.[21] They tried it several times on us to make us lose our balance, Serge and I, but I was still fit and the approaching countryside gave me strength. In that infernal race, as in American style cycling, the last ones are eliminated.

Finally we saw the first trees. We left Wittenberg for Apollensdorf. It was open countryside apart from a few isolated houses. The SS at the rear made a sign to us to leave. One said to me 'Leave or die'. Was it a final trap? We had no choice. After some deliberation the column fled half to the right, half to the left, simultaneously. I dashed to the right in the direction of a railway line and Serge gathered enough strength to follow me. In a few bounds across a sandy potato patch we reached the railway track and plunged down the other side of the embankment. A few shots indeed rang out but I think that if the SS wanted to kill us it would have been an easy matter as we presented a clear target against the setting sun. Those shots were designed to speed up our flight. The thirty-odd deportees split up a little further on just before the village of Griebo.

*

**

The toll of the death march was heavy. I estimate the losses of our column to be fifty per cent, taking various escape attempts into account, but in other columns it was higher. One marched for another day as far as Zieco after going through Coswig. As I mentioned, another dragged on to 27 April heading for Berlin. Considering that some were totally wiped out it is no exaggeration to state that, of the 3,000 evacuated, more than 2,500 died.

## Chapter 10

# From No Man's Land to the Russians

The silence in the darkness was broken by calls. I thought I recognised the voice of Vézier. We did not reply because we thought we could more easily pass unnoticed in pairs, rather than in groups of three or four.

The horizon was hidden in darkness but we also knew that it was due to the woods. After resting for an hour or two we crossed the railway line and blindly headed for what we took to be woods. The going was heavy on the recently ploughed sandy ground. On scratching the earth mounds dotted in the field we found them to contain recently planted potatoes. In a few minutes we had unearthed a dozen each, but what could we do with them without matches?

We did not know where we were heading and the sound of barking dogs told us that we were nearing a village, instead of reaching the edge of the forest.

I was very tired and slumped against an earth mound; Serge did the same. Suddenly the moon rose and in its light we were able to pick out large wooden supports criss-crossing above us, rising skywards, ending in an observation platform. We had crashed out under a watchtower! We immediately left this risky place for the edge of the wood which lay a few hundred metres away. There we dropped to the ground to finally sleep.

In the night it began to rain. To get some protection we stretched out my waterproof blanket and huddled inside Serge's blanket. We were awakened by a drenching. The weight of the collected water had undone one of the ties of our roof releasing the pool of trapped water onto us. Soaked through and shocked we dared not move. Towards midday we got up but although we were free our spirits were low. What was to become of us in this hostile world?

We tried to eat some pine buds and raw potatoes but knew we would not last long on that diet. I kicked myself for not thinking about this release and not thinking about fire. In the camp I could easily have got a flint lighter or some matches. And I had often read Rosny's *The Quest for Fire*.

From our hiding place we overlooked the plain. Further down there was a farm with dogs barking constantly as if they had got the scent of us and, beyond it, was a village. Everyday life had begun for the residents. On the road by the wood a Volkssturm with a rifle, or a farm cart passed from time to time. Once two staggering figures of deportees emerged from the edge of a clump of trees and moved towards a farm worker in a field. He took them to the village. Should we do the same?

At nightfall we went off in search of shelter but without map or compass we had no way of finding our way. After following the road bordering the forest we stopped to sleep in a shelter on which lay two bottles of compressed air. Serge thought they were to operate some anti-tank equipment.

The next day, 23 April, we woke up feeling weak, still wet, and we spent the day dozing, without stirring, in silence. We had decided to give ourselves up in the next village the following day, rather than die of starvation. My thumb was giving me sharp pains and had begun to go sceptic. The fleas that we had not hunted for weeks had multiplied so much that they openly spread over our rags. Serge, like me, was ravaged by those vermin. When we did not feel them moving we did not dare to move for fear of stirring them into action. That day of desolation and distress, one of the worst we experienced, was lit by a ray of hope by the sound of artillery in the evening.

Early on 24 April we emerged from the shelter as a farmer passed. He called out and asked us what we were doing there. After giving a garbled explanation we dashed into the forest and were surprised to come across a stream flowing into a pond. So we were able to wash and drink something other than muddy puddle water. Our ablutions were interrupted by the sound of approaching barking dogs and the silhouette of a soldier on the other side of the pond. The civilian must have raised the alarm and we had to flee.

In that hostile world it was no longer a question of surrender. After passing through thickets which tore bits off our ragged clothes, and walking through a stream to throw them off our scent, we emerged onto the potato field again with another village in the distance. The previous day's rest had given us a lift even though we had not eaten for three days.

While we pondered where to go we noticed a planked forest hut about one hundred metres distant. It was probably for the use of hunters or foresters. The door was off and the windows broken, but it offered suitable shelter. Inside were bunk beds, cupboards, a stove and some cooking utensils. We checked out the items remaining as it had already been ransacked and we found salt, ersatz coffee, some doses of 'Viandox,'[1] paper, mess tins, buckets and four unused matches that had fallen onto the floor by the stove. A veritable treasure! Finally there was hope of a meal. We were saved.

Ten metres from the hut was an underground shelter made of logs, well camouflaged, only recognisable by a tube sticking out of it. We went down into it and were surprised to find it occupied by an escapee from the Langenstein convoy: it was Paul, a carpet dealer from Toulouse. Being in worse shape than we were, he had not moved for three days and was slipping away with no will to live. According to him we were not far from the main road overlooking the village of Griebo. So in three days we had gone full circle and were back where we had started.

The shelter had a living area and a large bunk with room for three. Immediately Serge and I allocated tasks, namely fetching dry wood, finding water, and gathering some seed potatoes some 200 metres away. After lighting the fire and drinking a brew of Viandox, we cooked about five kilos of potatoes in a basin we found in the cabin. The hardest thing was getting the water. It took two of us, Serge and I, to bring back a bucket half full, from a water hole 300 metres away. Paul, unable to stand, was detailed to keep the fire going to save our matches.

We ate the potatoes without peeling them like animals at the trough, first one mess tinful then another. Feeling warm and replete we fell asleep on the straw until violent stomach pains obliged us one by one to go and relieve ourselves in the wood. After months of privation and several days of fasting our digestive systems could not cope with such an abundance of food.

The next day, 25 April, after a disturbed night and with still aching stomachs we were awakened by guttural accents: three escaped German civilian prisoners forced us at knife point to give them the coffee, the precious vegetables and the Viandox. They made me go and fetch water and wood for them to cook the potatoes. After drinking our coffee and Viandox and eating our potatoes, they left. In the evening I did the chores alone since Serge was unable to get up, being exhausted with diarrhoea. Cannon fire was nearer, each shot clearly heard. I seemed to hear the rat-tat of a machine gun. I once again cooked a bowl of potatoes and in the night the 'runs' began again.

On the morning of 26 April rifle and machine gun fire could be clearly heard coming from the road and the village. During a pause I went back to gather some seed potatoes, carefully following the row that I had already begun, when shouts in German behind me made me look back; it was a Volkssturmer on a bike with a rifle aimed at me. I had not seen him coming. I approached him, hands raised. He was an older decent fatherly-looking man and although he was shouting I was not afraid since if he wanted to shoot he could already have done so. He explained half in words half in gesture that if I dug out the seed potatoes nothing would grow. I answered 'Essen!' and via the international hand-to-mouth gesture I indicated that I wanted to eat. He made me walk in front of him for a hundred metres towards the village, rifle in hand, bike in the other, then changed his mind and gestured to me to leave. I ran to the wood, zigzagging and stumbling with my bag of potatoes bouncing on my back. Once in the wood, hidden in the brush, I watched him. He slung his rifle across his shoulders and calmly rode away to the village.

On my return to the shelter I told my story to my pals and made it clear that I was done with potato gathering, and then I set off, bucket in hand, to get water to cook them with. On my way back a bullet whizzed past my ear hitting a tree trunk a few metres from my head, followed by another without the crack of the shot being fired. I ran off towards the shelter, determined not to venture out again, spilling half the bucketful as I ran. It was probably a Russian sniper hidden in a tree. We cooked the remainder of the potatoes and after eating some mechanically as we were going off them, I hid the rest under the straw. I did well to do so because the bandits came back and searched the shelter again. Under our noses they ate a smoked ham they had brought, slicing off large chunks with their big knife, and on leaving they threw us the bone as if to dogs. It still had plenty of meat on it and one by one we gnawed it with our teeth, happy to be able to eat a morsel of meat.

As the day drew on I decided to explore the surroundings. On the road at the edge of the wood a group of German soldiers was moving in the direction of the village, seeming to be retreating there. After walking for fifteen minutes I noticed the smoke from a bivouac. I approached, crawling, and indeed saw that a number of deportees and Russian civilians had gathered in a clearing. The bandits were with them. As single shots became more frequent I went back to the shelter. At dusk a strange weapon began to fire with an odd moaning sound. It was on the move since the sound came from changing directions. We did not know what it was but that strange noise seemed frightening.[2] During the night trucks passed, their headlights illuminating our cabin. We were now in the front line.

On 27 April rifle and machine gun fire crackled and less than 300 metres away German soldiers unrolled field telephone cables. Serge and I decided to try to cross the lines. Paul, still incapable of moving, lay still. We took the bag of cooked potatoes and the remaining matches. We walked through the wood in the direction away from the waves of troops, when suddenly, on emerging from a thicket, we were faced with a line of soldiers five metres apart, coming towards us. Combing the wood they had seen us and we could not get away. We raised our hands and went towards them.

An officer gestured and a soldier took us to the rear, making us walk ahead along a forest path. I heard the click of a rifle being cocked. My instinct was to run and I said so to Serge. He begged me not to try it, saying that I could not reach the thicket without coming under fire. I asked him to run too since in that way one of us might make it but he had not got the strength. I stayed with him, tensed up ready to dash into the undergrowth. Suddenly we came into a clearing where around twenty civilians and deportees were rounded up, guarded by a few sentries. Gradually our group got bigger and we were even surprised to see Paul arrive, having claimed not to be able to walk.

At dusk we set off by the light of lightning and cannon fire mingling with the sounds of thunder. In the distance a big country house burned. After marching at a modest pace for some kilometres we reached Coswig, crammed with German troops and refugees. A French prisoner yelled to us that the Russians were eight kilometres away. The reinforced prison gate opened to let us in. Once inside we were in the trap. What was to become of us?

Guards piled us into cells which were already occupied and threw in mattresses and blankets into which we rolled up to sleep, to forget the nightmare which was restarting after one week of freedom. The thunder and the artillery fire had ceased. The silence of the night was broken only by the sound of heavy iron doors opening and closing, reminding me of the far-off days in Bonne Nouvelle prison. As in all prisons the next morning began with the commotion of coffee and ablutions. It was agreeable, but I unfortunately had to get back into my smelly clothes. At about 11 am they gave us a thick soup with meat and beans in it, such as we had not eaten for months.

Serge and I had lain down feeling replete! Suddenly near midday all doors were opened for a roll call. We went down into the yard where the guards were assembling the prisoners. They handed out more soup and a piece of bread. Then the main gate opened. Were we about to experience another evacuation march?

The first ranks went out and a joyous shout could be heard. No sentries, no SS! We were free. Serge and I with Paul behind us wandered in our striped rags into the town. Some German civilians came to shake our hands, others held out garnished slices of bread while the soldiers seemed to ignore us. An old man who spoke French told us that the Russians were in Griebo (six kilometres away) and the Americans in Rosslau (twenty kilometres away) which explained the local people's change in attitude towards us. As there was no bridge over the Elbe we decided to get to Rosslau and in the afternoon we reached the small village of Büro. There we met some Belgian prisoners who advised us to get a change of clothes. They put us up near the farm where they were working, not far from a potato silo in a house under construction, without doors or windows, that was already occupied by two Frenchmen freed from Coswig prison. They quickly supplied us with Belgian military uniforms as well as some straw boots. We burnt our prisoner uniforms, happily watching the fleas crackling in the heat.[3]

We decided to stay in Büro and wait for the arrival of the allied troops. The next day, Sunday, 29 April, as we were walking in the village we got to know some Spanish deportees, also hidden by the Belgians. The residents greeted us and an old woman called to us and handed us bread spread with margarine and meat paste, since, even if our clothes had changed, our faces had not and they were like visiting cards, tell-tale badges of camp inmates.

A group of very young soldiers, some no more than 14 years old, were in action near our house. Their heads were lost in their helmets which were too big for them and to give themselves a warlike air they were dragging an old machine gun from the Great War and were festooned in cartridge belts which touched the ground. In the afternoon they laid a telephone cable from the fields to the main road.

In the evening the Belgians brought us a big dixie of vegetable soup and slices of bread with meat paste.

The Spaniards, who had caught some hens and 'organised' some rice from an abandoned house, invited us to a meal of Spanish chicken and rice. They explained how they cooked the rice directly in the chicken fat. It was our first meal for years. What a pleasure, what a feast! But in the night I was racked with terrible abdominal pain and diarrhoea. Soon Serge, who was not really over his potato colic, suffered the same fate. If we were not to die of indigestion we had to learn to be reasonable.

In the morning of 30 April we were purged and pale. Paul, having weathered the shock better, described what was going on outside since we could not stand: disarmed soldiers passing by, coming from the banks of the Elbe; white sheets appearing at the windows of houses in the village… An unarmed soldier came to ask us for civilian clothes, which we gave him. He gave us a packet of tobacco.

Towards midday I went up to the main road in search of any food left by the retreating troops. Suddenly I saw an American jeep coming from Rosslau carrying two soldiers. They stopped next to me and asked,

'Rusky?'

'Français!'

'Good!'

Then they slowly made their way to Coswig and I rushed back to give my pals the good news. Now we were eight, three Spaniards and five Frenchmen. I was met with shouts of joy. This time we really were free. Our little band made its way to Coswig, overtaken by convoys of Americans who waved as they passed. In the town streets, which seemed deserted by their residents, the houses draped in white sheets as in Büro, the only people moving around were American patrols, unarmed German soldiers and foreign workers.

Less than twenty metres away before us staggered a German NCO as if drunk. Suddenly while still walking he pulled his revolver from its holster, put it to his temple and blew his brains out. Scenes of pillage began in the town. Civilians could be seen coming from abandoned houses with broken window panes, dragging big cartons, packages and suitcases. Some were loading small items of furniture, tins of goose pâté and bundles of clothes onto small handcarts.

When we reached the square, which was also the site of the American headquarters, another spectacle was taking place: German soldiers came to surrender their rifles, helmets, belts, and cartridge belts onto piles already two metres high, under the phlegmatic gaze of a few American soldiers. The latter authorised us to search them and help ourselves to whatever we found in their pockets or bags such as tobacco or food. From one of them I retrieved a superb pair of binoculars.

Shortly after that a delegation of Russian military arrived at the town and we were witness to accolades and toasts. The town swarmed with more and more foreign workers, especially Russians and Poles who had come to share the spoils.

In a street on the way back a terrible scene was being played out on the first floor of a bourgeois town house. Furniture and various objects crashed onto the pavement and a woman could be heard screaming, being abused, and possibly raped. It was, we learnt, the home of a particularly brutal foreman, where foreign workers were taking their revenge. On the edge of town a French prisoner was kicking an unarmed soldier calling him a bastard. Was he one of his former guards? For my part I could not have identified one of our torturers, so alike were they all in their uniforms and behaviour. Those sinister silhouettes, yelling, beating, pushing my comrades to their deaths in ditches, appeared to me then through a misty veil.

We went back to Büro, loaded with food piled into rucksacks confiscated from the Germans. Once again we had a gargantuan meal, without a care for the consequences. I stuffed myself with chocolate received from the American soldiers and catastrophe struck during the night: vomiting and diarrhoea. The next day, 1 May, I could not get up or go to the town with my pals.

On their return they related their adventures. Serge paraded in a fine pair of leather boots. In a street in the middle of town he had made a civilian take off and surrender his boots. In numerous places portraits of Lenin and red flags had replaced the white sheets since the Americans had been relieved by the Russians. Extraordinary rumours were circulating, such as that Berlin had fallen and Hitler was dead. Such an event deserved a celebration. Serge had brought a bag full of food from Coswig containing boiled pork, jam, sugar and chocolate. We decided to give some to the old lady who had given us bread on our arrival in town. She was not alone, chatting to a younger woman, possibly her daughter who had just arrived. With dignity she declined our offer to toast the end of the war and would not even take our gifts. Then we realised that for them it was a day of mourning.

At night in our house open to the winds we had no warmth and after some deliberation we installed ourselves, as if by right, in the very centre of the village, in a building that must have been a kindergarten or primary school. There was a well equipped kitchen where the Spaniards could cook the meals. In the rest room was a pile of about twenty little mattresses. Set side by side they made suitable beds. Everything was neat and tidy. We piled the toys in a corner and on the cleared shelves we stored our now considerable stock of food, such as canned duck, rice pudding with chocolate or honey, plus American rations, biscuits etc. In the evening the Spaniards prepared a right royal feast for a house-warming party comprising canned duck, and rice pudding with chocolate and honey. At nightfall about fifty Russian soldiers occupied the almost deserted village. Most of the residents, above all the women, had fled.

On Wednesday, 2 May, we met the officer commanding the Russian detachment, which was setting up an artillery battery on the Elbe facing the Americans. Some soldiers conversed with the help of gestures. Serge and I showed them our tattooed Auschwitz numbers and they spoke about their campaigns and showed us their scars and wounds. The Spaniards, being ex-combatants of the Spanish Civil War, knew a few words of Russian and also fraternised with them. They invited us to eat a soup of meat with pasta, and goulash, at their mobile canteen. Then they took us to a large state farm on the outskirts of the village, which was being looted by several of their comrades. Many chests had been emptied with their contents thrown on the floor and soiled. On the ground floor lay broken objects and photos, all smeared with vomit and excrement. I could not understand how civilised people could behave in such a way.

Serge had come across a superb officer's greatcoat with field grey lining which came down to his ankles. I found a magnificent hunting jacket in fine silk-like material with carved horn buttons. In another room on the first floor, still more or less intact, we found hunting and riding trousers trimmed in leather, silk shirts and other fine underwear. Our rucksacks were filled up. We changed clothes leaving the Belgian uniforms behind. I stayed as I had found a fur lined three-quarter length coat on a hangar. I was bending to fold it when I was seized by a bout of colic which bent me double. Try as I could I could not hold it and my diarrhoea exploded in the smart trousers. I had to leave them behind and changed clothes after wiping myself hastily with silk underwear. Fortunately this scene was not witnessed. I was ashamed to have done what I had criticised moments before and it is still one of the most humiliating memories of my deportation. Leaving the room I came across some Russian civilians. They tried to come in but retreated holding their noses, crying 'Bliadj! Kourva!'[4]

I was gradually going off the Spaniard's spicy food and chocolate even though I had dreamt of it for months. This lasted only while I was ill, since the next day, after a good night's sleep, I was ready to begin again, like a drunk turning back to alcohol.

From then on we went in search of food with a wheelbarrow. Every abandoned house had food stashed at the back of linen and broom-cupboards, and in cellars. In some modest dwellings there was food enough for several months. I thought back nostalgically to my parents' stash behind the curtain in the small bedroom. The Russian soldiers let us get away with it. On the other hand they arrested any German who pillaged a neighbour's house. The shelves of our school were so well stocked that one could have taken our premises to be a grocery store. How long did we anticipate staying there?

In the night of 3 May drunken Russian soldiers forced their way into our school. They searched every room including the attic looking for women. They looked under our mattresses, upturned the pile of toys and knocked over our piles of provisions hoping to find schnapps. At that time alcohol was the last thing on our minds, likewise for the village locals, since in all our searches we had not come across any.

This incursion made us very aware of the risks we ran amidst those undisciplined troops coming from the far reaches of the Steppes. So the next morning the Spaniards left us to try to get to the American zone by going along the Elbe. Serge and I were too weak to undertake a fresh march. In addition to our now chronic diarrhoea we were swelling from water retention. Our swollen heads felt as if we had mumps and the sight of my face in the mirror, even after a close shave, scared me. My dark sunken eyes in a moon-shaped face were more frightening than in a face of skin and bone.

Also the oedema starting in our ankles began rising up our legs. Pushing our fingers in the flesh swollen with water left an imprint as if in butter. We had to do something as no Russian doctor or medic had paid us any attention and we ran the risk of suffering the same fate as that of a Belgian prisoner, recently buried by his comrades having died of digestive stress.

The Russian soldiers behaved like children coming across civilisation for the first time. Some wore a watch for the first time in their lives; it was as if they were holding their first communion presents; they kept looking at them and putting them to their ears to hear the sound of their ticking. Many now were discovering bicycles, and in groups they practised keeping their balance in the village streets. From time to time one heard the metallic rattle of a crash followed by loud laughter.

Serge was as anxious as I, all the more so since the regiments passing on the road were identifiable by their eyes as coming from the Far East and looked less naive and innocent than our Russians in Büro. Thus we left our little school to go to Rosslau where, as a Soviet officer told us, we stood a better chance of being repatriated as there was a bridge connecting with Dessau in the American zone.

Our painful still swollen legs forced us to stop to rest every few kilometres. We also had our bulky rucksack to carry. After a walk of about six kilometres we stopped overnight in a small abandoned farm in the village of Kliegen which was down to the last stage of pillage, that is, all that remained was furniture that was too big to carry or beds without mattresses. What was not taken lay scattered on the ground which was carpeted with soiled linen, eggshells, peelings, tin cans, burst bags of flour and other refuse. With a manure fork from the farmyard I cleared out most of the filth and settled on the double bedstead. Serge only had a child's bed which was too short for him. No matter. With one solid kick he knocked off the end and his legs overhung by twenty centimetres. We had unhooked some miraculously intact lined curtains for use as bedclothes.

In the morning we were awakened by the weeping and moaning of a young woman, doubtless the owner of the premises. She was rummaging through the debris picking up here a sock, there a little bonnet. She was selecting whatever could be recovered. We tried to make her understand that we were not responsible for the destruction, and as she kept on weeping, we shouted at her to leave us alone. She went into the next room from where we could hear her exclamations and laments from time to time. We made a quick exit, being much unsettled by this incident. On the road we met up with five French PoWs pulling a four-wheeled cart on which they agreed to take our bags.

On entering Rosslau, on the road to the Elbe bridge, there was a roadblock and a Russian officer, next to an interpreter, pointed us in the direction of some barracks where all foreigners were housed. For the first time we had come across some semblance of organisation. We were put in groups in a very clean room furnished with four beds with blankets. The food was decent without being copious. It was the same as army food, that is to say meat, soup and bread. This time I was treated by a Russian major–doctor who pulled a face when he saw my thumb. He lanced it, cleaned up the cut, covered it in white powder, and put on a dressing to be changed every two days.

We found some pals, who had escaped from the march, billeted in the other room. Many had to be admitted to the barracks sick bay, some remaining there for months, so weak were they. We were lodged in that place for several days and well looked after by the Russians, but dispirited since we were not allowed out. Suddenly on May 12 towards 8 pm the authorities gave us instructions to pack up our things ready to leave.

We packed quickly, delighted at the thought that we would be going to the American zone. Even the sick wanted to be in the convoy, but only those able to walk were allowed to leave. We were a few hundred assembled to take the road. As soon as we left town we were met with an unpleasant surprise. The Russian officer leading the escorted column did not take the Dessau road but the one to Coswig.

Our long caravan of wagons, handcarts, vehicles of all kinds, and pedestrians burdened with overweight bags, dragged on for part of the night. Many lay down at the roadside without the risk this time of being shot, then after taking a break they set off again helped by Russian soldiers. Finally, some kilometres before Coswig we took a side road on the left leading to Zieco, and arrived at a former PoW camp with bunks and straw mattresses, similar to the Halberstadt camp.

The sleeping quarters were dirty, full of all sorts of waste left by the previous occupants, and the straw mattresses were flea ridden. As we cleaned it out the next morning and changed the straw the general mood was bad. We resented the Russians for parking us in this camp. Furthermore I was by chance separated from my friends, and I was lost in a crowd of French

STO workers who were in good physical shape and not very likeable. The next day I was able to swap groups and get back with Serge and four other pals from Langenstein, including a butcher from the north and a farmer.

Little by little our life became organised. The Russians set up offices and a kitchen. They served us plain meals, the same as for their troops, which just kept hunger at bay, but we dreamt of other dishes than pasta or meat soup. Given that we were free to come and go during the day (the camp gates were shut at night) we soon began to plunder the farms and houses roundabout. We organised searches, even of occupied houses. We found food hidden in cellars, attics, chicken pens and barns. Our little four-wheeled cart 'organised' from a farm was often full of tins of ham, duck or goose or jam. We even found live chickens hidden in cellars. Those were days for feasting on fresh meat!

One day when we had retrieved two chickens, our chef served them without legs! Faced with our incredulity, since we knew full well that he had eaten them on the side, he protested saying that it was a breed without thighs. This story raised a laugh in all the dormitories and on choosing another chef we rediscovered chicken with thighs.

A week went by without any talk of leaving. With our help our butcher friend caught animals in the fields, killed them on the spot, and we brought back the best joints. We were not the only ones to do so and we came across and smelled the carcasses of rotting animals in the fields.

One day as we were trying to catch a lamb, which was no easy matter, the owner came to see us and explained that if we were hungry he would give us a good meal. Indeed he took us to his farm and gave us ham, fried eggs, and jams. When we left, that did not stop us from killing the lamb and bringing it back after having butchered it on the spot.

Alarming rumours began to spread regarding the behaviour of the Russian troops. One in particular was that some prisoners, unable to remove rings from people, had cut their fingers off.[5] Serge thought this news came from 'agents provocateurs' and it spread rapidly and strengthened our will all the more to get to the American zone. In spite of several approaches to the authorities, our stay dragged on and friction mounted between us and the STO and other civilian workers who criticised us for our fleas. In spite of frequent changes of clothes and underwear they continued to hatch out. Worse still they had invaded and occupied the fresh straw so much so that our sanitary condition deteriorated.

Our farmer friend went from one farm to another early in the morning and brought us a bucket of milk that he gave to us with priority for our ex-Zwieberge comrades. Our group had grown to include a number of pals coming from Coswig or elsewhere (we numbered around twenty at that time), and to celebrate these reunions I decided to make pancakes with a bucket of milk, some eggs and a packet of flour from an attic. I mixed the flour in a large bowl when suddenly it began to harden: what I had taken to be flour was in fact plaster powder! This joke, like the one about the chicken legs, went around the camp.

Another day we spotted a pig on a farm near the camp. We had set out at daybreak pulling our cart but on arrival at the stable where the pig was hidden we heard the unmistakable sound of a cow being milked, and to avoid any incident with the person whom we took to be the farmer we returned to the camp. Perhaps thirty minutes later our pal returned with his daily bucket of milk and explained that it was he who was milking the cow, not its owner. We returned to the farm that evening and lay low in a nearby building. Towards 3 am we went into the stable where the pig was. It took umbrage at our intrusion and began squealing, all the more so as I could not finish him off with the first blow from the club we had brought. We thought we would have to face the farm residents armed with pitchforks ready to chase us off, but no one stirred and our butcher bled, scalded, gutted and calmly cut up the beast. We wrapped the pieces in underwear and after loading them on the cart we covered everything in straw to hide things from the Russian sentries since, from the day before, all pillage was banned on the orders of the sector commander. But what was left to pillage?

## Chapter 11

# A Difficult Return to Civilisation

On May 24 around 3 pm the order to get ready to go into the American zone finally came. There was an outburst of joy and in next to no time bags were drawn tight and vehicles were loaded. Led by a Russian officer our convoy headed south on the Berlin to Leipzig autobahn, which we had crossed farther south when we were on the march; the bridge over the Elbe had just been repaired. Some people pulled handcarts, others pushed heavily loaded cycles, and others like us pulled fourwheeled carts. An ex radio repairer carried radio valves that he had 'organised' from a shop in Coswig. We waited for hours to cross the temporary wooden bridge as we were behind an endless column of PoWs coming from Luckenwald. It was dark when we were allowed to cross.

The Russian soldiers parked us in a meadow between two branches of the river and informed us that we could cross over into the American zone only with what we had on our backs or in our hands. The rest, bicycles, carts and carriages had to stay there. Each of us sorted his things out and kept only what he could pack in a bag or suitcase. For Serge and me who were much weaker it came down to keeping the few clothes we had got from the state farm in Büro. All the rest was piled with the vehicles in the meadow on the banks of the Elbe. Our anger at not being allowed to take with us the things we had amassed was such that, when someone suggested setting fire to it, he was applauded, and soon, despite the intervention of Russian soldiers, our immense brazier consumed the cycles, carts laden with parcels, and even the radio valves which exploded like fireworks. What a waste.

Early in the morning of May 25, after sleeping in the grass, we were allowed to cross the border and were taken over by American soldiers. The

PoWs marched with a document pinned to their greatcoats, escorted by their own entrusted men. In spite of that, the vigilant American soldiers pulled out some from the ranks and put them with us who were without papers. Suddenly I saw a friend from junior school who lived in the next street to ours. He recognised me and I shouted to him to tell my parents.

With the other suspects and non-documented people we were taken to a hut to fill out questionnaires, giving date and place of birth, address, profession, reason for arrest etc. I met Felix, a trainee priest on STO service, with no papers. He had burnt them before the Russians arrived since he had been told that novice and practising priests had been sent to a camp in Siberia to be 're-educated'. He had joined a convoy of PoWs hoping to pass unnoticed among them, but the American soldiers had quickly picked him out and excluded him from the group.

We waited for a good hour more, then we passed before a commission with an interpreter. An officer asked me, since I was from Rouen area, the names of the bridges over the Seine. What was the statue in the town hall square? The address of the École Normale? What was the global teaching method?

Obviously I passed this test to go to the West as did Serge, Felix and most of our companions. On the other hand a number of those who had been interrogated at the same time as us were detained and taken away by military police, among them one Belgian and one Luxembourger. Then we were taken under escort to a former SS barracks in Dessau where we slept-in after having a meal of beans and lamb. The town had been almost entirely flattened but the barracks were intact. We were to leave the next morning by train along with the Belgians and Dutch.

We were ready early on 26 May, a Saturday, but there was a setback in store for us. The train had been marshalled the night before and it was said to be full. It was a convoy of cattle wagons with straw covered floors. At every door there was a group of civilians or prisoners on guard who said, 'We're full up here. Look further along.' None of them would squeeze up to let us in. It was close to departure time and there were about fifty of us remaining on the platform searching for a space. Suddenly I noticed, at the back of a wagon, a woman who did not look like a deportee. Felix and I went off to find an American officer on station duty to whom we explained the situation. With several MPs he did a check and a number of German and Polish women that the workers wanted to take back with them were removed from the wagons and we were thus able to get on. We were received in a hostile silence which lasted for some time into the journey, in spite of our explanations. We had nothing against those who wanted to take a woman home but we felt we had priority in the circumstances.

After passing through various cities in ruins, such as Köthen, Halle, Leipzig and Apolda, we arrived in Fulda on May 27 after a 36-hour journey. There the American health officials had us get off, powdered us with DDT and served us a hot meal, again beans with lamb, and they gave us a cold collation to take with us. Late in the evening of May 28 we stopped overnight in Hanau station, near Frankfurt. The next day the train slowly progressed behind other convoys heading for the Rhine. Along the track groups of German women from surrounding villages begged us imploringly for food, above all meat, in exchange for ornaments and jewellery.

During one of those frequent stops American soldiers did the rounds of wagons asking us to hand over our trophies, such as weapons, knives, and belts, since, according to them there would be a search at the border and anyone found in possession of such objects would be refused passage. Some civilians obeyed but most like me realised that the military were just acting out of self interest. So I hung on to my binoculars.

We rolled on cautiously at a speed of visual stopping distance as we neared the Rhine and as it was hot inside I climbed onto the roof with some pals during a halt and from there I could see with my binoculars the trains in front of and behind us. Suddenly an American soldier in overalls called to me and by gesture offered me a big packet of chocolate sweets and cigarettes in exchange for the binoculars. My pals urged me to accept since we had no more supplies. I made the mistake of giving him the binoculars before getting the packet. He told me to wait a minute but the train started without any sign of him. At the next stop I looked for him among the soldiers accompanying us and I found him in the locomotive. It was the driver. He pretended not to recognise me and I had to fetch the officer in charge of the convoy to ask him to sort it out. He gestured that he did not understand and the train started to leave. I went back to the wagon feeling gutted to have been thus cheated. How could I have been so naïve? Had life in the camps taught me nothing?

Our train finally crossed the Rhine at Mainz and sped on to France passing through Pfalz and Sarreland. On 30 May we arrived in Thionville. The Dutch and Belgians left us to take another train. Now we were on home ground. At Longuyon we could send a telegram to our families, take a shower and eat. After filling out some forms we were given a repatriate card and 1,000 francs for our immediate expenses. We were once again put with the ex–Langenstein inmates and we took a train to Paris, this time travelling in third class carriages.

When we arrived at the Gare de l'Est it was a riot of joy, with dense crowds, shouts, tears, and music. We were hassled by hundreds of people searching for a loved one. 'Where are you from? Did you know so and so?'

Some held out photos. What could we say to all of them? As we had to go through processing at the hotel Lutetia, our escorts put us on special buses laid on to take us there. On our arrival, French military counter-espionage staff recommenced questioning on the camps we had been in, reasons for arrest, resistance members, traitors we had known, dead comrades, and survivors still in hospital… For about two hours I gave all the information requested.

Serge was catching the train at St Lazare to go to Colombes and had waited for me. When we got there the train for Rouen had just left and I had a wait of several hours before the last one. Serge suggested I go with him to his place which was ten minutes away from St Lazare station. We took a suburban train and went through Colombes to reach his apartment. Passers-by turned round to look at us, Serge with his Russian style haircut in his long fur-lined German officer's greatcoat reaching down to his fine leather boots, carrying his enormous rucksack, me in oversize riding breeches over patent leather dress shoes, fancy hunting jacket, my three-quarter length fur coat over my shoulder and Austrian hat rammed on my head (I had deposited my rucksack in a locker at the station).

When we reached his home his wife and son threw themselves on him with kisses and I felt 'de trop' in that intimate moment of reunion. After some introductions and explanations Serge disappeared with his wife to get changed and I remained alone with his 12-year-old son in a heavy silence that I tried to fill with an account of our wanderings on the banks of the Elbe. Time dragged on.

Serge finally reappeared freshly shaven, in civilian clothes. His wife told him about the struggle for better wages, the attitudes of the trade unions, the price of food, and I felt that, once back in society, family and the Party, his story had come to its conclusion. The following day it would be the same for me. The prospect of family, job, society and routine whirled dizzily in my mind. Feeling so removed, would I be able to fit back into all that?

As it was getting late, I declined their offer to put me up there and I took my leave. Their son accompanied me to the station in Colombes to show me the way. Unfortunately when I got to St Lazare the last train for Rouen had left. I would have to wait for the express train in the morning. I tried to get a room but my outfit and general appearance did not open any doors and I returned to the station intending to sleep in the waiting room. I came across an ex-PoW alone in transit who had stayed in Paris to celebrate. He said, 'Do like me and me mates. The hotels are too expensive. We sleep in the trains.'

He took me to a train still in the station, where the other rejects like me were sleeping on the seats. I did the same. At daybreak I was awakened by the shouts of a cleaning lady. I was alone. All the others had left. She accused me of being responsible for the vomit and other mess that she had to clean up. I told her my side of the story and showed her my Auschwitz tattoo. She apologised and explained that she had to clean up the filth from vagrants and the homeless who invaded the empty trains at night.

I picked up my rucksack and took a seat in the train for Rouen. Now I was impatient to get home, to be with my family, to see my room, my accordion, the streets of Rouen and its cinemas. I suddenly felt a rush of excitement at being alive, but simultaneously a kind of anxiety about the predictable life ahead of me. I had lived through extraordinary events and it was all over. I knew that nothing would be the same and I would not get back my lost youth.

As we neared Rouen memories flooded back. In the distance I could see the tower of chateau Renault, at Andé the Manoir bridge, under whose arches I had fished for barbels, then came Tourville-la-Rivière, and my dear grandmother's house, Oissel bridge, the ruins of Sotteville, the Eauplet viaduct, the park gardens on the Route de Lyons, and at last, after the tunnel, the Rive Droite[1] station.

As soon as I got off the train I was stopped, along with some other returnees, by a group of plain-clothes police who asked me to wait in a station office. Once more I had to provide information about my resistance actions, reasons for arrest, and the camp I was returning from. Then I was free to go out of the station and I heard a loudspeaker announce, 'Paul Le Goupil, former département head of the Front Patriotique de la Jeunesse, arrested at Monville on 13 October 1943, repatriated from Langenstein, a Buchenwald kommando.'

I passed between two ranks of people who applauded then the loudspeaker announced other names of the repatriated and a band began to play patriotic music.

Suddenly I was surrounded and hugged. My sister was there with my resistance friend Marie Louise and her husband George Chopin, a former FTP organiser whom I did not know. He had been injured in action against the Germans. They had awaited my arrival for two days and my family and friends took it in turns to be present to welcome me. A special bus took us home where we arrived an hour later after the other returnees had been dropped off at their homes.

As soon as I got off the bus my parents rushed into my arms. I was shocked at how much they had aged. For them those months had seemed like years. My sister who was a teenager when I left had blossomed into a pretty young woman. I held back my tears of emotion at being back among my folk. I rushed up to my room to see my familiar things, my books and my accordion. I had pushed all that to the back of my mind during those long months of horror, in order to hold on, to think only about surviving, and suddenly the protective shell cracked open and I broke down in tears.

For the first day I spoke very little, but listened a lot. I expressed my concern about the traitor Prieur. My father related the enquiry he had carried out at Monville, how Madame Ragot had seen his real name on the cycle ID plate and told one of the investigations done during the occupation to trace him. One day, knowing that from time to time he visited his fiancée at Rue des Petits-Eaux in Rouen, my father had decided to kill him. He had taken my mother along to keep a look out and they waited until curfew, in vain. In fact the traitor, having lost his cover in the Rouen area, had been sent by the Gestapo to the Manche département, where he continued his trail of destruction and he had to flee to the north at the time of the liberation of France. My father had been around all the police stations in the region to make sure he was sought under his name or under the alias of Baudry, or Lefèvre. The police had often gone to his fiancée's house, in vain.

Some months after liberation Prieur turned up there. She asked him why the police were looking for him. He played the innocent and, to prove to her that he had nothing to hide he went to the police station at Saint Hilaire Square in Rouen giving his real name. He did not know that the police knew his true identity, and he asked what they wanted of him. The duty officer, somewhat surprised, did not detain him, then after he had left they consulted the files and realised their error. They picked him up a few hundred metres away and arrested him. Since that time the case was pending while the prosecutor awaited the return of the deportees, to be able to build a case against him.

Several times my parents had believed me dead. Firstly an informer known to my father and living near the shooting range had informed him that I had been shot. But he had got the wrong name, and my father, via one of his colleagues who liaised with the Gestapo, found out the next day that it did not concern me. But what a terrible night they must have spent. Hopes revived when they got my letters from Buchenwald. In April when the camp was liberated, photos appeared in the press showing the piles of bodies rotting in the camp, and the crematorium. Once more they gave up hope of seeing me again. They were overjoyed when my schoolfriend came to tell them he had seen me in Dessau and that I was alright, which was confirmed by the telegram from Longuyon.

In the days after my return I related my scarcely believable adventures to my family. I talked about my arrest, being in prison, about the camps, and the roads. Certain memories haunted me, the journey in the cattle wagon, Auschwitz and its death factory, Langenstein and the march, above all the march with its terrible scenes of comrades on the brink of death, struggling, reaching out to me, who could not help them, scenes that I relived every night. To unburden my mind of those memories I shut myself in my room and wrote *La Route des Crématoires*[2] in the space of a few weeks, first and foremost to be able to live normally again.

My wounds, a feeding ground for fleas, had healed over, but the scars were so sensitive that I still had the feeling that those creepy crawlies were on me and I continued to scratch myself. From time to time I would find one in spite of continually changing clothes and taking innumerable showers. The last one died two months after my return but the memory of them crawling over my skin will never leave me.

I was called to the office for repatriated persons, set up in the former École Supérieure in Rue Poisson which has since become Rue des Requis. There I received a repatriation grant, underwear, a suit, an overcoat, most of them second hand, clean but used, sometimes moth-eaten. I reported the deaths of Richard, Dubernard and of others that I had seen executed, with sufficient information to enable their families to be informed.

One week later there was a ring at the gate and an old man introduced himself. 'I am the father of Richard and the repatriation office told me you had news of my son.'

The office employee had not informed him that Richard had been shot on the march and the poor man, full of hope, had come to see me. I had to give him the sad news and tell him the circumstances around the fact. He left looking twice his age under the crushing burden that I had thrust on his soul, repeating the words, 'So! That's it! He's dead!'

The family of Michel Dubernard never got in touch with me, but were they contacted and informed?

One by one the deportees came back. Via comrades we already knew that some had disappeared. Thus I learned of the deaths of seven young people who had been arrested following the Monville case, including the Abbé Kerebel who died from typhus after the liberation of his camp. On the other hand I was overjoyed to be reunited with some others such as Rangée, Hochard, Néel, Castel etc. Most were very sick and had to be treated in rest homes or sanatoria.

After the wave of returnees in June and July the rest came in dribs and drabs. Even though a significant number of them had not returned celebration parties were in aid of them but the spirit was missing since many of the women who had volunteered to run the stalls and bars were still waiting for a son or husband to return. They still had hope. Alas how many were in mourning a few months later, or worse, they never were to know what had become of their loved one.

Newspapers published numerous 'missing persons' notices with texts such as 'last seen in an evacuation column heading towards...x, ...left Buchenwald camp, transported to Dora...' etc.

I received numerous letters from relatives or wives whose son or husband had been last seen at Auschwitz, Buchenwald or Langenstein. Sometimes a whole family of a missing person came to see me. I tried to give them hope, while keeping my real thoughts to myself.

I attempted to return to a normal life but the camps had turned me into a person crude in language and behaviour. I had forgotten how to eat properly and I attacked my food as soon as I felt hungry like a dog at his bowl. It was a sort of restriction to be in civil society; most of all I wanted to be alone. I withdrew to my room into long periods of silence. I had to relearn how to live in society and to be involved with others. To that end my sister helped me by presenting me to her schoolfriends to whom I appeared heroic, a figure returning from hell. That feminine company greatly helped me to get back to normal life.

Yves had been repatriated from Buchenwald before me and he invited me to his wedding. He hugged me for a long time when he met me. Gilles was there too. If only he had looked in my direction when he passed through Halberstadt!

On July 14 I was invited to Paris by the Aubine family that I knew via my aunt in La Cambe and by other friends who had come to Illiers for food. There were endless outpourings of joy in the streets with street dances, endless congas and magical firework displays. I took the opportunity to go and see Réjane who had been living in Paris since the liberation. She was a struggling young actress after attending acting school. She later gave me back my diary during a brief stay at her mother's place in Rouen. She had changed a lot, not physically as I still found her pretty, but in her manner. She was more mature, a blasé woman of the world. Our paths had diverged dramatically and between us the spark had gone.

The education authority gave me back-pay from June 1943 and despite the erosion of some of it through inflation I found myself with a capital of 60,000 francs. I set aside a major part of it to buy a vehicle. I decided on a motorcycle, a British army Triumph, picked out by my friend Miton at a government auction, for which I paid 37,000 francs (at that time a teacher earned 4,000 francs per month). After quickly passing my test and getting my licence, I spent the summer visiting all the family with my sister.

At Villiers I was guest of honour at my grandparents', uncles' and aunts' houses. I took advantage of the trip to greet the parents of the younger men I had met at Buchenwald small camp. None of them had returned. I was the last person to see them alive. I made a detour via Montlandon to go and hug my pal Davignon who had returned a short while before me. He introduced me as his saviour. He remembered the crusts of bread that I brought down to him from the main camp. As I had brought my accordion on the luggage rack of my motorbike, he took the opportunity to organise a benefit barn dance at his place, for the deportees of his commune (he was the only one!).

Then we went to my uncle and aunt's place at Saint-Floxel. They were thrilled to see me but my aunt who thought the resistance movement pointless said to me in her dialect, in all simplicity, 'If you hadda stayed at 'ome, all o' that wouldna've happened to ya.'

In her simple country language she was expressing the feelings of many inhabitants of the region who saw resistance actions simply as a cause of the wrath of the occupiers, resulting in road blocks, hostage taking, and various forms of reprisals.

However, being right in the landings zone they were not spared from misfortune. Shells had fallen all around the farm, causing damage and a number of cows had been killed; within hours the Germans had ordered them out of the farm in order to use it as a command post. They were obliged to take refuge in a stable in the middle of marshland and there they narrowly avoided being shot by the Americans for giving aid to a wounded German.

Old Aunt Justine aged 91 had stayed in her house and all through the fighting around Montebourg, she took her walk in the sunken lanes, checking up on the damage, counting the wounded or killed cows, or the apple trees smashed by shells. She would meet patrols, be they Americans or Germans, amazed to see this carefree wrinkled bent old lady making her way through the fields with the aid of her walking stick. She went to visit her son and his family, lying low in their barn, repeating in her dialect, 'You should be ashamed squatting there when your cows need milking. Hurry up out of there quick!'

It is true that no one looked after the poor animals, lowing, frightened by battle, sometimes wounded, often unwatered, suffering badly from swollen udders.

She even caught two German soldiers raiding her private room and chased them out with her stick, calling them 'Dirty Prussians'.

One of my cousins in the area had the experience of several German soldiers killed in her yard by an American patrol. Some days after the battle for Montebourg when it was no longer dangerous, she, with the help of her neighbours, dug a big pit into which the dead cows and bodies of Germans were piled pell-mell. Perhaps they are still there?

All my other relatives had suffered damage, sometimes more than once, but nobody had been killed or injured. In Calvados my cousin's farm in Grandcamp had been shattered by a 420 mm naval shell, but fortunately they had all taken shelter at my aunt's farm in Cambes which was much less vulnerable. There was one shadow over the story, namely, my father's half brother had lost his son, killed by the Americans while he was running towards them to greet them. After a final stopover with a cousin in Bayeux, we went back to Rouen.

Petrol supply was difficult since the allowance for a motorcycle was only ten litres per month. Even though the war had been over since 8 May, rationing was still in place and there was a flourishing black market. Some dealers were selling petrol at 2,000 francs per jerrycan of twenty litres.

Luckily my friend Miton and other friends working in local government sent me tickets. As they expired at the end of the month I had to buy the petrol and store what I did not use. At a second hand shop I came across sixty-litre carboys that had contained sulphuric acid. I put them in the cellar and gradually filled them with my excess petrol. My father moaned about the smell of petrol vapour which mingled with the taste of his mug of cider when he went down to have a drink, and most of all he complained about the risk of explosion. I had to find a solution so I bought jerrycans on the black market, at a high price, and lined them up this time in the laundry at the end of the garden which was better ventilated than the cellar.

Our stock of food behind the curtain in the small bedroom was still substantial, consisting mostly of dried beans and flour. The problem was how to preserve them; the flour was weevil infested and the beans were too hard so we had stopped eating them. Fortunately my father grew a lot of vegetables in his garden and Miton sent me bread ration tickets. In addition, as a repatriated person I had an allowance of supplementary rations.

In August I went to see Gilbert who had avoided all the Gestapo nets. He was a full time representative and belonged to the new organisation of the FPJ, FUJP (Front Uni de la Jeunesse Patriotique) which had become the UJRF (Union de la Jeunesse Républicaine de France) and which combined the forces of all the youngsters who had fought with us in the Résistance. It was spearheaded by the disbanded JCs (Young Communists) who had joined their ranks and had assumed a leading role in all associations and major groups in the département. For Gilbert they meant the rallying of youth around the Communist Party. For my part I was much less convinced. I soon realised that politics had tainted that fine youthful enthusiasm that had given its life for the liberation of France. Catholic youth had re-established its JAC and JOC, and the young socialists, who had stood aside from our movement, were now against it, considering it too enslaved to the Party. There were still a lot of unaligned young people in towns, villages, and in the country, who were in awe of the Résistance.

Most of my former comrades in the FPJ did not rally to the UJRF such as Rangée whose Gaullist ideals could not be reconciled with the new association.

In the département of Seine Inférieur the committee of the UJRF was in the grip of Roland Leroy, an orthodox communist who had become leader of the FUJP just before the liberation. He gave me a position in it and I was able to place my sister and one of her friends as student representatives. I became aware that I was not the only person objecting to the sectarian line of the leadership. Namely there was a Trotskyite and a young bourgeois (who was also Jewish) with no political leanings, but with a record of active resistance. What heated discussions took place in the UJRF headquarters in Saint Clément square! Leroy and his friends, being in the majority, forced the former to resign in disgust and the latter was hounded out as a 'young bourgeois class enemy'. The peak of political errors was reached when the *Avant Garde*, now the newspaper of the UJRF, ran its election edition under the headline, 'Vote for the Communist Party, the only defender of youth.' With my supporters I fought against this stance which was sabotaging the UJRF. I was defeated in the vote but I got the assurance that Leroy would report our opposition in Seine Inférieur to the congress platform. He dutifully carried this out but Raymond Guyot in his closing speech replied to the effect that 'Those in opposition have no place in the UJRF.' I drew my own conclusions and, with others of a like mind I resigned before being pushed out. One by one the associations lost their non-communist members; the country and village groups faded away and the UJRF became the Young Communists. The whole of the Résistance movement fell apart, riven with violent political quarrels. That was one of the most painful aspects of my return. I had joined the Communist Party, as an active member in the Roger Bonnet cell in Petit-Quevilly. That is where I met fine people, discreetly active in the Résistance, sticking up posters, distributing tracts, with workers who had struggled for an ideal of justice all their lives. We would meet in the dining room of one or another of us. The

Party signified that friendship and trust in comrades that I experienced in the résistance. We were far removed from the jockeying and power struggles of the leadership. I stuck with it a while longer for the sake of camaraderie although my political views had moved on.

During the summer there was also a general meeting in Rue Poisson with a view to setting up an association of the deportees. It was an excuse for the settling of scores which left many comrades feeling disgusted. First a speaker attacked André Marie in his absence accusing him, without proof, of taking money to organise safe passage. To the speaker's surprise Madame Marie was present and she let him have it in no uncertain terms, reducing him to silence. Then my former cell neighbour, having returned from deportation, was asked by the chairman of the meeting to leave. 'There is someone in this room who denounced his comrades. He has no place being here.' G…made for the door but was called back by some friends and stayed at the meeting.

Left and right there were rumours about Rue Borlainville and Rue Leroux and I knew that rifts were opening up among the deportees. Worse still, each resistance organisation recruited its members from those who had been arrested without reason, caught in sweeps, or suspected of activity. They had titles such as 'Front National' or 'OCM'. I heard a well-meaning lady say to a deportee, 'Ah you were socialist before the war so you must be one of the Libé Nord so we'll enrol you with us.'

I left before it ended. Was all our suffering just for that? Where were the ideals I had struggled to defend in the hope of seeing a new society emerge? Luckily that day I met up with some prison companions who had also returned, namely Charles and Nivromont senior (his son was still in hospital).

The public was hungry for deportation stories told first hand. Those photos of piles of emaciated bodies appearing in the newspapers, those 24-hour crematoria gripped the imagination of people and when anyone learned that I had been deported, questions came thick and fast. I was invited to friends and neighbours of my parents. It was hard to refuse those people who had given my parents moral support but I found it painful to be invited in order to have to give an account. At a given moment during a meal there was always the remark, 'Ah the things you must have been through. Tell us about it.'

And like a performer singing for his supper, I had to perform. Above all I could not omit the ovens, as inevitably someone would say, 'And the ovens! Did you see the ovens?', as if burning bodies had represented the height of Nazi brutality.

How could I explain to those good folk the true meaning of hunger, not of the stomach but of the mind which is in torment; talk of those hands clutching at you, that you thrust away to avoid being dragged down to a certain death; those deportees beaten by their comrades for a scrap of bread. How to explain to those people cocooned in a civilised world the depths that a man can plumb when he is reduced to his degraded animal state. Often I would stop mid-story and with those images flooding back from the world beyond civilisation I would say, 'Let's talk about something else.'

Some friends that I had contacted before my arrest and who had refused to help exhibited amnesia or pure hypocrisy: 'Why didn't you tell us you were in the Résistance? We were looking for a way to join.'

Others, claiming to have agreed to be in my organisation, asked for testimonials. I refused but came across them later at resistance meetings wearing badges labelled Libé Nord, OCM or even of a fictitious network. Out of complicity or often for political reasons of self interest, some ex-resistance leaders gave out what Rangée and I had always refused when justification was absent, that is, an attestation of resistance membership.

The case of the Prieur affair was developing and I was called by the prosecutor. After his arrest he had, in order to lessen the charge, denounced Roche as a member of the Gestapo. He clung to this contact saying he had met him at Rue Donjon and seen him in conversation with Alie. He also said that his controlling Gestapo officer had said to him, 'Roche has been flushed in Monville. You can take over from him.'

Roche's answer to that was that he had never set foot in Rue Donjon (the Gestapo headquarters) but that he had happened to meet his former colleague Alie in the street there by chance and had greeted him.

To give him credit, Roche knew about my activities for a month before the Gestapo intervened, but it was not their custom to leave a suspect on the loose. What is more, Roche was always broke whereas Gestapo agents were highly paid; and lastly, German police made multiple use of their informers and the name of Roche is not mentioned in any other affair.

The only case against him was the statement of Prieur, so the judge, lacking evidence, declared the charge inadmissible, after my deposition.

The residents of Monville nevertheless remained convinced of Roche's guilt, so much so that in July 1945, when he together with Prieur was brought to Monville to face witnesses who claimed to have seen them together at the entrance to the village on the afternoon of 12 October 1943, which was proved false, the crowd started to beat them up having first surrounded the gendarmes and cut the tyres of their van; their primary target was Roche. He had to be hospitalised and almost lost an eye (for his part Prieur had some hair torn out).

I found out from the file that Prieur, a pharmaceutical chemist, had gone to Germany as a volunteer, returning at the end of his contract to work for the city services. He went into the Vichy zone without trace for a while. Had he been trapped by the Germans? It remains true that he was recruited by De Mayer from the Gestapo in May 1943. He then met his fiancée and via her brother was introduced to the Stein-Blankarts. He had them do some photographic work for him including his fiancée's portrait and did them some favours by obtaining ID cards for people avoiding transfer who they were hiding.

The trap was set and was quickly sprung. In fact the Gestapo knew from denunciations that two airmen were hiding at the house of a certain Tarbe near Neufchâtel and Prieur was to use one stone to kill two birds. On 24 September 1943 he asked the Stein-Blankarts to provide him with the addresses of anyone able to put them up; he would then go and collect the airmen and place them with the hosts. Soon afterwards they were all arrested including the airmen. The Stein-Blankarts did not think to wonder why.

Then a sequence of events took place without any apparent link to the photographer's studio:

Arrest of Mr Dupré, pharmacist, sheltering a British soldier since 1940.

Arrest of Mr Corroy, secretary to the police commission in Darnétal, having been in contact with Prieur.

Arrest of Captain Bau and Mr Ragane to whom Prieur brought a so-called British pilot.

Then Prieur turned up in the département of Eure in Étrépagny at the Morand Hotel, claiming to be a member of the maquis from the forest of Lyons, then at Vernon at the home of Thoire, a bailiff, claiming to be a liaison agent, to whom he supplied ID cards. Everyone there was arrested.

He was then sent by the Gestapo to Besançon for a while to continue his trail of destruction there.

After Monville, by using the Stein-Blankart studio method he continued to get other resistance members arrested, such as the Leblonds.

Being too naïve and having outlived their usefulness, the photographers were also snared. The husband would die in Auschwitz and his wife would come back from Ravensbrück.

Once flushed out in the Seine Inférieure département, Prieur went to the Manche département. He was responsible for the arrest of Mr Guillaud, a pharmacist in Coutances, of Mr Souchon, director of the family welfare payment service, who would not survive deportation, of Mr Letan, a bailiff, of Mr Leménager, and of many others.

He was seen in Tourlaville, in Saint-Pierre-Église, in Sainte Suzanne where he tried to trap Mr de Hautecloque, in Pontorson, and in Saint Jean du Corail where, according to his statement, he tried to prevent the executions of members of the maquis.

Later he had to answer for his crimes before the Rouen Court of Justice, particularly on the charge relating to the Monville affair. To the end he kept up his accusations against Roche. He confessed to having gained from that affair (in addition to his monthly salary of 3,000 francs) the possession of the objects belonging to those arrested (in my case, my cycle, the leather overcoat and the 7,000 francs in my wallet) plus a travelling allowance of 1,000 francs. Being condemned to death, he was executed by firing squad shortly afterwards in spite of the desperate pleas of his lawyer who cited the tribulations of war and its pitfalls and the youth of his client: 'If you condemn him to death, he will be yet another victim of the German occupation.'

While waiting for the verdict a number of us survivors, especially Leblond and I, solemnly swore to execute him if he ever came out of prison, even twenty or thirty years later. For my part I believe I would have done it.

September came, bringing with it the start of the school year. I had been appointed to the Charles Nicolle School which was a few hundred metres from my home, but I did not feel the vocation to be a teacher. I would have preferred to have been a journalist or writer. I began to write rather bitter short war stories of those times that I submitted to review editors. I received encouraging replies but none of them wanted to publish my work. One review editor in chief wrote to me that he had never read anything as shattering, but that his readers had had their fill of that kind of narrative.

I made a final trip to Grandcamp for a spring tide and a cousin gave me a hundred buckshot 12-bore nine-pellet cartridges. He had found a boxful in one of his fields abandoned amidst other munitions which were probably intended for the resistance.

The hunting season was due to open but cartridges were limited, the allowance being a mere ten per hunting permit. That was enough for a few minutes' hunting. My father had paid a ransom for a hundred unearthed on the black market and he had bought a new gun. He gave me his 12-bore, which had been buried in his garden for the whole war. It was pitted and rusted inside and out in spite of being covered in a thick coat of grease. I had it refurbished to make sure it would not explode in my face.

Thus the big day, awaited for six years, arrived. The Illiers flat land was chock full of game. From the first moments after we rounded the cemetery going up to Meslier farm I saw hares and partridge scattering on all sides. In spite of double shots on the same game my father and I were still empty handed while my uncle and other hunters filled their bags. We began to have doubts. My father opened one of the cartridges with his knife bought on the black market: instead of lead they were full of sand! I switched back to using the buckshot given by my cousin which whizzed by the other hunters. Far off across the flatland I could see them gesticulating angrily. Towards midday a hare of about eight pounds came to a stop about a hundred metres away, hit by one of my cartridges. I had just bagged my first hare!

Six years had passed since the ruined opening of the 1939 season. Time, seemingly frozen, had begun its normal course again. Was it the joy of shooting my first hare or was it the feeling that this season's beginning was where I was to pick up the threads that had been severed for such a long time? For the first time since my return I had the feeling that a new life lay before me.

VALCANVILLE
March 1992

# Endnotes

## Chapter 1: Novice Teacher and Novice Resister

1. Translators's note: Newspaper founded by Jean Jaurès, initially organ of the Socialists then of the Communist Party, currently independent.
2. Translator's note: A scene from Victor Hugo's Les Misérables, in which Jean Valjean realises he has unintentionally robbed a young chimney sweep, having stepped on one of his coins. A morally ambiguous moment.
3. *Hope*.
4. Service Obligatoire du Travail/Obligatory Work Service, usually in Germany, abbreviated to S.T.O.
5. Francs Tireurs et Partisans, a resistance organisation created by the Communist Party which became militarily active after the invasion of The Soviet Union.
5. Libé Nord (Libération Nord), a major resistance organisation in Northern France.

## Chapter 2: Going to Ground

1. Jeunesse Ouvrière Française Travaillant en Allemagne (French Youth Workers in Germany).
2. People's House.
3. Insignia of Pétainiste France showing a double-headed axe.
4. Légion des Volontaires Français contre le Bolshévisme (Legion of French Volunteers against Bolshevism).
5. Translator's note: Organisation TODT, the civil and military engineering branch of the Reich.

6. Translator's note: Familiarity in French is expressed by the use of 'Tu' instead of 'Vous' (both meaning 'you'). The 'Tu' form is a mark of friendship and in non-family circles is a mark of trust.

7. Christian youth groups in agriculture and industry.

8. Hope for Young Norman Patriots.

9. Normandy's Future.

## Chapter 3: Turbulent Arrest in Monville

1. Translator's note: Alie was a notorious collaborationist police chief responsible for deportations. He was condemned and executed after the war.

2. A brand of handcuffs used by the Gestapo. We called them by this name in prison which is why I use this name.

3. I later learned that they were those of Loeber and Neel, two members of the Monville section.

4. For a long time, the inhabitants of Monville, awakened by the shouts and noises of all sorts, believed that the abbé and I had fought against the Germans and a sort of legend grew up around the affair. In his book *Rouen et sa région pendant la guerre 1939-1945*, Gontran Pailhes went so far as to write, 'In Monville, led by P......., who pretended to be a member of the Resistance, the vicarage was surrounded by the Gestapo. The Abbé Kérébel (a Breton), Mr Le Goupil, a Département leader of the Front Patriotique de la Jeunesse, and eight other persons were arrested. The operation was not unopposed since the courageous cleric rolled up his sleeves and fought so hard that the combatants had to be taken to Hotel Dieu [a hospital in Rouen].'

5. German military police.

## Chapter 4: Bonne Nouvelle Prison

1. Translator's note: maquis, impenetrable scrubland in southern France, became a synonym for résistance group(s).

2. In fact it was a forest warden from Maison-Brûlée who did the deed, on police orders. Later he and the customs officer were rewarded by the Germans.

3. The mayor, as well as the vicar and Loeber, were freed thanks to the intervention of an industrialist from Monville, originally from Alsace, who was friendly with some members of the Gestapo.

4. I was never able to confirm the layout of the cells since, despite several requests after the war, neither the penal administration nor the ministry of justice would give me permission to take photos of my cell door or landing. There was never any answer to my letters as if that prison was such a blight (I presume it remained as it had been) and that everything about it had to be brushed under the carpet.

5. I saw Christian Sénard 48 years later. He maintained that Leroy had not told him of my being in on their escape. On the other hand he remembered the condemned man on the ground floor whom they had left behind. He also explained that he had opened the slop trap door with his nails and not with a square key, and only did that at the time of the guard's round. They were not on the wall but hidden in the angle of the door which was the means of climbing onto the inner wall. It was a good thing for them that they had not used the ladder which would have attracted the guard's attention.

6. A Département of Normandy.

7. Attacks on isolated German officers.

8. It was the attack of 31 October 1943 on the Cinédit cinema, requisitioned by the Germans. Roland, going under the name of Claude in the FPJ, had replaced an absent comrade at the last minute. With the help of partisans he had thrown two British hand grenades into the exit lobby at the end of the show. Fleeing by bicycle he had been unbalanced by a German soldier, crashed into a shop window and broken his handlebars. Nevertheless he managed to get away.

9. After the war I was never able to find out if this story was true or was part of Nazi propaganda. On the other hand it is true that on several occasions French soldiers fired on crowds and that some detainees were tortured and shot.

10. Silence!

11. Why?

12. The German Navy in the 3rd Reich.

## Chapter 5: From Compiègne to Auschwitz

1. I later learned from my parents that my first parcel, which arrived the day following my departure, was returned to them.

2. Translator's note: The region of sandy pine forests south west of Bordeaux.

3. It is not my intention to describe here in detail the hellish journey of four days and three nights which led us to Auschwitz-Birkenau and the extermination camp as I have already done so in the two editions of *La Rroute des Crématoires* (1963 and 1983). I seek to recreate what my memory still retains after almost fifty years, commenting on the terrible contemporary facts as they come to mind. With the passage of time some details fade yet others emerge from that landscape of memories and sometimes I wonder if it really happened or whether it is just the trace of a bad nightmare during a night of fever.

4. Homage is due to all those unknown victims who disappeared in the cauldron of the camps, but who knew how to impose some order, in the wagons or at Birkenau, on the lamentable animal herd we had been reduced to.

5. They were buildings that had been German army stables.

6. The convoy arrived on 6 July 1942, being registered in the series numbered 45,000. It consisted of 1,170 French non-Jewish detainees, for the most part communist and trade union members; 600 remained in Auschwitz One and 570 were transferred to Auschwitz Two Birkenau to work on the construction of the camp. In April 1943 the survivors of the latter camp (fewer than twenty) were brought back to Auschwitz One and met up with the 100 or so survivors of the other half of the convoy (figures quoted by Louis Eudier in his book *Notre Combat de Classe et de Patriote*).

7. I since learned that Aspirin is contra-indicated medically in cases of haemorrhage.

8. They were all executed shortly after our departure.

9. A French Département.

10. Translator's note: this knowledge was based on research work Paul Le Goupil did after the war.

11. A dish of ham and beans from south western France.

12. On their return some comrades took the credit for saving our convoy from the gas chamber. But tattooing and registration had begun on the night of our arrival which proves that it was not to be our fate. Were we originally supposed to go to Buchenwald? Had we been directed to Auschwitz by way of reprisal, as had happened to male convoys of 5 and 6 June 1942, and the women's convoy of 23 January 1943? We did not know. Was it linked to the execution of Pucheu in Agiers? It seems unlikely. Perhaps it was due to a lack of space at Buchenwald which could not accommodate us, or an error of train routing? One day perhaps a historian will find the missing piece in that jigsaw puzzle; but for the moment, since no theory can be confirmed, none can be ruled out either.

## Chapter 6: Buchenwald, from Small Camp to Main Camp

1. Camp guards.
2. 'Road of Joy' – the author's preferred translation. (Translator's note: However, the German use of the Spanish *carajo* indicates 'din, fuss, and rush', evoking the loud forcing of arriving prisoners along this road.)
3. This sign is preserved in the camp museum.
4. 'To each his own'. (Translator's note: This quasi-biblical expression has become notoriously associated with Buchenwald, causing controversy whenever used in post-war Germany. The Nazi use signifies more probably, 'To each his just deserts'.)
5. A Département south west of Paris.
6. The Street was a Mohican cut without a crest. In this way escapees could be easily detected.
7. On their return these comrades were not entitled to a Deportee status card and were considered as common law offenders. They received no pension, no advantage or compensation, even from the German government, even though they had suffered the same privations as our men and had behaved in the camps with courage and dignity.
8. Block leader.
9. Get up!

10. On liberation, he declared at the Hotel Lutétia that he had been denounced by Paul Le Goupil, a teacher in Grand-Quevilly. I learned of it when I was nominated to receive the Légion d'Honneur in 1968. An inspector in the Renseignements (French State Security Bureau) was investigating my moral character: he read the Lutétia report to me and a recent report in which Nivromont junior had declared that I was in no way responsible for his arrest.

11. Office responsible for drawing up kommando lists, and their transports.

12. Defrance, through his action, was one of the first to be decorated, even after his arrest, with the Resistance medal in April 1944, awarded by de Gaulle in Algiers.

13. See Pierre Durand, *Les Français à Buchenwald et à Dora.*

14. Before 14 May, 11,429 Frenchmen had arrived in Buchenwald; 5,250 were sent to Dora. After this date, out of 11,918 only 3,200 left for Dora. While Frenchmen made up about a quarter of the final Dora workforce, they accounted for only one tenth the workforce of Langenstein-Zwieberge which was a very hard camp for underground work, commenced on 14 May 1944.

15. Archive centre in Germany holding all camp records.

16. 'piece, part, item', a term used derisively by the SS to refer to a prisoner for labour puposes.

17. Pierre Durand, *op.cit.*

18. *Rue de la Liberté* (*Road to Liberty*).

19. Emil, who received a heavy prison sentence in East Germany after his return for so-called 'deviationism'.

20. A Slovene who was involved in a Kominform plot and sentenced to five years' detention on 'The Naked Island' – Goli Otok. He was rehabilitated after Tito's death.

21. On reading my manuscript Yves explained that he was 'in' with a group of Spaniards who received Red Cross parcels from Algeria.

22. Get up.

23. Line up.

24. The uniform was copied from the Yugoslav royal guard.

25. Lacking trade knowledge I do not know what these numbers refer to.

26. After the bombing he was transferred to the Russian front and is believed to have died there of typhus. Translator's note: the author explains that 'Wineroot' was a drinker.

27. Get in line.

28. The one who was 'on' turned his back to the others, laying his right hand flat, palm-up behind his back, using his other hand to protect his head and neck. Then he would receive an almighty slap on the flat of his hand (from one of his pals) sometimes hard enough to make him stagger. He would then turn to name his assailant. If he was right, the named person would take his place, otherwise he would continue to be 'on'. The Russians laughed like schoolchildren at this game, accompanied by colourful oaths.

29. All present. Dismiss.

30. Brothel

31. See, among others, Christian Pineau *La Simple Vérité*, p. 461.

32. The French performances were directed by Yves Darriet.

33. In the 'canteen' there was no food, just toothbrushes, soap bars, and similar objects.

34. According to the official SS figures (the camp kommandant's report) there were 315 dead among the inmates, 525 seriously wounded (burns or amputations) and 900 lightly wounded.

35. Also where he is said to have written Egmont.

36. In *Mémorial de Rouen* dated 25 January 1850 there is a description in a second-hand book sale, item number 889, of *Constitution of the French Republic*, Dijon 1793, and one volume in format 16, bound in human skin. From 1792 to 1794 there was tannery for human skin in Mendon.

37. From an article in *Mémorial de Rouen*, 'The corpses retrieved from the Loire were burnt and the fat collected in barrels was sold in Nantes.'

## Chapter 7: Halberstadt and its Junkers Factory

1. Some comrades believe we then set off on foot over the heath overlooking the camp; others think we took a sideroad near Spiegelberge station; for my part I recall getting back in the wagon with Serge and Vézier, but can I rely on my memory?

2. When I met him after the war, Gilles indeed recalled going to play a match at Halberstadt while he was working in a factory in Blankenburg. In fact he did know some civilians in the Junkers factory and might have been able to help me. Luck was not with me that day.

3. Translator's note: This menu is a parody of a typical florid French menu, containing slang words and word play. As such much is lost in translation; an approximate rendering would be

   Munich Salad

   Braised Jerry Rissoles

   Gateau Carefree Barbed Wire

   Belotin Halberstadt Style

   Beer, Borngole Undertakers Special Brew (Borngole was a famous undertaker in Paris)

   Wine Vintage Twenty Per cent

## Chapter 8: Langenstein Zwieberge and its Tunnels

1. also Malachyt.

2. The figure varies from eleven to seventeen kilometres.

3. Translator's note: This refers to an almond tart served for Epiphany in which is hidden a ceramic charm representing one of the three kings. The person discovering it in their slice becomes 'king'.

4. A report by the Buchenwald kommandant cites a total of 1,308 dead for the period of 19 to 25 March for the whole camp and its outside-camp kommandos. In this global figure, Malachyt (Zwieberge) topped the list with 234 deaths, followed by SIII (Ordruf) 207, Leau 69 etc.

5. The leftovers were in theory dished out to each sleeping quarter one by one but there was preferential treatment and some huts were sometimes 'forgotten'. This is what probably happened on that day.

6. I saw him later in a town in western France where he was a scrap dealer and ran a stock car business. He pretended not to recognise me.

7. Translator's note: Didot, an alias of René Hardy.

8. After the war, commissioner Porte lived incognito for several years. He was sought by the DST [La Direction de la Surveillance du Territoire, a French government agency for homeland security] suspected of being responsible for the arrest of many communist resistance members who were later shot as hostages by the Germans. He believed that he was targeted at the time because of what he knew about the Caluire affair.

9. Translator's note: Red triangle designated political prisoners; a green triangle designated criminal prisoners.

10. Subsequently, on our return to France this affair had consequences. Before the Metz military court Jo was charged, in a case brought by X, with Grievous Bodily Harm. Jo asked several of us to act as defence witnesses to his services rendered. The case was dismissed.

11. I later found out that these parcels were sent from Algeria.

12. Forty-six years later I still bear some scars and for a long time after my return I still itched in some places as if the fleas were still under my skin.

13. The German army of the Federal Republic.

14. The East German secret police.

## Chapter 9: The Road to Hell

1. I have been able to reconstruct the itinerary of this evacuation route which led us beyond the Elbe after a march of 250 kilometres, noting in pencil the stages, the amount of food distributed and the main events, in a small notebook given to me by Jo. I had put them in a still intact pocket of my jacket, in case my knapsack was stolen. The details contained in it were confirmed more than forty

years later when, with a group of surviving comrades we took the same route in a bus. We found the approximate locations of our bivouacs. There one can find monuments marking the sites of mass graves where our executed comrades are buried. They hold only a tiny portion, perhaps a quarter of our dead. The others are buried here and there at the roadside, long ago forgotten without trace. Sometimes a farmer ploughing his field or a road worker clearing a ditch comes across a few bones which are then buried in a nearby cemetery. How many will be forever forgotten?

There were two sorts of reaction by local authorities after liberation: one was to find the bodies and group them in a decent mausoleum with fine monumental features, decorated each year on the day commemorating the victims of Nazism; the other reaction was, for fear of reprisal, to bury them hastily in fields woods, or at roadsides so as to wipe out all trace of those crimes.

2. These suffered differing fates: one disappeared, probably entirely massacred. Another was almost completely wiped out after a march of about 400 kilometres, 150 of them beyond Wittenburg, passing through Coswig, Renden, Wiesenburg, Ziesar, Genthin, Gusen... until 28 April at which point there remained only 24 prisoners out of 500! Our column, whose history I will trace, consisted of more or less the entire Junkers camp inmate workforce, with about one hundred Frenchmen, half of whom would never see their country again.

3. Valantin told me when I saw him again in the 1960s how he and his companions had managed to escape: his tactic was to slip directly behind one of the guards, with the effect that the following sentry thought that he was seeing the silhouette of his comrade in front of him, then suddenly he jumped over the hedge and lay still. Still seeing an outline in front of him the following guard took no action.

4. During our pilgrimage later we found in the cemetery of Rieder the grave of 'Two Unknown Poles'. Perhaps he rests there with the first victims of the evacuation march.

5. We found and immediately recognised this site – just the stadium entrance had been modified, passing via an adjacent side-street instead of along the

cemetery. On the site of the silo was a new house. The local mayor, who was 9 at the time, clearly remembered our passage. He told us that the village residents had collected food for us but the SS had prevented its distribution. There had been rumours in the column of this initiative. It was not the only time such an event occurred.

6. A popular expression in the camps meaning stolen. Other nationalities said 'comme çi, comme ça' accompanied by a sweeping hand gesture.

7. Some of these people claimed to have escaped so as to avoid the possibility of execution. On his return Serge had B and C banned from the Communist Party.

8. Forty years later we found this barn. It appeared at a bend in the road just as we imagined it at the crossroads, huge, isolated, with, in the background, the embankment of a disused railway line. It had recently been re-roofed. Opposite it a garden commemorated and marked the site of a communal grave, with a small monument which reads 'On 12 April 1945 17 anti-fascist resistance members were executed in Wiederstedt, 9 of them here find their resting place. 8 Soviet comrades were transported to Eisleben and buried in the Soviet cemetery of honour.' In almost all the villages we passed through there is a mass grave with a similar inscription. In Endorf for example, fourteen dead. In Quenstedt, 'Here lie 8 anti-fascist resistance members assassinated here in April 1945 by fascist adolescents.' In Harkerode, 'In glorious and honoured memory of the 16 victims of fascism who were executed here in April 1945 by the so-called Volkssturm and other fascists.' During the 'Black night' of 11-12 April large groups had slipped way from some columns but the next morning the mayors of the villages along our route had launched manhunts with the Volkssturm and had had whole groups of escapees executed.

9. For twenty years we believed him dead, when one day he appeared at a gathering of camp veterans. This is his story: 'On Friday, 13 April 1945, in the evening I was injured in both legs and the left hand from a shell burst. As I was unable to continue with my comrades in the column an SS guard tried to finish me off, leaving me for dead. I don't know by what miracle I am still

alive. On the morning of 15 April I was given first aid by a German or foreign woman who passed me on to the Americans who had occupied the village since the morning. I remained in the American hospital until 2 September 1945.'

10. The village of Hinsdorf was reached by the Americans around 11 am of the same day. Several columns of deportees were able to be freed in this sector but none came from Zwieberge.

11. According to the book *Histoire et crimes de la Gestapo parisienne* published by Belgo Suisse, his name was often cited as being a familiar figure in the Rue Lauristan, HQ of the French Gestapo. He was from the underworld of Marseille. He was executed at the beginning of the next leg and thanks to the information I was able to give at the research commission in 1945, his body was found in a grave containing four bodies in Trossin. He was identified by his press book.

12. For years I always wondered what became of the hundreds of bodies scattered along the route of our final stages. I was surprised to find out, during the later pilgrimage that I previously mentioned, that a number of the bodies had been gathered in extensive communal graves from Bitterfeld onwards, overlooked by municipal monuments tended and regularly garlanded with flowers. Thus on entering Bitterfeld there is a monument to 49 dead and, in the town itself, at the Neue Schanke restaurant, there is a plaque commemorating 'two prisoners who were executed on this spot'. A few kilometres after leaving Mühlbeck there is a monument to '68 Buchenwald prisoners assassinated during the evacuation march at Mühlbeck and its environs in April 1945'. Near the site where we spent the night in Sollichäu there is a small column by the roadside commemorating seven bodies with the inscription 'Never Again'. Finally in Kossa, the next village, there is another monument to '58 unknown prisoners executed during the Death March'. The German people were more affected by the executions than by the camps because we 'paraded' in those towns and villages in front of their populations who thus became witnesses to our distress and to our dead.

13. An evacuation column from the Neuestassfurt kommando had passed along the same road the day before and was decimated. Their dead rest with ours in the mass grave of Kossa.

14. 'Slow, slow!'

15. Panzerfaust, the German anti-tank weapon, equivalent to a Bazooka.

16. When I returned to the scene in 1988, I tried to find the house, printed on my memory but it was no longer there. In East Germany isolated farms had been demolished, with their occupants rehoused in villages. As for Richard's body, was it buried on the spot or does it lie in the communal grave in the cemetery of Prettin where there is a monument to '32 inmates executed in the town at the end of the Second World War, who were buried as they fell, and who were later transferred to the cemetery', or in the Lieben cemetery a little further along the route, where lie '19 Unknown inmates executed between Prettin and Jessen during the Death March'?

17. A large monumental sculpture by the artist Jurgen Woyski now overlooks this massacre site, with its mass grave, bearing he inscription, 'To the memory of 43 concentration camp inmates executed by the SS during evacuation march in April 1945.'

18. Some years later I learned from a survivor that most of the escapees were massacred and their bodies had never been found.

19. The town was hit around 2 pm when one of our columns was entering it. There were many casualties.

20. Translator's note: ironic reference to the SS executioners of the sick every morning.

21. Most of the victims of this final stage are gathered in a common grave outside town in Apollensdorf containing 488 bodies including foreigners killed in the bombing of Wittenberg. At the roadside on entering the town there is a grave 'For 11 prisoners executed on 21 April 1945' and another at the entrance to the cemetery 'For 7 unknown prisoners'. There are in addition scattered in all surrounding villages in the area, graves of prisoners who died of hunger or at the hands of the Volkssturm, in Hohndorf, Naundorf, Euper, etc.

## Chapter 10: From No Man's Land to the Russians

1. a meat extract sauce.

2. The sound of a German electrically-operated artillery weapon used late in the war.

3. I have often been asked why I did not bring back my deportee uniform. If I had been in a more decent camp like Buchenwald, where the clothes were decently maintained, I could have done so. But how could I keep those rags, in shreds, with gaping holes at the knees, whose stripes were invisible under layers of greasy dirt, still stained with machine grease from Halberstadt and the mud of Langenstein, all colonised by fleas. The textile weave, made from nettle plant fibre, had reached the end of its life and would have disintegrated in the first wash. My only regret is not to have kept the red triangle marked 'F' bearing my number. Happy were those who could bring back smart suits which they paraded in patriotic ceremonies; they had been in a better kommando.

4. Russian curses.

5. I do not know if any such cases happened. Personally I know of no example.

## Chapter 11: A Difficult Return to Civilisation

1. Rouen north bank station.

2. *The Road to the Crematoria.*